The Godfather and Sicily

SUNY series in Italian/American Culture

Fred L. Gardaphé, editor

The Godfather and Sicily
POWER, HONOR, FAMILY, AND EVIL

RAYMOND ANGELO BELLIOTTI

Published by State University of New York Press, Albany

© 2021 State University of New York

All rights reserved

Printed in the United States of America

No part of this book may be used or reproduced in any manner without written permission. No part of this book may be stored in a retrieval system or transmitted in any form or by any means including electronic, electrostatic, magnetic tape, mechanical, photocopying, recording, or otherwise without the prior permission in writing of the publisher.

For information, contact State University of New York Press, Albany, NY
www.sunypress.edu

Library of Congress Cataloging-in-Publication Data

Names: Belliotti, Raymond A., 1948- author.
Title: The Godfather and Sicily : power, honor, family, and evil / Raymond Angelo Belliotti.
Description: Albany : State University of New York Press, 2021. | Series: SUNY series in Italian/American culture | Includes bibliographical references and index.
Identifiers: LCCN 2020042935 | ISBN 9781438484310 (hardcover : alk. paper) | ISBN 9781438484303 (pbk. : alk. paper) | ISBN 9781438484327 (ebook)
Subjects: LCSH: Puzo, Mario, 1920-1999. Godfather. | Puzo, Mario, 1920-1999—Film adaptations. | Godfather films—History and criticism.
Classification: LCC PS3566.U9 G6293 2021 | DDC 813/.54—dc23
LC record available at https://lccn.loc.gov/2020042935

10 9 8 7 6 5 4 3 2 1

To Marcia, Vittoria, Angelo, and Alicia

Ha l'audacia di rischiare tutto? Per correre la possibilità di perdere tutto su una questione di principio, su una questione d'onore? È un siciliano?

(Does he have the audacity to risk everything? To run the chance of losing all on a matter of principle, on a matter of honor? Is he a Sicilian?)

Contents

Preface	ix
Acknowledgments	xi
Introduction	1
Chapter One The Passions and Limitations of Honor	5
Chapter Two The Sicilian Family Order	39
Chapter Three Power, Destiny, and Evil	77
Chapter Four Repentance, Atonement, and Redemption	115
Appendix A Summarizing *The Godfather*	165
Appendix B Summarizing *The Godfather II*	169
Appendix C Summarizing *The Godfather III*	175
Notes	179
Bibliography	195
Index	201
About the Author	207

Preface

On July 3, 2019, David Kyle Johnson, a scholar compiling an anthology on the topic of popular culture as philosophy, contacted me and solicited my participation, sweetening his invitation with a plum assignment: an essay on *The Godfather*. Kyle and I had never met or corresponded, but he was acting on a recommendation from a mutual colleague whom we both respected as distinguished and trustworthy, Bill Irwin. I accepted immediately, and Kyle designated December 15, 2019, as the deadline for me to submit my draft.

Bill suggested that Kyle assign me that topic undoubtedly because he knew I was an unapologetic Italian American flag-waver who would pounce at the chance to critically analyze the Corleone family and their Sicilian contemporaries. After all, these fictional icons immigrated to the United States at the same time as did my ancestors. Giuseppe Leonardo and Grazia Giordano Leonardo immigrated to this country from Valguarnera Caropepe, Sicily, in 1912. Angelo Belliotti, Gaetana Zaso Belliotti, and Rosario Belliotti arrived from Cerda, Sicily, in 1896. Rosario met and married Agnese ("Daisy") Rizzo, an immigrant from Alia, Sicily, in the United States, and together they raised five children, one of whom was my father, Angelo Belliotti. Giuseppe and Grazia raised nine children, one of whom was my mother, Luisa Leonardo Belliotti. These are my immediate predecessors in the generational chain that stretches from Sicily to the United States of America. I owe them everything. I would be nothing but for their unwavering courage, familial pride, grueling labors, fierce determination, and inexhaustible love. I aspire only to emblazon my link in the chain as honorably as they did.

By analyzing the fictional late nineteenth-century and early twentieth-century Sicilian immigrants portrayed in *The Godfather*, I could re-examine the Italian ethos that animated the spirits of my immediate ancestors and that cast an indelible shadow on my own psychology. As Fred L. Gardaphé insightfully remarks, "*The Godfather* has done more to create a national consciousness of the Italian American experience than any work of fiction or nonfiction published before or since. It certainly was the first novel that Italian Americans as a group reacted to, either positively or negatively, perhaps because it appeared at a time when Italian Americans were just beginning to emerge as an identifiable cultural and political entity."[1]

That the fictional Corleones were gangsters was relevant but not disqualifying. Only a miniscule number of Italian Americans were ever operatives within organized crime, and those who were constituted a small percentage of criminals in America.[2] The criminality of the Corleones was noteworthy but not essential to the wider matters of inquiry that I envisioned.

I aspired to examine *The Godfather* from a distinctive vantage point: as a fictional but well-researched narrative of the Italian American immigrant experience in America—as the struggle between nineteenth-century Sicilian cultural values and twentieth-century American individualism and industrialism. I composed my essay and delivered it to the editor on August 21, 2019. At that moment, I realized that my topics of choice merited and would reward a more thorough study. That realization is the genesis of this work.

Acknowledgments

Numerous people contributed to this work directly or indirectly. As always, my family comes first. Thanks to Marcia, Vittoria, Angelo, and Alicia for their ongoing support, enthusiasm, and love. My greatest accomplishment in life is to be a member of a family whose talents and virtues far exceed my own. But for Bill Irwin and Kyle Johnson I would not have undertaken this project. I am deeply grateful for their faith in this venture and for their encouragement. Thanks also to Alice Hodge, an expert of book formatting who corrected my numerous errors and prepared the final manuscript with peerless efficiency and grace. Additional thanks to James Peltz, SUNY Press Director, for shepherding the work through the peer review and editorial board approval processes under challenging circumstances; to the peer reviewers whose evaluations were insightful, edifying, and generous; to Jenn Bennett-Genthner, Production Editor, for taking the book but not its author seriously; to Anne "Maximum Alacrity" Valentine, Marketing Manager, for earning her new nickname; to Kate Seburyamo for assuming the final burden of marketing the work; to John Wentworth, Copyeditor, for bravely foraging through and improving my tortured prose; to Kirk Warren, for designing such a stylish cover; and to Sue Morreale for so efficiently and swiftly finalizing the work. Finally, I thank the following publishers for their permission to adapt or reprint short excerpts from my previously published work:

Seeking Identity: Individualism versus Community in an Ethnic Context. Lawrence: University Press of Kansas, 1995.
Why Philosophy Matters: 20 Lessons on Living Large. Newcastle: Cambridge Scholars, 2015.
Power: Oppression, Subservience, and Resistance. Albany, NY: SUNY Press, 2016.

Nietzsche's Will to Power: Eagles, Lions, and Serpents. Newcastle: Cambridge Scholars, 2017.

Jesus the Radical: The Parables and Modern Morality. Lanham, MD: Lexington Books, 2013.

Introduction

This is an interdisciplinary work that philosophically analyzes concepts such as honor, power, will to power, respect, atonement, repentance, forgiveness, and leading a meaningful human life in service of a distinctive interpretation of *The Godfather* as a novel and film sequence. Applying these analyses to the cultural understandings transported to America by nineteenth-century Italian immigrants to America casts fresh light on old-world allegiance to *l'ordine della famiglia* (the family order), *la via vecchia* (the old way), and the patriarchal ideal of *uomo di pazienza* (the man of patience), as well as the Sicilian code of honor. As such, this work exercises philosophical examinations to inform historical, sociological, and psychological findings, as well as literary and cinematic explanations of the novel and film trilogy.

On this reading, the narrative spun in *The Godfather* is much more than a lurid metaphor for the excesses of American capitalism or the story of problematic monarchial succession or the tale of a troubled dynastic family struggling for survival. *The Godfather* describes the existential conflict between two sets of values partially constituting competing prescriptive and descriptive visions of the world: a nineteenth-century Sicilian perspective grounded in honor and the accumulation of power within a culturally specific family order, and a twentieth-century American perspective celebrating individualism and commercial success. The two sets of values coalesce uneasily in the same cultural setting, and their conflict is irresolvable. Ultimately, the Sicilian perspective must wither away in the United States because, unlike the old country, the new world lacks its sustaining cultural conditions. This reading interprets *The Godfather* as, among other things, a commentary on the transformation of personal identity within the Sicilian and Italian immigrant experience.

Chapter 1 concentrates on two pivotal scenes: Amerigo Bonasera's solicitation of the intercession of Don Vito Corleone in punishing miscreants who brutally assaulted the undertaker's daughter, and Tom Hagen's discussions with film mogul Jack Woltz pursuant to securing a movie role for Don Vito's godson, Johnny Fontane. The substance and aftermath of these encounters illuminate the nineteenth-century Sicilian values that Don Vito embodies. Most strikingly, they demonstrate Don Vito's boundless regard for honor, respect, and power, for both measuring personal worth and protecting self and family in a hostile social environment. On this rendering, the accumulation of wealth is a means facilitating the realization of these higher values. The chapter provides philosophical analyses of the values of honor and respect, as well as critically evaluates their benefits and limitations for salutary living. As such, this chapter provides the foundation for understanding *The Godfather* as showcasing the existential incompatibility of nineteenth-century Sicilian patriarchal values and twentieth-century American culture.

Chapter 2 introduces and analyzes a critical human psychological and existential challenge: our relationship to others. We at once crave robust individuality and loving associations, two often incompatible aspirations. Much of our lives focuses on carefully navigating between these hankerings. The nineteenth-century Sicilian response was *la via vecchia*, the old way, and *l'ordine della famiglia*, the family order, which prescribed proper relations and a hierarchy of duties rooted in degrees of intimacy arising from biological connections and contractual loyalties. As always, under *l'ordine della famiglia* the values of honor, respect, and power are indispensable for crafting meaningful human lives. After philosophically analyzing the concept of a meaningful human life, the chapter explains the patriarchal ideal of the *uomo di pazienza*, the patient man, defined by meticulously designed attributes and actions. Approximating this ideal was required for worldly and tribal success in Sicily. After examining and evaluating the nineteenth-century Sicilian social ethos, which, among other things, distinguished mafia as a cultural accolade from Mafia as an organized crime syndicate, the chapter explores the historical roots of Mario Puzo's creation of Don Vito Corleone, as well as the connection between the Sicilian social ethos and the rise of the Mafia there.

The Godfather is a novel and a film that entertains. It bestows a grand story invoking classical themes of family allegiance, personal betrayal, calculated vengeance, lurid sexuality, merciless violence, peppered with sporadic plot twists. On a surface interpretation, *The Godfather* seemingly romanticizes organized crime, or at least the Corleone family, with scant regard for the pernicious reality of criminal activity. Chapter 3 begins by sketching supposedly subtler metaphors capturing the deeper allegorical meaning of *The Godfather*. All plausible interpretations, however, invoke the notion of power. Accordingly, the chapter continues by explaining why the protagonists of the film regard power as the ultimate prize and not merely as a means of securing wealth; provides a philosophical account of the concept of power; and analyzes Don Vito Corleone's will to power and its connection to his maximally affirmative attitude toward life.

The interplay of human destiny, personal choices, and resulting evil is next on the agenda. In the novel, Don Vito sometimes invokes destiny as the animator of a character's biographical arc. What does he mean? That our paramount life decisions descend from the stars and not from our hearts and souls? That one life-changing choice, sculpted by external circumstances beyond our control, can or must determine our future? Or something else?

Finally, the chapter discusses the personal degeneration of Michael Corleone, the significance of his exile in Sicily after the murders of Solozzo and McCluskey, how the context and events of *The Godfather: Part II* chronicle Michael's increasing alienation and estrangement, and the evanescence of *la via vecchia* in response to American social circumstances hostile to that tradition.

Much of the substance of Puzo's novel and Coppola's three films transpires from their refashioning of historical events. These virtuosos researched their subject attentively, and their findings are evident in their work. Chapter 4 begins by describing a host of ways that reality configured the novel and the three films. It continues by explaining and examining the role that rustic chivalry assumes in *The Godfather* genre and the distinctively Sicilian origins and significance of *Cavalleria Rusticana*, the one-act opera that forms the musical backdrop of *The Godfather: Part III*. The chapter then registers how the three films constitute a coherent narrative grounded in parallel segments. In the final film, Michael struggles with opportunities for repentance, atonement, redemption, and spiritual transformation. These phenomena of the soul are often invoked but rarely critically analyzed. To correct this deficiency, this chapter includes philosophical dissections of the concepts of repentance, atonement, and forgiveness, and their connection to salutary personal transformation. Finally, the chapter concludes by demonstrating why Michael Corleone's scattered clutches for personal redemption were doomed.

Chapter One

The Passions and Limitations of Honor

The Godfather describes the existential conflict between two sets of values partially constituting competing prescriptive and descriptive visions of the world: a nineteenth-century Sicilian perspective grounded in honor and the accumulation of power within a culturally specific family order, and a twentieth-century American perspective celebrating individualism and commercial success. The two sets of values coalesce uneasily in the same cultural setting and their conflict is irresolvable. Ultimately, the Sicilian perspective must wither away in the United States because, unlike the old country, the new world lacks its sustaining cultural conditions. This reading interprets *The Godfather* as, among other things, a commentary on the transformation of personal identity within the Sicilian and Italian immigrant experience.

This chapter concentrates on two pivotal scenes: Amerigo Bonasera's solicitation of the intercession of Don Vito Corleone in punishing miscreants who brutally assaulted the undertaker's daughter; and Tom Hagen's discussions with film mogul Jack Woltz pursuant to securing a movie role for Don Vito's godson, Johnny Fontane. The substance and aftermath of these encounters illuminate the nineteenth-century Sicilian values that Don Vito embodies. Most strikingly, they demonstrate Don Vito's boundless regard for honor, respect, and power, for both measuring personal worth and protecting self and family in a hostile social environment. On this rendering, the accumulation of wealth is a means facilitating the realization of these higher values. The chapter provides philosophical analyses of the values of honor and respect, as well as critically evaluates their benefits and limitations for salutary living. As such, this chapter provides the foundation for understanding *The Godfather* as showcasing the existential incompatibility of nineteenth-century Sicilian patriarchal values and twentieth-century American culture.

A Mortician Seeks Justice

"I believe in America. America has made my fortune."

—Amerigo Bonasera

The Godfather begins brilliantly with an aptly named undertaker, Amerigo Bonasera, petitioning Don Vito Corleone at the wedding of Constanzia Corleone and Carlo Rizzi. Knowing that, by tradition, a Sicilian father cannot refuse any reasonable request on his daughter's wedding day, Bonasera describes what Don Vito[1] already knows: two non-Italian boys forced the undertaker's beautiful, virtuous daughter to drink whiskey and then brutally assaulted her when she refused to submit to their sexual overtures. Bonasera swells with pride as he assures Don Vito that the girl kept her honor. However, she suffered a shattered jaw, broken nose, permanent facial disfigurement, and horrifying emotional distress. As a Sicilian craving desperately to become fully American, Bonasera brought charges through the criminal justice system. In the light of overwhelming evidence, the two reprobates pled guilty. The presiding judge scolded the criminals and levied sentences of three years each, which he promptly suspended. As the two malefactors left the courtroom they smirked when passing Bonasera, in effect rubbing his nose in dishonor. The mockery of legal probity besmirched the undertaker's faith in America and disgraced his entire family. Amerigo now asks Don Vito for the justice denied him by American jurisprudence. He whispers that he wants Don Vito to murder the boys and will pay any price for the service.

Don Vito, parceling out contempt and condescension in measured doses under the guise of explanation, informs Bonasera that although the Don's wife is the godmother (*commare*) to the victimized girl and a close friend of Bonasera's wife, the undertaker has avoided all contact with Don Vito. Amerigo has trusted in and been rewarded by the new country and has received his justice from the courts. Why does he now complain? He has garnered precisely what an unconnected Sicilian immigrant should expect. Now, Bonasera does not offer friendship. He ignores traditional Sicilian manners and protocol. Moreover, Don Vito is not a killer by contract and what Bonasera asks is a disproportionate response to the offense, not justice.

Translation: Bonasera, you thought America was different from Sicily—that judges were not corrupt, law enforcement was impartial, and you could ignore the family structure, allow a legal dispute to remain such, and thereby be rewarded for your civic rectitude. You have played the fool and you now reap what you have sown. Your courageous daughter retained her honor, whereas you have cast honor aside in deference to profit and assimilation. You have received that for which you bargained. You have assiduously shunned a relationship that was forged by my wife's sacred oath as *commare* to your daughter. You now seek to exploit my daughter's wedding day to gain your vengeful design. Instead of petitioning for forgiveness, demonstrating respect, and redeeming the relationship of our families, you regard this matter as murder for money—an arm's-length bargain between strangers or acquaintances. Bonasera, is there any Sicilian remaining within you? You know or should know the appropriate drill, but you reveal yourself as nothing more than a commonplace *stronzo*. You have earned your American fortune but squandered your manhood.

Bonasera gushes with an extravagant faith in the possibilities of the new world that has been rewarded. He has made his fortune in America and has achieved material security unavailable in his homeland to a person such as himself. Now, he has run afoul of a legal system manipulated by the wealthy and powerful and of licentious social customs that contributed to his daughter's victimization. This conflict forms the cornerstone of the dilemma all immigrants, including Don Vito, experienced at some level: Does individual aggrandizement, amplified personal freedom, and material success undermine the preservation of family cohesion? Can the family and the old value system survive in a radically different cultural context with relaxed standards of propriety? If not, what is to become of our identity, how may we define ourselves in the new world?

After lowering his demand for justice from killing the perpetrators to making them suffer comparably for what they inflicted on his daughter, Bonasera, stunningly, is so fearful of incurring a debt to Don Vito that he again offers money for the Don's services. Don Vito calmly but firmly excoriates Bonasera's Americanism. The undertaker has secured "his fortune" through dishonorable submission: he dances like a puppet at the end of strings manipulated by corrupt, American masters.

> You go to the law courts and wait for months. You spend money on lawyers who know full well you are to be made a fool of. You accept judgment from a judge who sells himself like the worst whore in the streets. Years gone by, when you needed money you went to the banks and paid ruinous interest, waited hand in hand like a beggar while they sniffed around [your affairs].[2]

The godfather wonders how he has offended Bonasera such that the undertaker reiterates such disrespect. He instructs Bonasera that should he vow friendship (pledge his loyalty) all his enemies would become Don Vito's enemies and Bonasera would become a feared man by association. At once, Don Vito scorns Bonasera's feckless understanding of power and asserts the range of his own agency. In the instant case, the culprits who terrorized his daughter would be suffering forthwith. Finally perceiving the obvious, Bonasera implores Don Vito for friendship while kissing his hand. These words and this gesture are performative: they constitute Bonasera's pledge of loyalty. Don Vito accepts and reminds Bonasera that there may come a day when the Don will request a service from his newly vowed friend.

The film omits some critical information from the novel. The two reprobates were Jerry Wagner and Kevin Moonan, presumably German-American and Irish-American, respectively. One of them was the son of a powerful politician, and the implication is stark: the sentences were suspended through political and legal corruption. The judge noted that the perpetrators were from "good families." Bonasera fatuously placed his faith in American justice, but the fix was in place at the outset. Don Vito is not surprised because his illegally obtained gains depend upon arrangements with corrupt members of law enforcement and government.

Amerigo Bonasera believes in America because the new world has provided opportunities for upward mobility unavailable in his place of birth, has allowed him to flourish financially, and has encouraged him to dream. But he must now seek Don Vito's intercession if he is to gain justice for his injured daughter and restore the honor of his immediate family. The mortician's belief in America is rewarded insofar as his interests do not conflict with those of higher social rank and their political collaborators. Owning and operating his funeral home are nonthreatening capitalist enterprises. Lodging criminal allegations against scions of the American establishment is quite another matter.

Curiously, Bonasera is one of the few characters in the film who speaks with an Italian accent. Despite his most profound yearnings, the self-styled American straddles two worlds. That Don Vito feels compelled to remind Bonasera that friends bear mutual obligations of assistance underscores the godfather's lack of faith in the undertaker's Sicilian allegiance. Of course, Bonasera would understand the terms of their relationship, the precise stipulations he had tried to avoid by obtusely offering money in exchange for the services he requested. Throughout the discussion, Bonasera forgets that the accumulation of money is merely an instrument for securing higher Sicilian values: power, respect, and honor. In his quest to assimilate, the mortician has confused a means as an end. He now pays the spiritual price.

Don Vito poses as a tradesman of justice. He refuses Bonasera's initial request of murdering Wagner and Moonan on the grounds of its disproportionality to their offense. This pose reeks of disingenuity: Don Vito had often retaliated disproportionally in the past and will do so in the future. For example, Don Vito responded disproportionately when he coerced the bandleader to renounce the personal services contract he had negotiated with Johnny Fontane. He will react disproportionately when he orders the murder of a union leader trying to shake down Johnny for fifty thousand dollars in return for smooth labor relations during a movie production. Suppose the two thugs had violated Constanzia Corleone prior to her marriage. Would Don Vito have not rendered them deader than the fish that will soon nestle in Luca Brasi's bulletproof vest?[3]

Indeed, his code of honor permits disproportionate retaliation to transgressions of honor. In the instant case, Bonasera has forsaken Sicilian honor in exchange for the pursuit of material gain, comfort, and leisure; he has become an American in aspiration if not fully in citizenship. Don Vito is unwilling to respond disproportionality in the name of a person who explicitly scorned the principles of the family order—Carmela Corleone is godmother of Bonasera's injured child, which should have cemented bonds of loyalty but did not—and who now, at most, totters uneasily upon a flimsy nexus of coerced allegiance. Bonasera does not rest within Don Vito's circle of intimacy; thus, only proportionate retaliation is appropriate. Bonasera lacks an intimate relationship with Don Vito, and therefore is devoid of the metaphysical bonds that might warrant disproportionately harsh redress.

The lessons of the film's opening scene include the primacy of honor—even Bonasera evinces pride at his daughter's retained honor and bristles at his own loss of honor in the courtroom—and the unwelcome consequences borne by Sicilians who renounce the family order by trusting naively in the tender mercies of the new world. Beneath the surface, the opening scene describes the conflict between two sets of values, competing descriptive and prescriptive cultural visions: those reflecting and sustaining the traditional understandings and imperatives of the Sicilian family order and those entrenched in the ideology of the United States of America. The conflict between these two competing sets of visions and values is irresolvable, even if their climatic battle can be delayed. The opening scene of *The Godfather* offers a minor skirmish within that ongoing conflict.

Ironically, Bonasera comprehends this viscerally, although not intellectually. He is prepared to shuttle the prescriptions of the Sicilian family order and embrace the new world's jaunty individualism seasoned by the solace of the nuclear family. He must "believe in America" because doing so has "made his fortune." However, vestiges of Sicilian honor are sparked by the torments inflicted on his daughter and the indignities ladled on him in the American courtroom. He must compromise his social blueprint and seek extralegal intervention. As in the old world, to attain justice Bonasera must transform a legal dispute into a private, personal matter. Bonasera, foolishly, approaches Don Vito with hopes of avoiding relational entanglement. He must have known better. Don Vito has no interest in orchestrating murders for money that are unrelated to his wider organizational network. Bonasera—given his wife's intimacy with Don Vito's spouse who is *commare* to Bonasera's only daughter—should be Don Vito's "friend," at least among his loyal associates. Instead, Bonasera presents himself as no more than a cordial acquaintance and desires no deeper relationship.

Later in the novel, Tom Hagen signals to Jack Woltz the significance of *commare* (godmother) and *compare* (godfather) relationships: "Mr. Corleone is Johnny Fontane's godfather. [To the Italian people that] is a very close, a very sacred religious relationship . . . Italians have a little joke, that the world is so hard a man must have two fathers to look after him, and that's why they have godfathers."[4] Much the same can be said about godmothers.

Bonasera, so desperately aspiring to Americanism, sprouts ethnic amnesia. He misunderstands Don Vito's standard, indirect Sicilian discourse; offers money for murder; evinces an uncomplicated faith in new world institutions; and must even be reminded that Don Vito's service entails future obligation. At the conclusion of the scene, Don Vito refuses to acknowledge his agreement with the undertaker. Instead, he advises Bonasera to consider "this justice a gift from my wife, your daughter's godmother."[5] Don Vito at once underscores the past bond that Bonasera has hitherto contravened and expresses a reservation about Bonasera's semi-coerced oath of loyalty to him. Don Vito grasps acutely that but for Bonasera's recent calamities the undertaker would have accompanied his wife and attended Constanzia Corleone's wedding but assiduously avoided the Don.

Later, Bonasera is terrified when he receives a telephone call from Hagen requesting a service on behalf of Don Vito. Of course, he cannot refuse. But the undertaker fears he will be implicated in serious criminality. Even if he escapes legal retribution, depending on the service he renders, Bonasera might be targeted by Don Vito's enemies. Fortunately, Don Vito's request is strictly legitimate: he asks Amerigo Bonasera to "use all your powers" to salvage cosmetically the bullet-ridden corpse of Santino Corleone. Don Vito again invokes his wife: "I do not wish his mother to see him as he is."[6] Even now, the exchange of services, although transacted by the men, flows most directly from their two spouses. Don Vito and Amerigo Bonasera, each suspended between two world visions in different ways, can never be more than transactional "friends."

Still, Don Vito understands intellectually that the Sicilian vision must perish in the United States, but he resists this truth viscerally. He refuses to assimilate gently or transform his sense of masculinity obligingly in the new world. Fred L. Gardaphé explains well the tensions that thereby ensue:

> From the very opening of *The Godfather*, it is apparent than an Italian sense of masculinity cannot survive transplantation to the United States . . . The problems that [Bonasera and the other petitioners] face wouldn't arise in Italy, or if they did, the men wouldn't have to face them alone. They would have their family members for support. To solve these problems in the United States, they must go to see Don Corleone, the head of the symbolic larger family . . . the central conflict of *The Godfather* is how to keep the family together and "Sicilian" for its own good in a land that has lost its dependence on the family unit for survival.[7]

A man of indomitable will, extraordinary mental toughness, and high ambition, Don Vito has steadfastly refused to act sycophantically with American power brokers, those political and social magnates who wield disproportionate influence over the terms of social life. These *pezzonovanti* (*pezzi da novanta*) masquerade as apostles of justice and goodness, but Don Vito knows all too well the genuine designs they harbor. They have helped him make his fortune, broaden his enterprises, and amplify his covert power. Nevertheless, Don Vito had expected that the most American of his sons, Michael, might become one of them: a senator, a governor. Don Vito was neither a warrior for social justice nor a dreamer conjuring a more egalitarian society. He accepted people for what they were and what he suspected they always would be. Don Vito would agree with the cynical adage that "In this world a person must either be a hammer or a nail." His choice was anchored and unblurred.

A Philosophical Analysis of Honor

To comprehend *The Godfather*, we must philosophically analyze the concept of "honor." Don Vito understands and presents himself as an honorable man. He does not perceive himself as a murderer, gangster, hoodlum, or common thief, all of which he most certainly is. More strikingly, he does not recognize himself as merely an exceptional businessman or successful capitalist. Instead, he is a talented, strong-willed, man of honor who refuses to dance like a vassal at the end of strings manipulated by the dishonorable *pezzonovanti* who otherwise define the terms of social life. Don Vito's signature value, then, is honor, and fulfilling the prescriptions of the code he has internalized is his greatest virtue.

Although the term "honor" has been used in a variety of contexts throughout history, a reasonable rendering of personal honor can be reconstructed.[8] A sense of personal honor, which is a measure of an individual's value, obtains if four components are in place:

1. A canon of behavior such that

    a. a set of imperatives (the "honor code") constrains an agent's choices and actions;

    b. the force of honor code imperatives cannot be destroyed or softened by considerations of expediency, utility, or personal advantage—the pursuit of honor and the satisfaction of such considerations are often conflicting aims; thus

c. living up to and complying with the honor code often involves personal risk or sacrifice to the agent up to and including death.

The power of honor codes is designed to trump considerations of expediency and personal advantage. The values embodied by the honor code are taken to have the greatest call upon the agent's allegiance in part because they are most definitive of personal identity. The Italian proverb illustrates that point: *Meglio onore senza vita che vita senza onore* (Better to have honor without life than life without honor). To live with shame is to eviscerate and betray the self, deny one's innermost values, and impoverish one's entire life. To die with honor is to enhance one's biography by validating one's inner worth and higher values. Fulfilling the imperatives of an honor code often conflicts sharply with short-term self-interest and preservation. Where the risk or sacrifice to the agent is greatest, the highest honor is merited. Thus, honor often conflicts with prudence, which weighs risks, tallies and compares advantages and disadvantages, and selects the course of action promising the greater probability of tangible gain.

The following imperatives partly constitute Don Vito's honor code: subordinate gangsters swear absolute obedience to their superiors; they do not ask for and are typically not offered explanations for their bosses' orders; the availability of subordinates—their willingness to carry out these orders and their effectiveness in doing so enhances their honor, which facilitates more opportunities for financial gain, information, and power; the interests of the crime family take precedence over all other interests, including those of a soldier's immediate household; those within the crime syndicate must be truthful with one another in order to nurture mutual trust; mutual loyalty is critical; individuals must make appropriate choices of spouses and act properly within marital relations; the principle of silence (*omertà*) must be strictly observed; a member's cache of honor is enhanced by the rectitude of his spouse; and compliance with the honor code vivifies a member's sense of professionalism, group identity, and shared system of values.[9]

Accordingly, Don Vito is willing to risk everything to comply with a principle of honor, often triggered by revenge. Considerations of expediency fade away under such circumstances because embodying and exemplifying honor partially constitute his self-understanding. His code of honor grounded in the imperatives of the Sicilian family order circumscribe his individual license.

2. A group affiliation promoting a sense of belonging such that

    a. the honor code arises from a group membership that the agent has either antecedently chosen or posteriorly accepted (internalized) as the agent's own;

    b. the honor code may but does not necessarily correlate to the wider society's professed moral principles, policies, and standards;

    c. the agent judges and evaluates himself or herself in large part in accord with how the agent perceives the way others who are capable—the group members who are qualified to assess—judge and evaluate the agent given the agent's compliance with the honor code, and how the agent judges his or her compliance with the honor code;

    d. a merited positive evaluation in that regard heightens the agent's self-esteem and pride and nurtures a more profound sense of belonging, whereas a negative evaluation implies that the agent has demonstrated weakness of character and has acted disreputably, which signals that the agent has betrayed the group ethos and thereby weakened his or her sense of belonging;

    e. a recognition by the group members qualified to assess that the agent deserves such a negative evaluation is typically followed by censure up to and including exclusion from group membership or even death unless the agent regains his or her honor;

    f. to have personal honor is to possess a right to be treated as having a certain value and includes the right to respect and to be treated accordingly within the group; to lose personal honor is to relinquish those rights by failing to live up to the honor code.

An honor code need not correlate to a nation's rendering of morality. As mentioned, groups try to define "honor" in accord with their distinctive values. As such, "honor" cannot be tied necessarily to the imperatives of conventional morality. Honor among felons is certainly possible. A criminal enterprise, such as the Corleone family, may define "honor" in terms of remaining silent when arrested and thereby protecting fellow criminals from prosecution; always responding, even disproportionately, to perceived slights, insults, and demonstrations of disrespect; manifesting respect to superiors within the enterprise by certain ritualized behaviors and by sharing with them the proceeds of criminal ventures; being careful to never inappropriately address or treat family members within the group; providing material and emotional support to the families of group members who fulfilled the honor code and are incarcerated by the authorities; and observing the rule that received benefits create obligations that must later be fulfilled as an expression of gratitude. In living up to such an honor code, a group member will often transgress conventional morality because of the nature of the honor group.

More specifically, the typical rules of honor informing a *Cosa Nostra cosca* (gang) include the following:[10]

1. The principle of *omertà* arises from the lack of public trust. Secrecy was required to ensure family, friends, and allies would evade oppression from corrupt state law enforcers. Conveniently, the principle also shrouded criminals from rightful prosecutions. Prior to widespread use of electronic surveillance, Racketeer Influenced and Corrupt Organizations Act (RICO) indictments, and witness protection programs, the principle of *omertà* sequestered executives of criminal families from prosecution as convicted associates and soldiers remained silent when pressed to disclose the felonies of their leaders.

2. Subordinates owe a duty of absolute obedience to those superior to them in the family hierarchy. Unlike the military, where the lowest ranking member is permitted to disobey an unlawful order from an institutional superior, in *Cosa Nostra* all orders flowing from above are regarded as sacrosanct. Leader infallibility rules. Moreover, allegiance to the crime family trumps all other obligations, including those typically associated with kin, friends, and intimate allies.

3. Respect must be accorded the wives, daughters, female relatives, and girlfriends of other crime members. This imperative facilitates internal crime family peace and avoids

feminine wrath that could undermine unity. Don Vito's honor code would surely endorse *Cosa Nostra*'s prohibition against affairs with the wives or girlfriends of other mobsters and duty to ensure their safety and well-being when their mates are absent due to mob business or incarceration. The penalty for failure to comply is often death. Pleas that retribution is disproportionate are summarily spurned.

4. Unauthorized physical violence against those holding the rank of soldier or above is strictly prohibited. Violations are first subject to negotiation at a sit down presided over by a capo. Typically, a rapprochement is seemingly crafted. But, as this is organized crime suffused by an honor code hypersensitive to insults, future congenial relations can never be assumed.

5. Soldiers and associates must seek and receive permission from their caporegime prior to undertaking business dealings, embarking on a vacation, or engaging in antecedently unauthorized activity.

6. Most families levy explicit prohibitions against drug trafficking. Since the onset of *Cosa Nostra* in America, crime bosses prohibited drug trafficking under penalty of death. The ban, however, was, at most, selectively enforced and even then invoked as subterfuge for vengeance for other offenses. Profits from narcotics are colossal, and violations of this imperative are frequent even among family bosses.

Don Vito's group membership consists of the general Sicilian community, wherein the imperatives of the family order reign, and the subgroup of organized criminals where those imperatives serve evil designs. The resulting honor code does not correlate to the normative principles prevalent in American culture. The Sicilian family order arose from a specific societal context, while organized crime cannot be officially endorsed by any government or nation.

The set of imperatives that structure a person's choices and actions is the honor code that arises from the group to which the person belongs.

The nature of the honor code varies in relation to time, place, group, and social setting. In each context, a group tries to capture the meaning of "honor" for its distinctive values. Sometimes people belong to a group by virtue of ratifying what originally were unchosen attachments such as the class into which they are born; the nation in which they were raised; their ethnic, religious, or racial inheritance; and the like. At other times, people choose their group affiliations by entering clubs and teams, or pursuing causes with others with whom they share purposes. In all such cases, the group affiliation becomes constitutive of personal identity insofar as it is connected to honor. Although many group affiliations are peripheral to a person's self-image and merely pleasing ways to pass time, what distinguishes an honor group is that ongoing connection to it is critical to a person's sense of self. This is true regardless of whether the person entered the group by choice or first discovered and later ratified his or her affiliation.

Most fundamentally, the code of honor reigning over Don Vito's world shapes the identity of all those subscribing to its imperatives and distinctive rules of behavior, which constitute modes often conflicting with those of dominant society.[11] The struggle for honor is a competition for social advancement, especially among those not fully cognizant of the intricacies of the capitalist market. Conflicts ensuring within the honor code mentality are zero-sum episodes: my increase in honor can occur only at a commensurate dishonor to another. Those amassing less honor than others will in some respects and social circumstances be dependent on those garnering more honor—thus Amerigo Bonasera's dependence on Don Vito to achieve what he takes to be his just purposes.

The importance of "honor," then, is intricately linked to a sense of self and to community. To breach the honor code, perhaps by turning state's evidence, fractures the extant solidarity and thus mars the integrity of the betrayer's character. Even when incarcerated, members must maintain a sense of dignity by adhering to the imperatives of the code.[12] While it is plausible that a person might conjure an individualistic, unique code of honor applicable only to himself or herself, typically the concept of honor is connected strongly to group or institutional roles. The person crafts his or her identity within such roles, and to separate or be severed from them is to alter the topography of the self. Accordingly, the notion of honor will glisten most brightly in settings that stress communal attachments, institutional roles, and social bonds.

3. An internalization of the canon of behavior such that

   a. living up to and complying with the honor code, which confers status, is tightly bound to the agent's sense of identity and self-worth;

   b. a positive evaluation in that regard is a source of deserved, deepened self-respect and pride;

   c. a negative evaluation, which follows from a known and recognized failure to live up to the honor code, is taken by the agent as a mark of disreputability, as manifesting a weakness of character and typically elicits shame, diminished self-esteem and reduced pride.

Those subscribing to an honor code evaluate themselves largely in terms of several vectors: Have I complied with the honor code? How do the group members, who are most qualified to assess my compliance with the honor code, evaluate my compliance? How does the group judgment influence my evaluation? How does my evaluation influence the group judgment? My behavior will manifest whether I embody the personal qualities that entitle me to honor, and qualified group members will recognize my inner worth or lack thereof by their assessments of my compliance with the code. My evaluation of my inner worth will depend greatly on how the relevant others perceive me. My sense of worth and honor does not depend on the perceptions of other people in general. Instead, I trust only those within the honor group, especially those who have proven themselves the most experienced and capable evaluators. I can retain my honor in the face of negative evaluations from outsiders, but I cannot do so when confronted by those I take to be most qualified to judge—those whom I respect as fellow members of our honor group.

Attributes of honor, then, are bound to complex relations and the interplay of several evaluations. No single assessment—whether by the agent or by the honor group—is sufficient. Each assessment is linked closely to other assessments. The overall evaluation embodies the dynamic tension of its constitutive units.

To have conferred and to confer upon oneself a favorable evaluation of one's honor is to cultivate a deserved, deepened self-esteem and pride, and a more profound sense of belonging to the honor group: I have lived up to a difficult set of imperatives, a set most other human beings would be unable to fulfill; I have placed principles over narrow self-interest and have renounced the easy path; I have kept the faith with my vows of compliance and thereby proved my worth.[13]

To have conferred and to confer upon oneself a negative evaluation of one's honor is to recognize failure and to lose status: I have failed to live up to the honor code; I have chosen expediency over principle; I have betrayed myself and the honor group; and I have demonstrated the poverty of my spirit. In such cases, the appropriate response is shame, a loss of self-esteem and pride, and a weakened sense of belonging to the honor group. My inadequacy and disgrace are evident to those qualified to evaluate my inner worth based on my failure to fulfill the imperatives of the honor code.

Once the group members recognize that a fellow member deserves a negative evaluation, they administer some form of censure up to and including exclusion from group membership or even death unless the agent regains his or her honor. To violate the honor code is to choose to risk forfeiting membership in the group. Depending upon the specific honor code at issue, a disgraced member may be punished or simply banished. Under the most primitive codes, punishment may mean death. Some honor codes permit shamed members to restore their honor through prescribed actions. Other honor codes insist that once honor is lost it is forever gone. Moreover, depending on the nature of the honor code and my connection to it, my loss of honor may also shame my family or the honor group itself.

To have personal honor is to possess a right to be treated as having a certain value and includes the right to respect and to be treated as an equal within the group. To lose personal honor is to relinquish those rights by failing to live up to the honor code. In addition, one's personal honor can be infringed upon by insults, which by themselves neither impair the agent's reputation nor diminish the agent's inner worth, but which fail to treat the agent commensurate with his or her status. The transgressor has failed in his or her duty to treat the honorable person in accord with that person's value. In such cases, honor codes typically include an imperative of response: if someone impugns the agent's honor, the agent must respond in the prescribed fashion; otherwise the agent's honor is diminished or destroyed.

As argued, Don Vito embodies honor as constitutive of the self, scoffs at Bonasera's loss of honor in pursuit of American identity and material gain, and bemoans the mortician's diminished self-esteem and shame. Still,

Don Vito understands that personal transformation, implying abrogation of the specific honor code to which he subscribes, will be required of the next generation. He, however, can remain authentic. Or so he presumes.

4. A principle of redress such that

   a. personal honor can be infringed upon by insults, even those that by themselves neither impair the agent's reputation nor diminish the agent's inner worth, but which fail to treat the agent commensurate with his or her merited value; and

   b. honor codes typically include an imperative of response: if someone impugns the agent's honor, the agent must respond in the prescribed fashion; otherwise the agent's honor is diminished or destroyed.

Those subscribing to a code of honor are typically more easily insulted than are ordinary citizens. By placing heightened value on the personal standing linked to a code of honor, agents become sensitive, often overly so, to words, gestures, and actions that do not wholly affirm their standing or code. Moreover, the principle of redress underwriting an agent's response to perceived insult rarely embraces strict proportionality. Few honor codes include paeans to retributive justice. Redress under most honor codes is frequently disproportionately harsh.

In the case of Don Vito, his refusal to murder the young reprobates who viciously assaulted Bonasera's daughter arises from the undertaker's metaphysical distance from the mortician. Amerigo has acted as if he were only among Don Vito's acquaintances, not as an intimate friend. His induced pledge of loyalty places him, at most, within the loyalists who are regarded at best with attenuated affection. Don Vito's obligations to him are formal and fragile. He will not murder the punks who viciously assaulted Amerigo's daughter, but he will have them thrashed appropriately.

Also, when Don Vito forswears vengeance for the murder of Sonny and sues for peace, he seemingly dishonorably violates his code and demonstrates weakness that his rivals exploit. However, when Don Vito repeats a Sicilian proverb that "Revenge is a dish that tastes best when it is cold,"[14] he underscores his conviction that vengeance delayed is not vengeance denied. Michael will serve as his avenging agent and restore Don Vito's honor posthumously.

Although their role in mob negotiations is merely alluded to in the film, in Puzo's novel the fictional extended Bocchicchio clan exemplify a stunningly fierce, primitive commitment to the honor code.[15] Even by nineteenth-century Sicilian measures, the Bocchicchios' unshakeable allegiance to family solidarity, the principle of *omertà*, the sanctity of vendetta, veneration of honor, and unadulterated ferocity were remarkable. In earlier times, the Bocchicchios were significant players in a small segment of Sicily. Trading in protection and a monopoly in flour mills, they controlled the water supply in their corner of the island. The success of their enterprises depended only on the clan's primary excellences and allegiances. The Bocchicchios were ruthlessly straightforward and unrepentantly aggressive, but were devoid of the cunning, subtlety, and subterfuge exercised by more capable Sicilians. Still, by understanding their strengths and remaining within their areas of competency, the Bocchicchios flourished.

The adage maintains that our most debilitating shortcomings arise from the exaggerations and distortions of our most glorious capabilities, and our worst vices spring from the amplification of our greatest virtues. The Bocchicchios provide a sad example of the truth of these maxims. When Benito Mussolini seized political control of Italy, he vowed, among other things, to destroy organized crime in Sicily. For what is the point of being a Fascist dictator if you lack a monopoly on the exercise of violence? He declared the equivalent of martial law on stilts in Sicily and authorized Cesare Mori, notorious as the "iron prefect" and "the man with hair on his heart," to eviscerate the Mafia. Given the Bocchicchios open, defiant, and guileless perpetration of their craft, they were early and easy targets of Mussolini's project. When confronted by overwhelming Fascist forces, the Bocchicchios responded in trademark fashion. As was inevitable, their aggression and overt resistance—their most outstanding strengths—facilitated their self-destruction given the circumstances at bar. Almost half of the extended clan were killed in combat, while almost the entire remaining half were imprisoned. Around two dozen or so survivors immigrated to the United States by way of Canada.

The Bocchicchios eventually settled, as a unit, outside of New York City and made their way in the sanitation industry, employing their distinctive capabilities. Unable to compete successfully in mob enterprises such as prostitution, gambling, narcotics, and government fraud, the Bocchicchios, relatively simple but relentless, eased into their underworld niche as hostages during crime negotiations between warring families. A Bocchicchio would stand as surety when a significant sit-down was scheduled. For example, when Michael Corleone met with Virgil Sollozzo and his bodyguard, Captain McCluskey, the Corleone family demanded that Sollozzo pay for and provide a male Bocchicchio as insurance against treachery. Should harm befall Michael, the Corleones would murder the Bocchicchio hostage, and the remaining Bocchicchios would exact vengeance against Sollozzo, the proximate cause of their tribesman's death.

As a matter of honor, the Bocchicchio hostage would accept death, and his surviving family members would execute their vendetta against the treacherous party who had betrayed them. No appeal to expediency, no offer of reparations, no public atonement, no cost-benefit analysis, no threatened punishment would dissuade the Bocchicchios from murdering the traitor responsible for their clansman's death. Bocchicchio hostages were renowned as the ultimate insurance policy during crime negotiations. In the new world, the Bocchicchio brand, grounded in straightforward adherence to a code of honor leavened by primitive ferocity, glistened with currency. A Bocchicchio hostage would never accept money to harm the party who held him hostage; would never resist death should that party have justification to kill him because its representative had been injured during negotiations; and the extended family could never be swayed from fatal retaliation in the event the hostage was slain. Simple, primitive, rigorous adherence to such an honor code engendered safe, reliable negotiations among warring crime families.

What is not even alluded to in the film but chronicled in the novel is the role the Bocchicchios play in the return of Michael from Sicily. After Don Vito brokers peace among the five crime families of New York City, at a palpable loss to his prestige and honor, in order to secure Michael's return, one glaring obstacle remains. The police have only one prime suspect in the murders of Virgil Sollozzo and Captain McCluskey: Michael Corleone. Relief emerges from a Bocchicchio who is already convicted and condemned to die for a classic Bocchicchio revenge killing. After being supplied details of the murders that will render his admissions credible, he agrees to confess to the murders of Sollozzo and McCluskey in exchange for significant money for his survivors. Once a Bocchicchio had successfully avenged a slight to his honor—after all, the entire clan was Sicilian in the requisite sense that they would risk everything for a principle such as vendetta—and was sentenced to death as a result, he might as well turn fatal adversity into practical advantage for his heirs.

The Bocchicchios lived in a black-and-white world lacking exceptions, fine print, and thin distinctions. They had transformed their old world ferocity into new world value. The indefatigable combatants had become instruments of peace, at least insofar as their employers complied with the same code of honor. As ever, they represent unsullied, agrestic allegiance to honor.

The Case for Honor

Reliance upon honor codes, other than in the military, police, criminal organizations, and the like, strikes most contemporary thinkers as anachronistic. The notion of "honor" conjures images of knightly combat; duels arising from perceived insults; ongoing vendettas whose originating causes have been long forgotten; and murders resulting from husbands who have been cuckolded or fathers whose daughters have been sexually violated. Invoking "honor" recalls class-based societies in which personal identity was closely allied with social roles—times when the only honor available to women centered on retaining chastity. Even the vestiges of honor in paramilitary and criminal enterprises underscore the masculine, violent, antagonistic foundations of such codes. Such vestiges remind us that much of the history of honor is bound to male bravery, machismo, and eagerness to avenge all perceived insults, aspects of social life that may strike us now as recklessly out of place. We might well be tempted to conclude that the virtual disappearance of honor codes and invocations of honor are events to be cheered.

For example, years ago, in an academic unit at my institution, a professor, whom I will call Giordano, opposed a colleague's application for promotion to the rank of professor. Although Giordano held that colleague in high esteem, his evaluation was based on the colleague's failure to publish a book. In the history of this academic department no faculty member had been promoted to the rank of professor without having published at least one book. Although this requirement was not expressed in any written document, it was longstanding tradition and transmitted by word of mouth. In Giordano's letter of evaluation he argued that to accept a promotion only because others were willing to confer it even in the absence of one of the longstanding necessary conditions brought no honor to the candidate. Moreover, that others were willing to confer the promotion under such circumstances brought no honor to them.

Giordano's argument was grounded in the conviction that the other evaluators and the candidate were breaking the department code of honor in the interests of expediency: having no stake in opposing the will of the majority and having insufficient regard for the value of traditional scholarship anyway, the institution's management would endorse the majority position and grant the promotion. Understanding this, the other evaluators seized the opportunity to advance the interests of a valued member of the academic unit. Thus, the highly regarded, likeable colleague would receive the promotion under a lower standard than previously employed by the academic unit. In Giordano's judgment, such a promotion marred the honor of the recipient and those who championed his cause. In Giordano's view, they had placed expediency and a colleague's short-term interests above principle. Also, they had rendered no long-range service to their colleague by not requiring that he accomplish what he was fully capable of attaining. Having read Giordano's evaluation, the Dean was taken aback by the reference to "honor." He dismissed it as irrelevant, and his remarks stressed that he perceived no place for such a consideration in academe or anywhere else. The Dean's comments tracked clearly what is the predominant contemporary assessment of invocations of honor: they are pernicious remnants of historical periods that have been rightfully eclipsed.

That honor in the past has been most closely associated with patriarchal prerogatives, aristocratic privileges, and violent reprisals is undeniable. But nothing in the concept of "honor" requires such linkages. As stated previously, the history of "honor" is the effort of various groups to capture the term for a specific set of values and virtues.

The case for nurturing a sense of honor is compelling. Allegiance to a notion of honor and cultivating the character traits required to behave in ways consistent with that notion connect a person to wider community. Assuming that the values embodied by the notion of honor at issue are worthy, they vivify personal identity and fulfill the human need for intimate bonding with others. A salutary honor code provides imperatives that are not subject to barter or considerations of expediency. Such imperatives infuse life with meaning and purpose. For those who are firmly convinced, as I am, that if there is nothing worth dying for then there is nothing worth living for, a sense of honor frames a person's bedrock convictions. The right to be treated as having a certain worth is most resplendent when it is conditioned on the demonstration of the personal qualities that entitle a person to that right. That others within the honor group—those who share allegiance to the imperatives of the honor code—recognize that a fellow member has the requisite personal qualities reinforces the sense of that person's inner worth. In opposition to the Stoics, how other people judge us does and should matter to our own evaluations and understandings of who we are. In opposition to those with an impoverished sense of self who are vulnerable to all external evaluations, only the judgments of some other people should matter—those who are most qualified to render fair, accurate assessments, and those who are the other people who matter most to us. Popular opinion in and of itself bears little recommendation.

The notion of honor connects the individual to a project that transcends the narrow concerns of the self. People with a sense of honor privilege the imperatives of the honor code and take compliance with those imperatives as one of their higher values. In societies where the yearning for individualism has amplified dangerously into self-indulgence, narcissism, and the pursuit of popularity, the notion of honor provides a communal antidote by championing a sense of duty, sacrifice, and merited reward. Compliance with the imperatives of an honor code can motivate us to act contrary to strictly personal desires in deference to community obligations. Connection to honor codes is thus one way to distance ourselves from a purely atomistic notion of the self.

A sense of deserved pride is the reward of fulfilling the requirements of a worthy honor code. Justified pride in our accomplishments and in our personal characters animates the quest for excellence. Yes, if exaggerated, pride amplifies into arrogance and vanity: an unjustified sense of superiority that exalts the self by diminishing others. But if justified and measured, pride is seemingly the basis of self-esteem that is presupposed in our ability to love self and others. Is not pride, if deserved, merely a justified sense of self-worth? Moreover, even from a religious standpoint, pride seems necessary to maximize our highest potentials and thereby glorify God's bestowed gifts. Without pride and the desire to excel, we court passivity and slothfulness. Indeed, pride ignites heroism and underwrites most great attainments in the world. In short, a healthy pride spurs our best efforts, vivifies our quest for meaning and purpose, and protects us from resignation when adversity stings us.[16]

The case against pride is primarily biblical (Proverbs 16:18–19; Luke 4:1–11; Luke 18:9–14; Romans 5:6). Pride corrodes judgment and facilitates sin. By luxuriating in our attainments and savoring our development, we jeopardize our connection to wider community and to the divine. We set ourselves apart, regarding ourselves as special or even unique, while evaluating others as less capable. We incline toward excessive love of self and of objects that glorify the self—such as fame, awards, and social station—instead of focusing on spiritual goods. The most horrifying human acts bloom from the soil of pride. Wars, murders, rapes, terrorism, and the like are perpetrated not by the self-effacing and apathetic, but by those fueled by an inflated sense of entitlement and excessive self-worth. Worse, pride supplies an unworthy motivation for performing deeds that seem from an external standpoint to be virtuous. We are all familiar with the charity worker who benefits the disenfranchised more from a sense of superiority than from genuine concern for their welfare: "Hey, look at me, I am doing what the better people always do, helping my social inferiors."

Still, the indictment against pride is excessive. Religious tradition instructs us to love our neighbor as ourselves. This presupposes that self-love as such is not sinful, but a requirement of fulfilling our duty to love others. Accordingly, pride, insofar as it is self-love, is necessary for discharging moral obligation. Pride, as justifiable appreciation of the self, would appear to be unavoidable and even recommended. Pride requires robust communal connections to secure its value. What justifies pride is personal excellence, stellar achievements, and uncommon worth. Such achievements need not be historic. Small tasks done with exceptional skill and diligence give rise to justified pride. Intelligence, creativity, determination, imagination, overcoming significant obstacles, and maximizing one's highest potentials help constitute that skill and diligence. Recognition by others and the acclaim of the masses often accompany such skill and diligence but are unnecessary to their existence.

Accordingly, a sense of honor and a connection to an honor code can facilitate a justified perception of pride and sustain robustly meaningful, valuable lives. Preserving the jewel of honor in the family of virtue sparkles with value. The critical questions center on the type of values and virtues that should capture the meaning of "honor" and the appropriate imperatives that should define a beneficial honor code. Unfortunately, too many codes of honor have embodied and evinced noxious patriarchal prerogatives, toxically violent principles of redress, insular tribal understandings, and racial, ethnic, religious, or class imperialism.

Capitalism and Honor

"This is business, not personal."

In 1969, when I first read *The Godfather*, several characters intoned "this is business, not personal," or some variation, ostensibly to calm listeners and transport them to a more reasonable position than they had advanced.

I was jolted by this doltish locution. How could Mario Puzo, otherwise so perceptive, invoke an expression that entirely missed the mark? The protagonists in the novel took themselves to be men of honor. Surely, Puzo must know that people bearing such a self-image invariably take more words, gestures, and actions personally than do other human beings. Sadly, I concluded that Puzo must have been striving for a memorable phrase, one that, like "I'll make him an offer he can't refuse" and "A lawyer with his briefcase can steal more money than a hundred men with guns," would earn enduring renown. Or perhaps he was trying to underscore how the novel was a metaphor for the excesses of capitalism and big business.

Then an epiphany. Tom Hagen is counseling Michael Corleone to reevaluate his offer to murder Virgil Sollozzo and Captain McCluskey. He points out that McCluskey's breaking of Michael's jaw was "business, not personal" and Michael should not factor that injury into his calculus. As I was about to bellow, "Not again, not this witless phrase." Michael responds:

> Tom, don't let anybody kid you. It's all personal, every bit of business. Every piece of shit every man has to eat every day of his life is personal. They call it business. OK. But it's personal as hell. You know where I learned that from? The Don. . . . That's what makes him great. . . . He takes everything personal.[17]

Alleluia! Finally, the truth. As a man of honor, Don Vito would take much more personally than other human beings. Under my account, Puzo in effect reveals that the business metaphor is inadequate to understand his novel. That the notion of honor underwrites Don Vito's mission is at this point clear.

Michael's assertion is not included in the movie. In Coppola's screen notes, scrawled in the margins of the pages of his copy of the novel, he remarks, "I never really got into this, though I understand it. Ask Mario" and "? Think about this." [18] Given Coppola's conviction that the story "was a metaphor for American capitalism in the tale of a great king with three sons"[19] that the primacy of honor might elude him is unsurprising.

At the peace conference attended by the leaders of American crime families, Don Vito confirms the personal nature of events when discussing the return of Michael from Sicily.

> If some unlikely accident should befall my youngest son, if some police officer should accidentally shoot him, if he should hang himself in his cell, if new witnesses appear to testify to his

guilt, my superstition will make me feel that it was the result of the ill will still borne me by some people here . . . that ill will, that bad luck, I could never forgive.[20]

To ignore the intersection of the Sicilian family order, the importance of honor, and the ambivalence of the immigrant experience, or to immerse them in wider metaphors of American business or capitalism, is to bypass willfully the more philosophically rewarding dimensions of the novel.

A Man of Business Is Overwhelmed

> "Is he a Sicilian?"
>
> —Tom Hagen

The movie omits another paramount passage invoking honor. Tom Hagen returns from his turbulent sessions with Jack Woltz. He informs Don Vito that Woltz is unwilling to grant his request to cast Johnny Fontane in Woltz's upcoming movie. Prior to determining his response, Don Vito must evaluate Woltz's character. He asks Hagen, "Does this man have real balls?" Hagen interprets the inquiry sharply and quickly. Sure, Woltz has strong character, a determined will, the courage to call bluffs, the willingness to suffer financial losses and inconveniences in the face of labor strikes or embarrassing exposures of the excesses of one of his stars. But Hagen suspects the Don already understands this and is searching for something more profound: "Did Jack Woltz have the balls to risk everything. To run the chance of losing all on a matter of principle, on a matter of honor; for revenge?" He responds to Don Vito, "You're asking if he is a Sicilian."[21] Don Vito nods. Hagen assures him that Woltz is not a Sicilian in this or any other sense. Now, Don Vito can conjure his treachery against Woltz.

Coppola's screen notes merely repeat, "Would he *risk* everything on a matter of honor? No. But the Don would."[22] Again, on my account, the contrast between the successful, intelligent, powerful businessman and the old-world man of honor within the structure of *l'ordine della famiglia* (the family order) is palpable.

Jack Woltz is not merely an uncommonly successful businessman. He is deeply connected to governmental power brokers: he boasts of a friendship with J. Edgar Hoover, director of the Federal Bureau of

Investigation, and alludes to his influence in the White House.[23] Woltz, not Hagen, loses his temper, sputters threats, and vows retaliation should Don Vito continue to press his request. Woltz will never cast Johnny Fontane in his upcoming movie, even knowing that his acting would enhance the film, because Johnny had once stolen the heart of one of Woltz's movie starlets, a young girl Woltz had groomed professionally and enjoyed sexually. Hagen is stunned that Woltz would reject what was in his business interests because of a private matter wrapped around the beauty and sexual allure of a woman. In the remorselessly patriarchal realm of the Coreleones, disputes over women were significant only in marital and family contexts.

Don Vito, relying on Tom Hagen's evaluation that Woltz would not risk everything on a matter of honor or revenge, has the movie mogul's prize race horse race killed and its head placed in Woltz's bed while he sleeps. (We must suspend judgment on how all this transpires so quietly and efficiently.) The value of the stallion is around $600,000, as measured by Woltz's purchase price, but we must suppose that Woltz has insured the horse's life for much more, as Khartoum's stud value would far exceed that amount. Thus, the murder is not significant as violence to Woltz's financial bottom line. The sheer barbarity of the enterprise, however, brings Woltz to his knees: Don Vito is willing to risk everything for what he takes to be a matter of honor. Don Vito's extralegal power amplified by his boundless resolve is far greater than the force of Woltz's legal and governmental connections. As always, Don Vito prizes power and honor supremely, while using money as his instrument to amass and exercise them.

Puzo allows readers a rare glance into the inner life of one of his character's. Thus, Woltz muses:

> The ruthlessness, the sheer disregard for any values, implied a man who considered himself completely his own law, even his own God. . . . People didn't have any right to act that way. It was insane. It meant you couldn't do what you wanted with your own money, with the companies you owned, the power you had to give orders. It was ten times worse than communism.[24]

Well, yes. Don Vito and those of his ilk pose a unique, intractable threat to Woltz's comforting inspiration: the ménage à trois of big business, government, and law. Woltz is too obtuse, however, to perceive how Don Vito's family partially overlaps and influences that relationship. Moreover,

Don Vito can bestow benefits, fulfill destinies, and perform secular miracles largely because he is a man who will risk everything on a matter of principle and honor. He is not "completely his own law," because he, like all people of honor, is constrained by the imperatives of his code, but he will surely not permit society's conventional understandings to circumscribe his methods or objectives. He is "his own God," then, within the boundaries of the code of honor to which he subscribes, a code that partially constitutes his identity.

Puzo, who steadfastly and disingenuously maintained that he only told stories and did not moralize, stacks the deck against Woltz, who is a thoroughly unattractive figure: arrogant, loud, threatening, abusive, exploitive, and, worse, a serial statutory rapist. Johnny Fontane is neither entitled to nor deserves the movie role which he seeks. Woltz's refusal to cast him is neither unjust nor unfair. Although everyone concerned admits Fontane would do a terrific job, countless other actors would perform as well. Don Vito ensures that Johnny is cast because he has given his word at his daughter's wedding to his godson. Armed with multiple inducements of his code of honor, Don Vito will risk everything to fulfill that promise, even after calculating Woltz's considerable personal, professional, and governmental resources. In the margins, we contrast Don Vito's sexual rectitude with Jack Woltz's ongoing sexual perversions. Don Vito, an unapologetic gangster, responds disproportionately and unjustifiably, yet viewers and readers cheer—at least those willing to overlook the mutilation of an innocent animal.

A Philosophical Analysis of Respect

The notion of respect permeating *The Godfather* is extrinsic, evaluative, and comparative, a depiction that is not the only or automatically the ideal rendering of respect.[25] On this depiction, respect is extrinsic in that it cannot be claimed merely by membership in the human species or based on possessing sentience or because something is a natural object; it is evaluative because it demands an assessment of worth or merit measured by specific criteria; and it is comparative because not all human beings will earn such respect, and even those who do will deserve respect in different degrees. Thus, this form of respect involves appropriate recognition and evaluation of facts about and dispositions embodied by a person; should that person qualify as a figure of respect then others should regulate their behavior appropriately; and such evaluations of respect are neither indefeasible nor incorrigible.[26]

To define and understand what I will term "warranted evaluative respect" in the context of *The Godfather*, Vito represents the person being respected, Amerigo the person bestowing respect, and excellence is the measure of worth or merit that warrants the respect bestowed.

1. Vito is entitled to warranted evaluative respect from Amerigo based on Vito's possession and exercise of excellence.

2. Excellence is the possession and efficacious exercise of power-over (to oppress subordinates; or to paternalistically advance the interests of subordinates; or to empower subordinates by aiding their personal transformation)[27] within the imperatives of the honor code defining the subcommunity within which Vito and Amerigo function primarily. Excellence is not an overall moral evaluation of Vito from the standpoint of conventional morality.

3. For Amerigo to have warranted respect for Vito, Amerigo must assess accurately that Vito possesses and efficaciously exercises excellence, and Vito must positively value this excellence. If Amerigo's s assessment of Vito regarding this excellence is positive but inaccurate, then Amerigo's respect for Vito is unwarranted. If Amerigo does not value this excellence, then Amerigo will not respect Vito, at least on this basis.

4. Vito's entitlement to respect is independent of Amerigo's pre-assessment desires, interests, and purposes beyond the imperatives of the honor code defining the subcommunity that the two men share. Amerigo's evaluation is governed only by his observations of, beliefs about, deliberations concerning, and conclusions relating to Vito's possession and exercise of excellence. Thus, Amerigo can have warranted respect for Vito while concluding that Vito is overall an unworthy human being and while personally disliking Vito.

5. For Amerigo to value this excellence and judge accurately that Vito possesses and exercises it sufficiently to warrant respect is also to *feel* respect for Vito. Should Amerigo not

value or be indifferent to this excellence, then Amerigo's accurate judgment that Vito possesses and exercises it would not imply the Amerigo feels respect for Vito.

6. Amerigo might still *act* respectfully toward Vito without having or feeling respect for Vito. (Perhaps Amerigo is motivated only by fear of Vito's retaliation, or Amerigo is trying to fool Vito into believing he has respect for Vito, or Amerigo is manipulating Vito for other purposes.) To express respect for Vito through behavior and action, Amerigo must be motivated by his recognition that Vito embodies this excellence, which Amerigo values.

7. Amerigo's respect for Vito constrains the range of his behavior toward Vito. Amerigo could respect Vito but never outwardly manifest that respect. (No observable behavior.) But should Amerigo interact with or behave toward Vito, Amerigo would do so in ways consistent with the respect he bears for Vito.

8. This behavioral dimension includes acts and omissions to act consistent with Amerigo's evaluation that Vito has and exercises an excellence that Amerigo values and the feelings thereby induced: fear, admiration, deference, esteem, subordination, obedience, awe, and all the rest. Amerigo's behavioral range will be shaped by the respect he has and feels for Vito.

Accordingly, Amerigo's having respect for Vito is constituted by an epistemic dimension (Amerigo's beliefs, observations, deliberations, and evaluations relating to Vito's relationship to the excellence described); an attitudinal dimension (Amerigo's feelings of respect for and valuing of that excellence); and a behavioral dimension (Amerigo will be motivated to circumscribe his actions toward Vito because of his respect for Vito).

In the case of Don Vito, his possession and exercise of power-over (his capability and disposition to affect the outcomes and/or interests of subordinates by controlling or limiting the alternative choices or actions available to them) within the imperatives of the honor code that partially defines his subcommunity grounds his entitlement to respect. He enhances his claim to respect when he recurrently exercises that power efficaciously.

His claim to respect diminishes when his exercise of power-over fails and when he infringes the code by dishonorably submitting to the power of others. Don Vito's claim to respect glistens in proportion to the difficulty of the occasions in which he exercises power-over auspiciously and to the obstacles he overcomes and the challenges he undertakes in service of the honor code.

In nineteenth-century Sicily, possessing land and accumulating wealth were not ends as such. Material prosperity was a mark of honor and a demand for respect, the genuine goals of enterprising Sicilians. Being a landowner and being wealthy liberated a person from the brute struggle to survive and the obligations of everyday labor. On this cultural notion, evidencing one's status as a person worthy of honor and respect required that wealthy landowners distance themselves from the property they possessed. This narrative explains why absentee estate ownership was so prevalent in the areas surrounding Palermo. Moreover, the story also underscores why mafiosi who acquired land could not distance themselves from their holdings. Acquiring their material wealth through extortion and expropriation, mafiosi understood that criminal competitors were eager to initiate strikes against them. Thus, they could not abandon their property to socially signal their preeminence. Instead, mafiosi established their honor and amassed respect through their often violent expropriation and defense of land and wealth.[28] What is significant is that material possession as such in the Sicily of this time is not the ultimate value. As always, honor, respect, and power form the trinity of highest distinctions, the ultimate signifiers of personal worth. Legitimate landowners and criminal usurpers, however, employed different means of staking their claims to those distinctions and emitted different social signals to establish those claims.

The salient conclusion is that Don Vito's value system differs strikingly from the dominant measures of twentieth-century American capitalistic individualism. For Don Vito, amassing wealth is a means, not an end; personal stature arises from honor, respect, and power; and family prerogatives and personal identity grounded in a wider subjectivity than the self are paramount.

The Limitations of Honor

By embodying, exercising, and complying with the imperatives of the honor code, the fictional Don Vito, unlike real gangsters, is a man of principle. He is connected to and is concerned with the interests of his community; he must occasionally, perhaps often, sacrifice his immediate desires to larger purposes; he is prepared to accept the consequences of his actions within a framework of mutual accountability and without lodging unpersuasive justifications or hollow excuses; his connection to the honor code vivifies his sense of self and significantly constitutes his identity; and he must often cooperate with others to facilitate his compliance with the honor code. The honor code itself is internally coherent; and his compliance with and exercise of the honor code are accompanied by emotions such as pride, shame, outrage, affection, and guilt; loyalty is venerated as the highest virtue; and clearly defined occupational roles and hierarchies of authority structure normative guidance. Don Vito explicitly and squeamishly brandishes an extralegal life of adventure, danger, and violence rather than subsist in banal, quiet desperation. The honor code to which he subscribes transforms legal disputes into personal transactions.

Moreover, Don Vito enjoys a network of relationships grounded in the honor code. Depending on a tightly bound complex web of relatives, friends, and loyal acquaintances, Don Vito operates within a system of cooperation, fixed expectations, and recognized standards of excellence. Although his honor code marginalizes the practical currency of individual conscience, Don Vito's life sparkles with meaning and significance.

Yet such a life is neither moral nor ultimately defensible. Don Vito does not recognize all other human beings or sentient beings as equal subjects of experience whose interests must be considered. His tribalism draws bright-lines between those whose interests must be calculated when determining actions and the much wider throng of human beings viewed as irrelevant or as obstructions to be overwhelmed in attaining the Don's ends. Being a person of principle, such as Don Vito, is necessary but not sufficient for being moral. That the Don's honor code is internally coherent and that he fulfills its imperatives consistently and assiduously are not enough to establish the code's or the Don's moral credentials. The extreme partiality of the code and its vigorous resort to disproportionate responses disqualify it from moral imprimatur.

The honor code brought to the United States by Don Vito and his compatriots emerged from a Sicilian culture that lacked the communal enterprise, social and economic institutions, educational influence, and civic virtue to mollify the oppression of centuries of foreign domination; that struggled with unreliable religious influence and capricious administration of law; that distrusted police and other governing authorities; and that was bereft of wide mutuality among citizens and firm allegiance to federalism. For example, the bedrock conviction of the principle of *omertà* is that legal and civic disputes are better resolved by personal, private interventions. Vigilantism grounded in vendetta was socially ratified. In the absence of appropriate civic education to offset extant customs, culture, and institutional distrust, prospects for significant change in the old world expired.

Complying with the imperative of *omertà* and resolving disputes extralegally glistened with social currency in nineteenth-century Sicily. Responding to perceived insults was obligatory in defense of personal dignity, honor, and preservation of self-respect. To resort to state intervention or legal authorities was an admission of fecklessness and impotency. In effect, the person who solicited police intercession in such affairs of honor publicly divulged impuissance and invited future assaults.[29] This cultural canon of manliness also reflected and sustained the Mafia's wider hegemony in clandestine dispute resolution. The honor code mandates retaliating against a *sfregio* (gash or defacement)—literally a wound or disfigurement, but the broader Mafia usage connotes a calculated personal insult designed to inflict profound humiliation, manifest disrespect, and injure reputation.[30]

In the words of Raimondo Catanzaro:

> A husband who does not react when his wife is seduced becomes an object of contempt and mockery. A man who is unable to respond with violence to *sfregi* (insults) he has suffered will forever be the objects of such insults. A man who reports an injury he has suffered to the judicial authority and the police is regarded as a spy and a traitor.[31]

Moreover, in the Sicily of this day, the security and flourishing of a person's family depended on the patriarch's standing. To be respected as a man able to retaliate against offenses perpetrated against the family, to subvert an enemy's reputation and material well-being, was to assert and reinforce one's own power and claim to deference from others.[32] Luigi Barzini observes that

> [The honor code] was particularly useful in Sicily, where the distances were vast, the roads few, the public institutions practically non-existent, the police and courts impotent, all governments discredited as having been for a long time instruments

of foreign oppression, and a man had to look out for himself. He could expect aid only from his relatives. The family was the source of his strength. His duty was to protect it, make it prosper, enlarge it by producing vigorous male children, widen its sphere of influence by allying it to other families, and cultivating influential friends.[33]

Of course, the imperatives of defending and avenging oneself only through one's own power and those of intimate allies, undermines salutary government, impedes the functioning of law enforcement, spurns the rule of law, and forestalls the remediation of corrupt elements in the state.[34] The cycle of private reprisal and public distrust was deep, dark, and dense.

Don Vito's honor code and the values it embodies directly affect their subscribers' self-esteem. Although the excellence that Don Vito possesses and exercises within and pursuant to that code is objective, evaluators must accurately perceive and assess that excellence and bestow upon Don Vito what he has earned. As such, recognition of Don Vito's distinctive dispositions and merits is vulnerable to the misperceptions and faulty judgments of others. As the excellence at issue is Don Vito's capability of possessing and exercising power-over within the imperatives of the honor code, his self-esteem is conditioned on maintaining a favorable power differential; his standing is recurrently dependent on preserving his relative power advantage. Should competing crime families become stronger or acquire more daunting allies or uncontrollable and unfavorable fortune beset the Don, his power superiority may evaporate, and his self-esteem will wither. The point is that Don Vito's self-value is grounded entirely in extrinsic considerations, circumstances, and advantages, not in his intrinsic value. As the cliché attests, when a person is convinced that in the world as presently constructed a person is either a hammer or a nail, and that person envisages himself or herself as a hammer, countless situations and other human beings are regarded as nails. A consequence of his general zero-sum game perception of and approach to life, Don Vito must oscillate between the euphoria of victories over formidable rivals ("the most excellent hammer prevails") and the despondency of defeats in the face of unforeseeable misfortune or overwhelming enemies ("even the most excellent of human beings must fail in the end").

The comportment of Don Vito—his disdain of narcotics, puritanical sentiments regarding sexual relations, veneration of family values, and dignified temperament—along with Michael's calamitous investiture into the family business, a consequence of unfavorable circumstances and his love for his father, seemingly elevate the Corleone family above the vile criminals with whom they joust: "Criminal acts, including murder, can be interpreted in the story line as necessary expedients to enable early Italian immigrants and their descendants to obtain a measure of equal justice, financial success, and dignity in a hostile American culture and environment."[35]

This interpretation caresses a scintilla of truth and magnifies it into a glob of confusion. Don Vito's business is grounded in extortion, labor racketeering, loan sharking, illicit gambling, physical mayhem, corruption of public officials, and murder. The overwhelming number of Italian Americans made better lives for themselves, their children, and grandchildren without resort to criminality rationalized by ethnic disadvantage. Michael was lured into malefaction only because he inherited and amplified the sins of his father. Yes, Michael's biographical arc oozes with tragedy; we can imagine a more glorious existence for him but for Sollozzo's deranged avidity for harming Don Vito and Santino Corleone's response to Sollozzo's initiatives; still, Michael crafted his soul and carved his destiny from a context shaped largely by his father's systematic maleficence and his own unwillingness to transcend the cycle of violence. At most, the Corleone crime family is different only by degree but not in kind from the Barzini and Tattaglia *cosche*. At bottom, none of these criminal syndicates represents the necessary or typical Italian American experience.

Denying the equal moral standing of others, relating to them in that impoverished spirit, and subscribing to a nineteenth-century Sicilian honor code exacts a distinctive cost: Don Vito is more dependent on external events than one might first suppose, and his self-esteem remains hostage to those events, as well as the perceptions, evaluations, and actions of others. An ancient Italian adage advises *chi fonda in sul populo fonda in sul fango* ("He who builds on the people builds on mud"). Perhaps he who rests self-esteem on establishing and preserving power advantages and on dominating others, instead of recognizing their equal standing, builds a life on sludge. At his core and despite his understated glamor, the fictional Don Vito is a stone-cold racketeer preying upon his fellow citizens.

It is in this spirit that we should examine and evaluate the honor code to which Don Vito subscribed within the context of the Sicilian family order. The family order is the critical cultural institution that accompanied these immigrants to America. The family both fostered self-worth and sustained devotion, while hampering energetic assimilation into the new world. To the Sicilian family we must now turn.

Chapter Two

The Sicilian Family Order

This chapter introduces and analyzes a critical human psychological and existential challenge: our relationship to others. We at once crave robust individuality and loving associations, two often incompatible aspirations. Much of our lives focuses on carefully navigating between these yearnings. The nineteenth-century Sicilian response was *la via vecchia*, the old way, and *l'ordine della famiglia*, the family order, which prescribed proper relations and a hierarchy of duties rooted in degrees of intimacy arising from biological connections and contractual loyalties. As always, under *l'ordine della famiglia* the values of honor, respect, and power are indispensable for crafting meaningful human lives. After philosophically analyzing the concept of a meaningful human life, the chapter explains the patriarchal ideal of the *uomo di pazienza*, the patient man, defined by meticulously designed attributes and actions. Approximating this ideal was required for worldly and tribal success in Sicily. After examining and evaluating the nineteenth-century Sicilian social ethos, which, among other things, distinguished mafia as a cultural accolade from Mafia as an organized crime syndicate, the chapter explores the historical roots of Mario Puzo's creation of Don Vito Corleone, as well as the connection between the Sicilian social ethos and the rise of the Mafia there.

Leading a Meaningful Human Life

Throughout history, many writers have argued that internal tension is at the heart of human experience: our yearning for intimate connection with others and the recognition that others are necessary for our identity and freedom coalesce uneasily with the fear and anxiety we experience as others approach.[1] We simultaneously long for emotional attachment yet are horrified that our individuality may evaporate once we achieve it. If we experience too much individuality and a deficient measure of community, we risk alienation, estrangement, and psychological isolation. If we experience insufficient individuality and an inordinate amount of community, we court emotional suffocation, loss of self-esteem, and unhealthy immersion in the collectivity.

This disharmony may never be fully reconciled once and forever, and so we find ourselves making uneasy compromises and adjustments during our life's journey as we oscillate along the continuum whose endpoints are "radical individuality" and "thorough immersion in community," respectively. This internal tension replicates itself at numerous levels: the individual confronts family, the family confronts wider community, communities confront society, society confronts the state, and the state encounters the international community.

The individual confronts others, of varying numbers and powers, at many different levels. As we meet others at institutional and not merely personal levels, the stakes rise in some respects. Our need to retain individual freedom and resist coercion intensifies when our relations are impersonal, where we experience less direct control over our destiny, and when entrenched bureaucracies seem ready and able to usurp our autonomy. Our dilemmas deepen as we choose and mold the appropriate forums in which to live out the human drama of individualism versus community. The aggravated dangers accompanying societal and state levels recommend strategies to moderate the perceived threats and amplify the potential benefits. As ever, our sense of possibility will be a major player in our solutions. Circumscribed by socioeconomic reality, the relentless socializing of the established order, and the inherent inertia of the masses, our sense of possibility resists extinction and thereby celebrates the human craving for going beyond our current context.

The notion of honor underscores the importance of our yearning for community and healthy attachment to institutional roles. Whereas philosophical movements such as existentialism and libertarianism extol the human need for freedom and transcendence, honor groups provide balance by highlighting communal values. Reaching an accommodation within our conflicts between individualism and community is critical for human well-being. An appropriate appreciation for honor can aid that accommodation.

The fictional Don Vito Corleone transports a nineteenth-century cultural mindset from Sicily to America. Part of that ethos was directed at narrowing the boundaries of community and locating salutary individualism only within those confines. In sum, the nineteenth-century Sicilian response to living a meaningful human life under the challenges of the individual-community conundrum was *la via vecchia* and *l'ordine della famiglia*, leavened by the patriarchal ideal of the *uomo di pazienza*. For Sicilians, living a meaningful human life was possible only within the shadow of the values of honor, respect, and personal and familial power.

In the mid–twentieth century, Luigi Barzini identified the heroic aura sheathing that ethos.

> The Sicilians' best virtues . . . are obviously not those of the anonymous organization man of today, but those of the ancient hero fighting, with his little group, the rest of the world . . . the Sicilian can reach unbelievable heights of fortitude, generosity, selflessness, and fearlessness. He can even accept death with open eyes or deal death impassively, without hesitation or regret, whenever he thinks there is nothing else to do, in defense of his particular, strictly Sicilian ideals.[2]

In my view, a sense of honor and a connection to an honor code facilitate robustly meaningful, valuable lives. In that vein, I offer the following analysis:[3] A human being is leading (at least) a *minimally meaningful* life if and only if

1. that person has and participates in a network of (or a single, overriding) interests, projects, purposes, and commitments that flow from or are adopted freely by that person; and

2. these interests, projects, purposes, and commitments fuel the person's connection to, zest for, and faith in life (active engagement or positive visceral response); and

3. these interests, projects, purposes, and commitments block claims that the person's life is not worth living—that it is less than a human life (they demonstrate that the person retains or has potential for leading an autobiographical life); and

4. these interests, projects, purposes, and commitments are not based on radically false beliefs—they are connected to reality.

The notion of a meaningful human life is an interpretive concept. We are not merely applying a fixed idea to specific situations and drawing conclusions. Instead, when we invoke "meaningful human life" we are arguing for a specific interpretation, a rendering that is persuasive yet contestable. I arrive at my view of a (minimally) meaningful human life, by considering a life that many would agree is not worth living and might well be better off ended. A life that is biologically extant but autobiographically bankrupt.

Given this structure, I ask what lives are not worth living because they are utterly meaningless and without potential for positive change? Such lives might well be candidates for voluntary euthanasia based on the person's prior stated desires or proxy conferred on loving family members or associates. The obvious candidates are those human beings locked in an irreversible coma; elderly human beings who suffer in the final stages of dementia; perhaps those enduring excruciating, unreliable pain who are unable to pursue any tangible interests, projects, or purposes. In short, human beings who are not capable or no longer capable, and in the best medical judgment will never be capable, of an autobiographical life. Those people whose agency has been extinguished by the cruelties inflicted by age or disease. (Note: I am not arguing for or against the moral permissibility of voluntary euthanasia here. I am, instead, trying to isolate what can reasonably be viewed as human lives not worth living.)

In my view, lives that are not worth living in that they no longer can embody and exercise agency are meaningless. While they may nevertheless offer meaningful projects for others—caretakers, loved ones, and friends who rally around the situation—the lives of such human beings are not themselves meaningful and are not worth living as such. Thus, in my judgment, a (weak) necessary condition of a meaningful human existence is the present or potential capability for embodying an autobiographical life, which blocks as unjustified any claim that the life at issue is unworthy of continuing or amounts to a life not worth living as such. (Of course, if one believes in capital punishment a miscreant's exercise of agency may lead to justifiably ending that life as punishment.) The lack of such current or future possibility for exercising agency is sufficient for concluding that that life lacks worth and meaning as such (whether the life should in fact be ended is a further question).

Although I do not require that an agent's projects, interests, purposes, and commitments gleam with objective value, I do reference epistemological and metaphysical objectivity: an agent's meaning in life must not arise from convictions and beliefs so radically mistaken that they sever the person from reality, and the network of meaningful pursuits must arise from or be adopted freely by that person. My rendering of meaning in life, then, requires a positive visceral response grounded in reality, arising from volition, and realized through agency. The relationship between an agent and her projects, understood broadly, presupposes an active engagement and affirmation that vivifies the person, who has freely created or accepted and now promotes and nurtures the projects of her more intense concerns.

Meaning in human life does not require that an agent's creations and attainments endure permanently; or that agents accomplish their paramount goals; or manifest grand creativity and originality; or embody overall happiness (understood as a predominately positive state of mind) or a balance of pleasure over pain; or commit to inherent cosmic meaningfulness. Also, establishing a fixed maximum or minimum percentage of human beings who must or may live meaningful lives is imprudent and unwarranted.

Meaning in life, then, is one of a passel of vectors relevant to evaluating human lives. A fruitful examination of the relative importance of meaning to other (typically overlapping but distinct) evaluative dimensions such as moral rectitude, general health, happiness, social impact, creativity, self-realization, bequeathing a legacy, maintaining a robust network of personal relationships, and the rest, must extend far beyond this work.

A human life is robustly meaningful when that person's network of interests, projects, purposes, and commitments, grounded in reality, are more complex, offer wider possibilities, and nourish the person's affirmative attitude toward and visceral connection to life more intensely, thereby enhancing the person's autobiographical life. A human life is valuable when it is robustly meaningful, significant regarding its worldly impact, and bound to moral values.[4]

Throughout this work, I will occasionally refer to biological, biographical, and autobiographical lives. Our biological life is measured from our birth to our death, our earthly existence. The idea of biographical life revolves around human life as a narrative, a story. We are a series of stories in that we understand and identify ourselves through a sequence of events, choices, actions, thoughts, and relationships. Our biographical lives, including value and meaning connected to our death and events thereafter, extend beyond our biological lives (and, more contestably, may precede our biological lives). In general, a person's biographical life consists of a sequence of events or set of facts in which the person is a subject. These events include, among other things, states of affairs in which the person has interests but may not experience. Our autobiographical life encompasses the span of our human agency, our participation in crafting our biographical life.

For example, Niccolò Machiavelli's *biological* life began in 1469 and ended in 1527. The *autobiographical* life of Machiavelli—as measured by his exercises of freedom, his choices, and deeds—began sometime after or during 1469 when he developed requisite human agency and perished in 1527. The *biographical* life of Machiavelli began at least by 1469, perhaps earlier, and continues to this day and beyond. A person in an irreversible coma retains a biological life and a biographical life as his or her story continues but lacks an autobiographical life—lacking all significant cognitive capabilities, the person lacks human agency and can no longer participate in writing his or her life story—even though the person's biological and biographical lives continue. In most cases, our biographical lives continue beyond our biological lives, but our autobiographical lives can vanish earlier than our biological lives in those cases where human agency vanishes although our earthly lives continue.[5]

By providing a set of nonnegotiable principles, a subculture of subscribers, imperatives of evaluation and redress for behavioral failures, criteria structuring personal identity and self-worth, and goals toward which to strive, an honor code anchors a person to a network of interests, projects, purposes, and commitments connected to reality that constitute that person's active engagement with and positive visceral response to life. On my rendering, such a life will be meaningful and perhaps significant even when it falls short of moral rectitude.[6] To be a valuable life, however, moral propriety is required.

Accordingly, critical questions center on the type of values and virtues that should capture the meaning of "honor" and the appropriate imperatives that should define a beneficial honor code. *The Godfather* highlights the paradoxes of honor and the individual-community continuum within the nineteenth-century Sicilian *la via vecchia* (the old way), *l'ordine della famiglia* (the family order), and the male ideal of the *uomo di pazienza* (man of patience).

L'ordine della Famiglia

> A man who doesn't spend time with his family can never be a real man.
>
> —Don Vito Corleone to Sonny

Personal relationships in *The Godfather* reflect cultural understandings prevalent in the old world. The disenfranchised sons and daughters of the *Mezzogiorno*[7] brought to the Americas an unwritten but deeply ingrained system of conventions, *l'ordine della famiglia*, prescribing their relations within and responsibilities to their family, and appropriate conduct toward those outside the family. *L'ordine della famiglia*, nowhere more profoundly entrenched than in Sicily, apportioned the world into four morally significant spheres of social intimacy: *famiglia, comparaggio, amici di cappello,* and *stranieri*.[8]

Unsurprisingly, *la famiglia* is the social group of paramount value. The family consisted not only of immediate members (the nuclear family) but also of relatives often extended to the third or fourth degrees. The exact degree of kinship determined reciprocal duties and privileges. Principles of proportionality guided these relationships of blood: the closer the genetic connection, the greater the duties owed and the more solicitudes expected. The welfare of the family, taken in this extended sense, was the primary responsibility of each of its members.[9] The presumption was blood as the ballast of community.

The next degree of intimacy was embodied in the system of *comparaggio* that, among other things, served as a limited check and balance over family policies and practices. This sphere can be subdivided into *compare* and *commare*, and *padrini* and *madrine*. The former duo were literally "coparents," typically one's peers and intimate friends, and often the godparents to one's children. New parents did not choose godparents lightly. To offer a friend this role was an immense compliment; to refuse the offer was a burning insult likely to alter drastically the relationship between the parties. Godparents became, then, indispensable ancillary family members.

For example, in Sicily, baptism not only cleanses infants from original sin, substantiates faith, and welcomes a new member of the church, it also inaugurates a new godfather (*compare*) and godmother (*commare*) into the family. Understood in terms of *l'ordine della famiglia*, the co-fathers and co-mothers are obligated, among other things, to fulfill all reasonable requests from their cohort.[10] Thus understood, the relationship between Carmela Corleone and the spouse and the daughter of Amerigo Bonasera gains clarity. That Bonasera has eschewed all contact with Don Vito Corleone divulges a significant breach of the protocol of *comparaggio*. John Dickie notes:

> The institution known as [*comparaggio*] was a kind of social glue; it extended the family bond further into society, encouraging peace and cooperation. Two men at daggers drawn might decide to bury their differences and become *compari* in order to avoid a violent dispute that would only harm both of their families. A laborer might enlist a more influential man as the godfather of his child, offering him deference and loyalty in the hope of favors in return.[11]

Padrini and *madrine*, by contrast, were venerated elders prized for their demonstrated wisdom, prestige, or power. These positions were earned by demonstrated talents, effective service, and merited status. Strikingly, the system of *comparaggio* admitted few vicissitudes: intimate friendships were permanent. Marginal adjustments could be negotiated between the parties, but their intentions to rescind their relationship, even if reciprocal, could not sever what were taken to be enduring bonds. Such relationships were constitutive of personal identity and thus not easily discarded.

This second sphere of *l'ordine della famiglia* expanded for those engaged in business, whether legally or illegally, or those requiring an extended social network for other purposes. Reminiscent of the ancient Roman structures of *amicitia* and *clientele*,[12] systems of friendships and patronages that fostered mutual advantage, Sicilians recognized non-genetic alliances for reciprocal benefits. These associations neither implied nor precluded significant emotional attachments. Within this domain, the term "friend" lacked the warm psychological connotations and expression of intimacy accompanying that term within the system of *comparaggio* proper. To be a friend on this level implies only a firm pledge of loyalty. Furthermore, relationships grounded in *amicitia* and *clientele* were neither inalienable nor incorrigible. The tests of loyalty and mutually beneficial quid pro quo exchanges were ongoing tests of these continuing associations.

The third sphere of concern involved *amici di cappello* (those to whom one tips one's hat): polite acquaintances who remained outside the scope of intimacy. Here arm's-length cordiality prevailed. The parties recognized each other but were under no mutual obligations. More important, those within this circle acknowledged the absence of adversarial tension.

The final, and by far the largest, group is composed of *stranieri* (strangers), everyone, whether known or unknown, who fell outside the three other classes. Among known strangers, some could bear malicious intentions, others benign indifference, and still others might seek closer relationships under appropriate circumstances.[13] Today's stranger might well become tomorrow's loyal associate or despised enemy depending on the turn of events.

This sense of family was not experienced merely as an impersonal network serving self-interest. Instead, it was felt as constituting a wider subjectivity: one's identity was related directly to social context. For a Sicilian of this time period, to be without family was to be *un nuddu miscatu cu nenti* (a nobody mixed with nothing). Under *l'ordine della famiglia*, a person experienced his or her well-being as part of a larger organic entity—as part of a family in the wider sense sketched above. Sicilian peasants had no opportunity to extend their horizons by interacting significantly with those of different backgrounds and outlooks.[14] Lacking the means to communicate with and observe the world outside their village, residents of the entire *Mezzogiorno* lacked the correlated opportunity to develop a more cosmopolitan moral vantage point.

Barzini observed:

> The family extracts everybody's first loyalty. It must be defended, enriched, made powerful, respected, and feared by the use of whatever means are necessary, legitimate means, if at all possible, or illegitimate. Nobody should defy it with impunity. Its honor must not be tarnished. All wrongs done to it must be avenged. All enemies must be kept at bay and the dangerous ones deprived of power or destroyed. Every member is duty-bound to do all he can for its welfare, give his property if needed, and, sometimes, when it is absolutely inevitable, sacrifice his life. . . . The strength of the family is determined by many factors—wealth, connections, alliances, prestige, rank, luck—but, above all, by its inner cohesion and ramifications.[15]

Local and regional governments had been archaic, corrupt, and distant from the problems of the *contadini* (peasants). Under such circumstances, self-reliance and smaller group affiliation instinctively replace allegiance to official authorities. More strikingly, there was great hostility, founded on experience, toward wider institutions: *la legge va contrai cristiani* ("the law works against the people").[16] The context is, however, more nuanced. Although it is tempting to idealize *l'ordine della famiglia* as a bastion of personal virtue in an otherwise heartless atmosphere, such sentimentality obscures part of the picture. It is inaccurate to view the family code as a reaction to the separate and larger social atmosphere; in fact, the family code was partly constitutive of the wider social arena.

The Sicilian family underscored the individual's connection to communal values and existential meaning beyond the preservation of the self. Providing solace after disappointments and failures, and supplying support and collaboration for paramount projects, the family was the foundational institution in Italy against which all other social structures were measured. Larger cultural institutions such as government, law, and police functioned well only if their operations were compatible with family prerogatives. The Sicilian family, then, was at once the cement ordering society and the primary obstacle stymieing the ripening of independent, vigorous political institutions.[17]

The family code hampered national and world identifications at the same time it nurtured the extended subjectivity of the family unit; while it posed an obstacle to civic virtue, it conferred strict understandings and a workable moral system for family members; as it mocked genuine nationalism and the social welfare, it sanctified family loyalty as true patriotism; while in times of war the code produced soldiers who were sometimes only minimally committed to the national cause, it generated people who, at their best, in peacetime would endure draconian sacrifices and unspeakable dangers for the sake of their immediate and extended families. In this fashion, through narrowly circumscribed spheres of concern, carefully understood burdens and privileges, and assiduously cultivated self-identities, *l'ordine della famiglia* both promoted and repressed the cardinal moral virtues.

L'ordine della famiglia was at once simple and complex, protective yet isolating, humanistic but distrustful. Its simplicity is apparent in the clear-cut demarcations among people: one is either part of the family, an intimate friend, a loyal ally, a polite acquaintance, or a stranger. Little nuance or ambiguity was recognized. The code was clearly protective in that it created, at least in theory, an intimate shield, a zone of security, against the oppressive economic and social structure of the *Mezzogiorno*.

But the isolating and parochial implications of the code were equally stark: *stranieri* were neither to be trusted nor consulted; *amici di cappello* were to be regarded at a distance with cool politeness. Not only was there no concept of an international brotherhood and sisterhood, there was little appreciation of those outside one's village. Yet the code reflected a deep humanism, often demanding strenuous sharing and contributions to joint interests within one's circle of intimates. Such parochialism, however, simultaneously deepened and legitimized existing cynicism toward outsiders: "In the outside world, amidst the chaos and the disorder of society, [Italians] often feel compelled to employ the wiles of underground fighters in enemy-occupied territory. All official and legal authority is considered hostile by them until proved friendly or harmless: if it cannot, it should be neutralized or deceived if need be."[18]

Accordingly, to portray this situation one-dimensionally is dangerously easy: innocent, noble peasants at the mercy of avaricious, unfeeling local land barons and exploitive northern politicians. In fact, much of the problem involved the deeply entrenched social system in the *Mezzogiorno*, a system in which common people were thoroughly implicated. As with most social situations, the characters in the drama of *Mezzogiorno* cannot accurately be clothed definitionally in either white or black hats.

The moral irony of *l'ordine della famiglia*—its simultaneous promotion in the family and repression on other social levels of the cardinal virtues—is accompanied by a psychological irony: on the one hand, the code provided spiritual sustenance and the foundations of personal identity in an otherwise hostile world; on the other hand, the code facilitated lingering dependencies and helped ensure that the outside world remained hostile.

Don Vito applies the fundamental understandings of *l'ordine della famiglia* when crafting his crime syndicate. The highest values of the Sicilian family order were the mustering and exercise of power, honor, and respect. The accumulation of wealth was often a means to attaining these ends. The element of organized crime pollutes these values and means with evil. Money and influence are, then, means to higher ends: family security, perhaps preeminence, and social standing grounded in successfully embracing and fulfilling the recognized code of honor. This in part accounts for why Don Vito's home and belongings are unostentatious rather than glitzy. The ultimate prizes to which he aspires are internal fulfillment and increased familial opportunities arising from his possession and exercise of excellences underwritten by a code of honor, not elegant chandeliers and precious china.

The Ideal of the *Uomo di Pazienza*

Don Vito harbors no illusion that his nineteenth-century Sicilian descriptive and prescriptive vision is compatible with twentieth-century American culture. He accepts rationally that his children will be better served in the new world by becoming the *pezzonovanti* whose disproportionate influence in setting the terms of social life he otherwise repudiates. Much like contemporary Americans who sneer contemptuously at the overly privileged one percent, but who burst with pride if one of their offspring enters that circle, Don Vito bristles at the pretension and corruption of the commercial and political *pezzonovanti* in America, yet he aspires for his children to rise to their ranks. He does so without allegiance to social justice and radical cultural transformation, which he deems utopian, but from the vantage point of zero-sum understandings (human beings are either hammers or nails) and increasing generational opportunities. What was denied Don Vito given his educational and geographical deficiencies is available to his American children in no small measure because of his industry and indefatigability, employed criminally.

Puzo crafts the character of Don Vito Corleone in the tradition of the *uomo di pazienza*, a man of patience who conceals his inner thoughts, bides his time, refrains from expressing anger, who much like a crafty poker player seeks a competitive edge while retaining a surface amiability. As Richard Gambino attests:

> In the old value scheme of Southern Italy, the ideal of manliness did include non co-operation with authorities and silence in the face of inquiries by *stranieri*, especially official inquiries. In a land where outsiders and authorities were for centuries synonymous with spoliation, exploitation, and oppression, the code of silence was necessary, sane, moral and wise . . . a man strove to be an *uomo di pazienza*—a man of patience in a special sense of the term. . . . This includes a man's cultivation and control of his own capacities and special skills—self-reliance and self-control . . . The ideal of *pazienza* is an ideal of control of life . . . an ideal of inner control, of reserve.[19]

Numerous actions and sayings that Mario Puzo assigns to Don Vito illustrate the understandings of the ideal of the *uomo di pazienza*. For example,

On the primacy of family: "A man who is not a father to his children can never be a real man."[20]

On the importance of friendships grounded in loyalty: "Friendship is everything. Friendship is more than talent. It is more than the government. It is almost the equal of family."[21]

On the need to act decisively but only in the proper moment: "Revenge is a dish that tastes best when it is cold."[22]

On the need to conceal inner thoughts: "Never let anyone know what you are thinking . . . Never get angry. . . . Never make a threat. . . . Reason with people."[23]

On the demand for respect: "We are all men who have refused to be fools, who have refused to be puppets dancing on a string pulled by the men on high . . . we are not responsible to the *pezzonovanti* who take it upon themselves to decide what we shall do with our lives."[24]

On the wisdom of calculation and restraint: "There are men in this world who go about demanding to be killed. . . . They quarrel in gambling games, they jump out of their automobiles in a rage [at the slightest provocation] . . . they humiliate and bully people whose capabilities they do not know."[25]

Michael on his father's purposes: "He doesn't accept the rules of the society we live in because those rules would have condemned him to a life not suitable to a man like himself, a man of extraordinary force and character . . . his ultimate aim is to enter that society with a certain power, since society doesn't really protect its members who do not have their own individual power."[26]

Puzo describing Don Vito's self-control: "The Don considered a use of threats the most foolish kind of exposure; the unleashing of anger without forethought as the most dangerous indulgence. No one had ever heard the Don utter a naked threat, no one had ever seen him in an uncontrollable rage. It was unthinkable."[27]

Puzo explaining Don Vito's calculated, delayed response: "[Don Vito] had long ago learned that society imposes insults that must be borne, comforted by the knowledge that in this world there comes a time when the most humble of men, if he keeps his eyes open, can take his revenge on the most powerful. It was this knowledge that prevented the Don from losing the humility all his friends admired in him."[28]

Puzo summarizing the principle of *omertà*: "Faced with the savagery of this absolute power [of foreign exploiters, land barons, the hierarchy of the Church, and their instruments of enforcement, the police], the suffering people [of Sicily] learned never to betray their anger and their hatred for fear of being crushed. They learned never to make themselves vulnerable by uttering any sort of threat since giving such a warning insured a quick reprisal . . . *Omerta* became the religion of the people."[29]

Puzo describing Don Vito's reasonableness: "He never uttered a threat. He always used logic that proved to be irresistible. He always made certain that the other fellow got his share of profit. . . . Like many businessmen of genius he learned that free competition was wasteful, monopoly efficient."[30]

Puzo chronicling Don Vito's methods: "He consolidated this power with a far-seeing statesmanlike intelligence; by helping brilliant boys from poor Italian families through college, boys who would later become lawyers, assistant district attorneys, and even judges. He planned for the future of his empire with all the foresight of a great national leader."[31]

One might speculate that Mario Puzo carefully researched the ideal of manliness in the *Mezzogiorno* and scripted Don Vito as its fictional exemplar in the context of criminality. Gambino adds that in nineteenth-century Southern Italy,

> One is taught to reserve his resources . . . to wait and plan for the moment when he may express his stronger emotions and expend his most pressing energies. . . . The code of reserve, of patience, of waiting for the moment, of planning for the event, and then of decisive, impassioned action, serves life. It was the manly way of life in the *Mezzogiorno* because it well served the conditions of life there, whereas impetuous, ill-controlled behavior meant disaster.[32]

Santino Corleone, indulging his emotions without reflection, was cascading toward tragedy. Frederico Corleone lacked the guile, self-understanding, and inner strength to attain the ideal. Despite his intellectual gifts, personal integrity, and firm loyalty, Tom Hagen was not a war-time *consigliere*. He was gulled into complacency when the enemies of the Corleone family decelerated their bellicosity and his misplaced sense of security was a causal factor in the massacre of Santino. Even he recognized his shortcomings as a martial counselor, especially when compared to the sparkling generalship of Genco Abbandando. At bottom, Hagen's deficiencies arose from the reality that, the education he absorbed from Don Vito notwithstanding, he was not a Sicilian in the requisite sense: he was unable or unwilling to risk everything on a matter of principle or in service of an imperative of honor or for the satisfaction of revenge.[33]

Michael Corleone twinkled with many of his father's excellences: personal charisma, understated force and intelligence, undeniable leadership capabilities. But he would ultimately, perhaps because of his American context, degenerate into a coldness and estrangement so debilitating that it would frighten him into desperately and futilely pursuing personal redemption. At the end, Michael was alienated from himself as his self-examinations unfavorably measured the person he had become against the person he had once imagined himself to be. Whereas Don Vito dies whispering, "Life is so beautiful," Michael dies after falling out of a chair as he struggles to put on his spectacles. A dog sniffs about his body, underscoring Michael's estrangement and suggesting the Italian proverb that those who violate the family order, *"fa la morte di un cane"* (will die like a dog). As we journey through the three films, the Sicilian ideal of the *uomo di pazienza* deteriorates into the worst image of American atomistic individualism: the alienated, estranged, isolated, incorrigible, irredeemable soul.

Puzo presents Don Vito as a quasi-divinity whom his offspring yearn to emulate. Fredo bemoans his failure to be more like his father. Santino beams when Michael accuses him of talking like their father when he assails his younger brother for joining the Marines and risking his life for strangers. Constanzia reconciles with Michael at their mother's wake when she recognizes that Michael's motivations for actions replicate their father's: protect the family and ensure its flourishing in a hostile world. Once he takes command of the family, Michael is schooled by his father on the intricacies of leadership. Later, when he senses that he is losing his family, Michael beseeches his mother: "What did Papa think deep in his heart?" Tom Hagen, never formally adopted but reared by the Corleones, benefited from Don Vito's instructions on nineteenth-century Sicilian thinking and tradition. He rises to family *consigliere* only because he absorbed his lessons well. Don Vito does not merely preside over his family, he structures tribal understandings during his life and his influence persists well beyond his death.

As Michael Corleone intones, "I do renounce Satan" at his nephew's baptism, his hit men are murdering family enemies. Puzo and Coppola underscore the uncomfortable union of religious piety and criminal mayhem. They obliterate the romance of organized crime at the conclusion of *The Godfather*: Michael lies to his wife about the murder of Carlo Rizzi;

he dismisses his sister perfunctorily; he sequesters himself with his most trusted criminal confederates; and his legitimacy has evaporated while his criminal power escalates. Michael has fallen from grace, embracing Satan while verbally denouncing him at his nephew's baptism.

Still, the benevolent aura of Don Vito lingers. Don Vito, the exemplar of the ideal of the honorable *uomo di pazienza*, the paternalistic mender of injustice, the strait-laced family man, and benefactor to all those who pledge loyalty, hovers as a spiritual reminder of founding principles and values. What fades away is the reality that Michael's vengeance is executed in Don Vito's name and according to Don Vito's intrigues. Don Vito has sworn to keep the peace, thereby relinquishing a measure of honor and power, but during the remainder of his life he instructed Michael on the most effective ways to exact the revenge he had foresworn.

Understood as a fable spun from Puzo's undoubtedly romanticized, distorted conviction that nineteenth-century Sicilian crime leaders were or could be the highest exemplars of the ideal of the *uomo di pazienza*, the novel and three films imagine the zenith of that ideal in twentieth-century America and its inevitable transformation and collapse when impugned by changing social and cultural conditions.

The unsympathetic or unsuccessful male figures in *The Godfather* either stray radically from the ideal of the *uomo di pazienza* or shamefully contravene the imperatives of the code of honor. Don Fanucci is a glitzy, arrogant, blowhard who casts an illusion of power without cultivating its substance. Moe Greene angers easily and overestimates his capabilities. Jack Woltz is an accomplished businessman with political connections, but also a serial pedophile and an unrepentant bully. Santino Corleone manifests several excellences in accord with the honor code. He is a strong, courageous, generous, great-hearted protector of the community defining his sphere of influence. A young Sonny pulls Tom Hagen off the streets and urges the Corleone family to shelter and raise him. Later, during inter-family hostilities, Sonny is a merciless, ruthless, effective urbane warrior. But Santino labors under two fatal shortcomings: he can neither control his passions nor conceal his thoughts. His judgment is erratic, he is quick-tempered, and he will not subjugate his aggressive pride to family prerogatives. Fredo Corleone lacks the required inner strength and calculating intelligence to attain the manly ideal or keenly grasp the imperatives of the code of honor. Portrayed as a bumbling simpleton in the films, Puzo sketches Fredo with more nuance in the novel. There he is burly, reasonably tough, dutiful, and loyal, but lacking charisma and bereft of leadership capabilities. Carlo Rizzi is dishonorable to his core, a cheap hustler and opportunist who left to his own devices could aspire to little more than operating as a barroom Romeo. Rizzi also assaults his wife, on one occasion as a contrivance to lure Sonny to his death. Like Woltz, Rizzi commits infamies regarding women. Don Vito is invariably strait-laced about sexual matters. Captain McClusky is a hypocrite whose honor is readily purchased by the highest bidder. In *The Godfather*, Don Emilio Barzini and Virgil Sollozzo come closest to the Sicilian ideal of manliness and the imperatives of the honor code, and they unsurprisingly prove to be the Corleone family's most daunting enemies.

Not only does Puzo romanticize and glamorize Don Vito, he also elevates *la via vecchia*, the old way, the Sicilian traditions that vivify the novel and film. Obscuring the daily frauds, acts of violence, and thefts that constitute Don Vito's livelihood, Puzo and Coppola present him as a benevolent patriarch, who because he exemplifies the Sicilian ideal of manliness, presides over his affairs more wisely, effectively, and judiciously than the corrupt governmental, corporate, and political *pezzonovanti* holding sway in our republic. Moreover, Don Vito was not born into white privilege. A child driven out of Sicily by thugs galvanized to kill him; arriving at Ellis Island with no resources, lacking formal education, and suffering from smallpox; consigned to the mean streets of Little Italy in New York City, young Vito Corleone was one of Sicily's contributions to Emma Lazarus's slogan. He was tired, poor, one of the huddled masses yearning to breathe free, nothing more than wretched refuse from Sicily's teeming shore.

As a uniquely American success story, Vito demonstrates that those of iron resolve and boundless audacity can rise to "kingly" stature forthwith—if they practice *la via vecchia*, exemplify the ideal of the *uomo di pazienza*, and remain true to the requisite code of honor. Puzo contrasts the utter rottenness and poverty of mainstream society to the sacred traditions, honor, familial intimacy, and rituals of respect of *la via vecchia*. In so doing, he at once glorifies the old way that collaborated in Sicily's enervation and caricatures America as nothing more than a bastion of hypocrisy and corruption. What is transparent is the utter incompatibility of the nineteenth-century Sicilian ethos and twentieth-century American culture.

As illustrated in Don Vito's reluctance to partake in Virgil Sollozzo's narcotics initiative, organized crime's approach to drug trafficking was and remains ambivalent. As Sonny Corleone and Tom Hagen insist, the potential profits are enormous and deliver remarkable power advantages to practitioners. As Don Vito cautions, however, government officials more vigorously oppose the sale of drugs than they do other illegality, and drug marketers are less likely to be judged leniently. Harsher prison sentences pose a sterner test for allegiance to the principle of *omertà*. Also, even if silence is maintained by incarcerated members of crime families, a greater loss of manpower ensues from convictions for drug trafficking and from operatives who became addicted to their own palliatives. Moreover, public opinion vigorously opposes the sale of dangerously addictive narcotics, and that judgment is loudly and frequently expressed. Unlike the pernicious effects of labor racketeering, gambling, corruption of government officials, loan sharking, and protection enterprises, the lugubrious harvests of drug trafficking are typically stark and unavoidable. Also, some family bosses share the public's antipathy toward drugs. Finally, the drug trade breeds tension between two different clusters of professional criminals: narrowly territorial, family-bracketed racketeers functioning as a shadow government within the confines of their turf; and rapacious, enterprising scoundrels whose business interests and smuggling networks traverse family and national boundaries.[34]

Still, in the calculations of incorrigible miscreants, the sirens of money and power bray while the apostles of caution skulk away. From its earliest glimmers in America, drug trafficking has fueled criminal ambitions. For example, the legendary Salvatore Lucania ("Lucky Luciano") (1897–1962) was arrested for selling heroin to undercover agents in the early 1920s. Although some crime families issued explicit prohibitions against drug trafficking, those imperatives were often ignored by family soldiers and, at most, were unevenly enforced by criminal hierarchies.

Clinging to collective amnesia regarding the details of Don Vito's business, we can reasonably interpret *The Godfather* as nothing less than Mario Puzo's fairy tale of old-world virtues and excellences unsustainable in the new world. Who needs flawed, but powerful ethnic symbols such as Cabrini, DiMaggio, LaGuardia, Marciano, Basilone, and Zamperini after Puzo's mythical portrayal of Don Vito Corleone?

The Historical Roots of Don Vito Corleone

Prior to 1920, extortion rackets orchestrated by Italian Americans were designated as *La Mano Nera*. The Black Hand was a remnant of Sicilian criminality and spawned a simple yet menacing logo. *Unione Siciliana*, once an honorable, mutual aid organization for Italian immigrants to America was infiltrated and corrupted by gangsters. But neither The Black Hand nor the Sicilian Union approached the sophistication and unification of *Cosa Nostra*, ruled by a commission, as it was conceived and refined by Salvatore Maranzano and Lucky Luciano. Luciano's orchestration of the murder of Maranzano in 1931 marks the time when the *Cosa Nostra* in the United States broadens into an Italian American, as contrasted with a strictly Sicilian, syndicate. *Cosa Nostra*, however, was never equivalent to or synonymous with organized crime in America. Each *Cosa Nostra* family in the United States is roughly organized along similar lines: the boss of the family consults with his *consigliere* and his underboss; subordinate to these criminal executives are *caporegimes* (capos) who directly supervise soldiers (made men) and associates.[35]

Speculation as to the criminal models that inspired Puzo's rendering of Don Vito Corleone remains rampant. The two mobsters most frequently mentioned are the raspy-voiced, Italian American Frank Costello (1891–1973), who gained unwelcome notoriety as a witness at the Kefauver senate organized crime hearings in 1950–1951, and Sicilian-American Carlo Gambino (1902–1976), who was secretive and cunning, while nurturing a low public profile.

Costello (born Francesco Castiglia in Calabria, Italy), comfortable interacting with Jewish and Irish mobsters, was known as "King of the Slots" and organized a network of bookmakers that spread and transferred their handle for mutual advantage. Suffering a brief setback when Mayor Fiorella LaGuardia cracked down on illegal gambling in New York City, the resourceful Costello transferred many of his slot machines to New Orleans, a more congenial locale for illicit gaming. Surviving LaGuardia's run as reformist, Costello was a major influence in the politics of the Democratic Party in New York State for decades, running Tammany Hall patronage and political appointments. Occasionally displaying promise as a conceptual analyst, Costello observed that "a racketeer is a fellow who tries to get power, prestige, or money at the expense of entrenched power, prestige, or money."[36]

Also dubbed the "prime minister" because of his reasonableness and abhorrence of gratuitous violence, Costello allegedly acquired more political connections and influence than any other Mafia crime boss. Rejecting the narcotics trade, Costello dealt fairly with his soldiers and associates, and built a host of legitimate businesses, including poultry and meat firms. He retired after enduring a failed assassination attempt, enjoying influential and peaceful golden years, excelling as a gardener while continuing to advise his peers on criminal strategy.

Gambino, despite rising to become the most influential member of *Cosa Nostra*'s central commission after the 1957 Apalachin convention and compiling an arm's-length list of felonious activities, was convicted only of tax evasion early in his career, receiving a suspended sentence. In 1976, Don Carlo died of a heart attack in his bed after watching the New York Yankees win the American League pennant. (His passing spared Don Carlo the agony of observing the Cincinnati Reds sweep the Yankees in four games in the World Series.)

Although the commission did not recognize a *capo di tutti capi* (boss of all bosses), Gambino was the most powerful crime leader of the 1960s to mid-1970s. After ascending to power by orchestrating the murder of Albert "The Mad Hatter" "Lord High Executioner" Anastasia, Don Carlo commanded the largest and most powerful *cosca*. He assiduously avoided indictments, and those that were filed resulted in dismissals or were successfully appealed. Don Carlo was about as flashy as an Amish farmer on the sabbath. Cultivating an undaunting appearance, living abstemiously, and skirting gratuitous violence, Gambino died peacefully. His criminal career was marked by innovation as he engineered infiltration into unions and legitimate business where risks were minimal and financial rewards soared. In the old-world spirit of resolving disputes without resorting to legal processes, Don Carlo gratefully received major kickbacks from companies as payment for ensuring tranquil labor relations and reasonable collective-bargaining agreements.

Gambino reflected the ideal of the *uomo di pazienza*. For example, in 1974, Dominick "Mimi" Scialo, a hardnosed soldier in the Colombo family, was inebriated and, spotting the aged Gambino at an Italian restaurant, publicly insulted and harassed him. Don Carlo maintained his poise and refused to retaliate in kind. Soon thereafter, however, Scialo's corpse was discovered encased in the concrete floor of Otto's Social Club in Brooklyn.

Under Don Carlo's gracious but always self-serving hand, trucking, construction, waterfront, and sanitation unions were firmly controlled. Molding his self-image as the embodiment of the qualities of the lion and the fox, Gambino was never reluctant to exert force when necessary.[37]

Both Costello and Gambino approximated the ideal of the *uomo di pazienza* in that they were long-range strategic thinkers who rarely displayed their emotions publicly; they dressed conservatively and eschewed splashy displays of wealth; yet when the occasion required, they understood how to transmit wider messages through murder.

I must offer, though, two other Sicilians as possible candidates for the mobster who inspired Puzo in creating Don Vito Corleone. Don Vito Cascio Ferro (1862–1943) was the master and innovator of the extortion racket. Prior to 1914, he endured indictments for extortion, arson, and kidnapping, all of which ended in acquittal. He wielded power based on a network of relations extending over two continents. In 1901, he illegally squirmed his way into the United States. Don Vito extolled his methods and philosophy in Palermo and in New York City, where he enjoyed a brief sabbatical with the notorious Morello family in New York City. In 1903, he, Giuseppe "Piddu" Morello (1867–1930), and Giuseppe Fontana belonged to a group of counterfeiters arrested by the legendary detective Giuseppe Petrosino. Suspected of complicity in a murder soon thereafter, Don Vito scampered back to his homeland after taking brief refuge in New Orleans.[38]

At first blush, the protection scam seems uncomplicated. But keenly appreciating the aesthetics of proportion and appropriate measure, Don Vito is credited with abrogating short-time avarice for long-term profit. He reasoned that demanding smaller, affordable amounts over a longer period was preferable to coercing large, unreasonable sums of money that could result in unpayable bills and even bankruptcies. Cascio Ferro's approach inspired the expression, "*Fari vagnari a pizzu*," an extortionist's demand to wet his beak (score a relatively small portion of the victim's take rather than seize the entire swag), an appeal Fanucci levies on young Vito Corleone in Puzo's novel.

Luigi Barzini detailed Cascio Ferro's perceived excellences:

> There was a natural aura of authority about him: people of all kinds found themselves obeying him and asking for his advice and consent for their projects without knowing why . . . Don Vito ruled and inspired fear mainly by the use of his great qualities and his natural ascendency, His awe-inspiring appearance helped him. He was tall, spare, elegantly but somberly dressed. . . . His manners were princely, his demeanor humble but majestic. He was well loved by all . . . he never refused a request for aid and dispensed millions in loans, gifts, and general philanthropy. He would personally go out of his way to redress a wrong . . . he was a king of sorts: under his reign,

peace and order were preserved. . . . He admitted having killed one man in his long life . . . not for money, but for the honor, prestige, and preservation of the *società*.³⁹

Don Vito undoubtedly underestimated the notches on his *lupara*, but the one person he admitted to killing was Petrosino, illustrious head of the Italian squad of the New York Police Department, who arrived in Palermo to investigate the connections between the Sicilian Mafia and New York City's *La Mano Nera*. Given that Petrosino's investigations in New York City precipitated Don Vito's return to Sicily, we should conclude reasonably that a strong personal element entered Don Vito's murderous calculations.

Piddu Morello, "The Clutch Hand," specialized in extortion, loan sharking, the numbers game, robbery, and counterfeiting, laundering his illegally acquired money through legitimate businesses. In America, Morello, thought to be the boss of all mafia bosses in America until around 1909, is credited with fashioning his protection racket around small, regular extortions instead of exorbitant demands that jeopardized the solvency of his clients. Whether he learned this from or taught this to Cascio-Ferro is unclear. Don Vito may have murdered or arranged the murder of Petrosino in Italy on Morello's request.

During his career, Don Vito was arrested on over five dozen occasions without a conviction. His luck ran out when Cesare Mori, Mussolini's iron prefect, arrested him under apparently flimsy or concocted charges. Given the broad brush of the original indictment—Don Vito was charged with a score of murders, numerous attempted murders, multiple robberies, dozens of acts of extortion, and over fifty miscellaneous violations involving physical violence—the likely explanation is that the state lacked sufficient evidence to sustain convictions, so the prosecutors invoked a different, single murder charge from the distant past. Don Vito insisted until his death that he was not guilty of this slaying.

Mori's policy was simple, clear, and unwavering: arrest and repress first, ask questions later. Within three years, he and his force arrested about 11,000 people, almost half of which resided in the province of Palermo. Mass trials ensued under intimidating conditions leavened by censorship of the press. Due process and proportionate sentencing became archaic ideals. Hundreds of Mafiosi emigrated from Sicily to America to elude Mori's relentless bulldozing.⁴⁰

Convicted and sentenced to fifty years, Don Vito presided over the Ucciardone prison in Palermo, serving as judicious arbiter of all disputes and as counselor to troubled inmates. He died while in prison, leaving the following adage etched on the walls of his cell: "Prison, sickness, and necessity reveal the real heart of a man."[41]

Don Calogero Vizzini (1877–1954), Mafia boss of the province of Caltanissetta in central Sicily and older brother of a priest, rose to power as a clever liaison brokering commerce between peasants and owners of wheat mills. Working with rural brigands, he also protected landowners from peasant revolts. During World War I, Don Calò collaborated with the Italian government, requisitioning horses and mules for the federal cavalry and artillery. However, he was indicted, found guilty, and sentenced to twenty years in prison for fraud, rustling, corruption, and murder while discharging his duties. The powerful political connections he had cultivated ensured he did not serve even a day of his sentence. Don Calò was amiable, approachable, and invariably undersold his talents, adroitly presenting himself as everyone's addled, ineffectual, but lovable uncle. He dressed simply even by peasant standards. Depending on where opportunity resided, he in turn championed the interests of landowners, peasants, Sicilian separatists, Fascists, Christian Democrats, and the United States military during World War II. He was always well connected to prominent church authorities.

The bosses of organized crime do not share any ideological or political allegiances. They are economic and political opportunists sharply exploiting perceived advantages as they emerge. That Don Calò collaborated with several different, competing political programs and championed the interests of peasants, landowners, and government sequentially is unremarkable. All such enterprises were fueled by Don Calò's assessment of where his own benefit resided.

The allied military government appointed him major of Villalba, as well as an honorary Colonel in the United States Army. Don Calò exploited his position artfully and orchestrated the post-war black market, as well as securing large portions of real estate.

Barzini, who knew him well, described his manner and method:

> Peasants, old women with black veils on their heads, young *mafiosi*, middle-class men. They all walked along with [Don Calò] in turn, explaining their problems. He listened, then called one of his henchmen, gave a few orders, and summoned the next petitioner. . . . His magnanimous and protective manners, the respectful salutes of passersby, the retinue surrounding him,

the humility of the people approaching him, the smile of gratitude on their faces when he spoke to them, all reminded one of an ancient scene, a prince holding court and administering justice in the open air.[42]

Prior to the end of his life, the Don summarized his life and career: "The fact is that every society needs a category of person whose task it is to sort out situations when they get complicated. Generally, these people are representatives of the state. But in places where the state doesn't exist, or is not strong enough, there are private individuals."[43] The self-proclaimed simplifier of the complicated, benefactor to society, and surrogate of the state, Don Calò died peacefully in his nephew's arms, reportedly uttering "How beautiful life is!" with his final breath.[44] Thousands of peasants and hundreds of politicians, priests, mobsters, and government officials attended his lavish funeral. The Villalba town hall and Christian Democratic headquarters closed for a week out of respect.

The church pinned the following requiem to its door: "Humble with the humble, Great with the great, He showed with words and deeds that his mafia was not criminal. It stood for respect for the law, Defense of all rights, Greatness of character: It was love."[45] Perhaps Don Calò's greatest gift was public relations wizardry. How a man who self-interestedly ordered scores of murders, orchestrated countless robberies and extortions, and perpetrated a legion of frauds could summon such an elegant silhouette to supplant reality must forever remain a mystery.

Francis Ford Coppola offered other candidates as the inspiration for Don Vito Corleone: "The character [of Don Vito Corleone] was a synthesis of [real-life mobsters] Vito Genovese and Joseph Profaci, but Genovese ordered soldiers not to deal in drugs, while he did just that on the side; Profaci was dishonorable at a lot of levels."[46] In one sentence, Coppola manages to assert then refute his own conviction. Vito Genovese was a notoriously brutal crime family boss who was serially disloyal. The most distinctive personal attribute he and the fictional Corleone share is their first name. Profaci was far more miserly with subordinates and materially ostentatious than the fictional Corleone. He did, however, peddle olive oil, as did Don Vito, as a cover for his illegal activities. The Italian-born American mobsters, Gambino and Costello, are much closer in temperament and comportment to Vito Corleone than are Genovese and Profaci, as are the Sicilian Mafiosi, Vizzini and Cascio Ferro, especially given the mythology encasing their legends in the old country.

Although Puzo claimed that observing his mother's attributes and mannerisms played a major role in his depiction of Don Vito Corleone,[47] the accounts of the lives of Don Vito Cascio Ferro and Don Calogero Vizzini, and to some extent those of Frank Costello and Carlo Gambino, contain too many similarities to Puzo's romantic rendering of Corleone for interpreters to dismiss them as coincidental. Puzo researched his topic well.

Sicilian Culture and Organized Crime

Accounts of the origins of the Mafia as an organized crime syndicate are wrapped in fables shrouded by mysteries encased within fantasies. The following amounts to a nonexhaustive inventory of overlapping yet distinct explanations.

Roman Oppression

The earliest speculation about the Mafia's origins hearken back to the days of Gaius Verres (120–43 BC), a "Roman magistrate notorious for misgovernment of Sicily [circa 70–73 BC] and to the alleged ethnic dialectic between the western, Carthaginian section of the island and the eastern Greek section."[48] Cicero successfully prosecuted Verres for his excesses and won great acclaim in Sicily that followed him until his death. Verres's malfeasance presumably occasioned western Sicilian disdain for government and the formation of small cadres of resistance fighters who mutated into more organized gangs. This account too facilely conflates rebellion against governmental oppression with the formation of sustained organized crime units.

The Sicilian Vespers

Others locate the origins of the Mafia in the thirteenth-century Sicilian Vespers, an uprising animated by a French soldier's sexual violation of a young Sicilian woman.[49] The origin of the term "Mafia," on this rendering, is as an acronym for *"Morte Alla Francia Italia Anela!"* ("Death to France is Italy's Cry!) This strikes me as far-fetched for several reasons, one of which is that the country was far from being united enough for a palpable Sicilian allegiance to a nation called "Italy." Moreover, that a single incident spurred a causal chain culminating in the Mafia as it was understood in the nineteenth century and thereafter is highly unlikely. Magical episode theories such as this are facially implausible.

A variation of this theme: the Mafia began in earlier times, perhaps in the thirteenth-century Sicilian Vespers, precipitated by the rape of a peasant girl by foreign occupiers of Sicily. The father's screams of "ma fia, ma fia" presumably rallied male neighbors to collaborate on appropriate retribution against the perpetrators.[50]

We should distinguish the origin of the term "mafia" from the genesis of the organized crime syndicate the term denotes. Several writers observe that the term bore currency in Sicily distinct from references to crime. For example, Barzini recognizes behavior extolled by mafiosi that mirror general cultural understandings:

> [Sicilians] must aid each other, side with their friends and fight the common enemies even when the friends are wrong and the enemies right; each must defend his dignity at all costs and never allow the smallest slights and insults to go unavenged; they must keep secrets, and always beware of official authorities and laws. These principles are shared by all Sicilians.[51]

Salvatore Lupo, citing a nineteenth-century Sicilian physician, folklorist, and politician, reports the use of the term "mafia" in the general culture:

> [Giuseppe] Pitrè claims that the term *Mafia* was regularly used even before 1860 in the working-class quarters of Palermo as a synonym for "beauty" and "excellence," and that therefore a *mafiusu* would be a man of courage, and *mafiusedda*, a beautiful and proud young woman. This is supposedly a term of "old" Sicily, which after 1860 lost its "original" and positive meaning, and took on another significance, murky but in any case negative, close to that of brigandage.[52]

Lupo also notes the first recorded manifestation of the term: "The first known mention of mafiosi appears in 1862–1863, in a highly popular play intended for a broad audience. The play was entitled *I mafiusi di la Vicaria*, and it was set in 1854 among the *Camorristi* imprisoned in the Palermo prison."[53]

John Dickie echoes the theme of "mafia" as a general cultural attribution:

> In Palermo dialect the adjective "mafioso" once meant "beautiful," "bold," "self-confident." Anyone who was worthy of being described as mafioso therefore had a certain something, an attribute called "mafia" . . . a mafioso was someone who fancied himself.[54]

In any event, the expropriation of a cultural encomium in service of the mob's self-image and propaganda is part of organized crime's stock in trade. Mafia defines itself in the same terms as prevalent cultural norms: bold and fearless individualism, devoid of squalor, evil, and criminality—a way of life and form of behavior, as an expression of traditional society. "Every eminent Mafioso makes a point of presenting himself in the guise of a mediator and resolver of disagreements, as a protector of the virtue of young women . . . a power group that expresses an ideology meant to create consensus on the outside and coherence and compactness on the inside."[55]

Accordingly, we must separate the search for the origins of the term "mafia" from the investigation of the genesis of the Mafia, as well as the self-presentations of mafiosi from their reality.

The End of Feudalism

In Sicily, the feudal system was abolished by decree in 1812. The provisions of that decree included a passel of conditions that differed from the statutes governing the mainland of southern Italy: "As early as 1875, Leopoldo Franchetti identified this as a decisive point in triggering the process of 'democratization of violence,' whereby the right to use force, originally the exclusive privilege of the aristocracy, was legally transferred to the state, while sustainably remaining in the hands of private citizens."[56] The train of thought seems to be that under the feudal system a monopoly of legalized force resided with the aristocracy. In the early nineteenth century with the abolishment of feudalism, the state formally seized sole legitimate power, but it was unable or unwilling to exercise that power effectively. Thus, substantive power percolated to private citizens willing to combine interests and exert it to their advantage. As with other renderings in this inventory, this explanation identifies a causal factor in the eventual rise of the Mafia but exuberantly amplifies that factor into the efficient and the final cause of the Mafia's existence.

Protecting Wealthy Landowners from Desperados

On this account, the Mafia arose from the practice of wealthy Sicilian landowners hiring private forces to defend their estates and families from rural brigands. These private armies exacted primitive, extralegal justice where federal allegiance and institutions were weak. The absence of adequate policing, the lack of a reliable legal system, and centuries of foreign oppression that cultivated distrust in central authorities were critical in triggering the cycle. Originally the enemies of marauding bandits, these private forces became more powerful and the line distinguishing criminal and law-enforcer more attenuated. Soon thereafter, the private forces spawned the protection racket: they extorted money from those not seeking their services voluntarily in return for not damaging their property. As such, the Sicilian Mafia "is believed to be also a spontaneous way, developed by the people themselves through many centuries of misrule, to administer a rough and archaic form of justice, a way to keep one kind of peace and ensure the safety of the inhabitants, an *ersatz* of legal government."[57]

Much of the poverty of Sicilian peasants arose from absentee landowners who leased their estates on short-term agreements to *gabelloti*, overseers who were unconcerned about long-range viability. They worked peasants mercilessly for immediate gain. The typical *gabelloto* was ruthless, driven, and avidly competitive. These avaricious supervisors needed to protect their person, contracted property, and livestock from brigands and rustlers. They either allied with or dominated the brigands, often joining the mafia to achieve these aims. The Mafia had connections in Palermo, where most of the absentee landowners lurked, and the armed forces to dominate uppity peasants and uncooperative brigands.[58]

In this vein, Alessandro Camon observes:

> [The Mafia] flourished in Sicily, which was at the time a distinctly non-industrialized, precapitalist area where the economy (and the social struggle) revolved around the land. The Mafia's first large-scale business was the protection of the Sicilian latifundio, the vast landed estates that the local farmers worked but couldn't claim. Members of the dispossessed class were recruited by the landowners to protect by means of prevarication an antiquated status quo . . . belonging to/owning the land is the original form of [the Mafia's] identity.[59]

This rendering discards magical episode theory and locates the rise of the Mafia within a wider network of cultural and social circumstances. As such, it exudes greater discursive power, although leaving several transitions unexplained.

As Accompaniment to Italian Unification

This narrative locates the rise of the Mafia during the time of Italian unification, around 1860, during the exponential growth of the citrus fruit industry. The leaders of the *Risorgimento*, the story goes, recognized the captivating beauty of inner Sicily but were repelled by its economic exploitation: expansive estates owned by an exploitive, wealthy elite, overseen by callous bosses, and worked by hordes of desperate peasants. Enlightened Italians perceived the Mafia as spawned by primitivism, poverty, and ignorance. They were convinced that once Sicily joined the Italian nation, cast off superstition, revitalized formal education, and extinguished their old ways, the island would regenerate. But in the words of Dickie:

> The mafia's origins are not ancient . . . mafia based their power on running protection rackets in the lemon groves. They could force landowners to accept their men as stewards, wardens, and brokers. Their network of contacts with cart drivers, wholesalers, and dockers could either threaten a farm's produce, or ensure its safe arrival at the market. . . . Once in control . . . the mafiosi could steal as much as they liked . . . killing people and getting away with it, and by organizing itself in a unique way that combines the attributes of a shadow state, an illegal business, and a sworn secret society like the Freemasons.[60]

On this account, although brigands and desperados plied their trades for centuries, the Mafia has a nineteenth-century genesis, grounded less firmly in the protection of land as such and more solidly in the rise of the citrus industry with its national and international horizons. This narrative prudently signals the economic, political, and social links facilitating the rise of the Mafia. It also implicitly underscores the inability or unwillingness of the state to exercise its formal monopoly of power. Surely, the time at which we pinpoint the origins of the Mafia and the events we posit as spurring the Mafia's ascension depend heavily on what we take the Mafia to be. Lupo understands the Mafia thusly:

> The basic function of the Mafia, can be identified in the racket that protects a legal institution, the business enterprise, using violence to ensure a monopoly for itself—specifically the verbal and physical intimidation of thieves, traitors, witnesses, and competitors . . . [it] presupposes a disorder that needs to be organized and kept firmly under control . . . it helps to create the widespread sense of insecurity on which it battens and which it exploits.[61]

The genesis of the Mafia at the time of *Risorgimento* presumably obscured its indefensible criminality and enhanced its romantic myth. Grass-roots resistance in Sicily in the 1860s against Bourbon oppression and, later, the excesses of Italian unification was diverse and often indistinguishable. Unapologetic republicans, disgruntled clerics, counterrevolutionary Bourbons, rabid Sicilian separatists, self-seeking brigands, and representatives of the skittish ruling economic class registered distinct but overlapping dissatisfaction with both the status quo and the imminent political future. In the words of Raimondo Catanzaro: "All this confusion provided the embryonic Mafia with moral credentials. Its appearance as a sort of spontaneous rebellion against the injustice of the constituted order surrounded the mafiosi with a romantic aura of popular heroes and conveniently for them, characterized their actions as morally ambiguous even as late as the 1950s."[62]

Catanzaro describes the Mafia Geist of this period:

> Mafia can be defined as criminal silence, brazen courage, imprudent mendacity, betrayal of intimate personal relations, [and] resistance to all moral and civil laws . . . it is fame that bestows imprudent courage on the man who, through criminal deeds and the swift use of physical force—through intelligence and personal connections—has been able to subject those who know him by name and personally, so that he can brazenly commit crimes with the assurance of impunity, since everyone is afraid of him and no one dares to react to his brazen demands by accusing him.[63]

At this stage of development, mafiosi are not portrayed as constitutive of a large, hierarchical organization demanding obedience from subordinates and evincing an ambiguous relationship with extant government. Instead, they are envisioned as those able to meet the Sicilian cultural ideal of defending and avenging oneself only through one's own power and those of intimate allies seasoned by a thorough disdain of moral rectitude and legal mandates. When the Mafia matures, it aspires to economic and political hegemony—monopoly, if possible—over the projects it undertakes; it consists of a loose organization consisting of numerous *cosche* (gangs or crime families); with a subculture grounded in the race for respect, honor, and power; which achieves its goals through collaboration with and corruption of politicians and law enforcers underwritten by threats of violence.

As An Economic Industry Focused on Private Protection

On this portrayal, the Mafia employs violence as a means of advancing its purpose, which is providing protection from worldly dangers not adequately parried by legal forces and from damage that the Mafia itself threatens. The Mafia flourishes where mutual trust is unsteady and the state's law enforcement mechanisms are unreliable or tendentious: "In both legal and illegal markets [not involving direct extortion] those who enlist Mafiosi to sort out their disputes, to retrieve their stolen property, or to protect their cartels from free riders and competitors do not perceive their protection as bogus."[64]

Foreign dominators in Sicily, especially the Spanish Hapsburgs, deliberately poisoned public trust through divisive policies and punishments in Sicily, thereby nurturing a narrower private trust vested in family, friends, and allies—resulting in the solidification of the tradition of *l'ordine della famiglia*. The absence of public trust generated profitable opportunities for private protection enterprises. Seizing such opportunities required a supply of potential paladins for such enterprises: "vigilantes, former soldiers, private guards, bandits, and prison inmates are typical of the groups that traditionally nurture the skills a person needs to become a 'protector.' During the nineteenth century all these types were plentiful in Sicily, and through a highly specific set of circumstances both the supply of and demand for protection intersected and flourished."[65]

Those who succeeded in forming protection enterprises emerged as independent suppliers seeking monopolies or, at least, local hegemonies. In western Sicily, social tensions intensified due to absentee landlords, a disjointed economic ruling class, and greater hostility toward Italian unification. Therefore, in western Sicily "at least three protection functions were in short supply: the policing of the peasantry; the enforcement of property rights over land, livestock, and produce under threat from competitors and bandits; and the regulation of ill-defined or extralegal rights of priority and exclusivity in the allocation of resources related to the land."[66]

On this account, the Mafia's protection industry did not attain the autonomy required to establish it as a unique enterprise until the nineteenth century: "The earliest date, therefore, at which the mafia might be said to have come into being is 1812, the year when feudalism began to be dismantled in Sicily, and the latest 1875. . . . In this encounter of rural and urban, force and cunning, lower and middle classes lies the secret of the mafia's origins, the energy that turned it into an industry."[67]

The Mafia's Self-Image

Retrospective falsification oozes from organized crime's self-image. Most descriptions of the Mafia's origins and virtually all published reports from members of the mob warmly recount the days when men of honor, surrounded by treacherous enemies and acting within a state ruled by oppressive foreigners, mediated private disputes judiciously, skirted the incontinence of the legal system, benefited the impoverished and powerless while holding the haughty accountable, and engaged in only proportionate and merited violence. This is in effect the myth that Puzo's Don Vito Corleone represents in *The Godfather*: the Golden Age of criminal administration.

The probabilities that such an epoch existed are slim and none, and, as they say, slim is receiving extreme unction. Even if the Mafia did woo Camelot, the flirtation was sloppy, nasty, and fleeting. Still, the myth stirs romantic fantasies and promotes self-serving propaganda allowing the syndicate to bask in comforting illusions centered on its immaculate founding principles and royal pedigree. Typically, the myth continues by indicting the avarice, hostility, and wrongful aggression of outsiders, or the betrayal, weakness, and selfishness of a relatively small number of dishonorable insiders as the source of the Mafia's fall from grace. Just as the purity of Adam and Eve was compromised by the loathsome treachery of a serpent, so too, the Mafia as agent of peace and justice was tragically undermined by reprobates unworthy of and ungrateful for its excellence. This world was not constructed to abide a federation of such beauty, or so it would seem to the apostles of the founding myth. In the absence of an independent, reliable historical chronicle of prevenient Mafia activities, self-admiring inventions of men of honor protecting the defenseless and thumping the oppressive abound.

Salvatore Lupo observes:

> [*Cosa Nostra* and Mafia mobsters who publicly revealed their activities such as] Valachi, Gentile, Bonanno, Buscetta, and Calderone all portrayed themselves and their friends as wise men who applied the rules, who sought to mediate conflict, and who avoided illegal violence, turning to bloodshed only as a last resort, in order to apply the rational and carefully weighed deliberations of the organization. At the same time, they depicted their enemies as treacherous individuals, unwilling to respect the laws of (their own) society, always ready to engage in betrayal, killing at the drop of a hat, and verging on the brink of sadism and insanity . . . if their adversaries were to speak, they might well tell the story from a diametrically opposed point of view.[68]

In any case, cultural conditions in Sicily, in the nineteenth century and earlier, offered fertile soil for the Mafia's flourishing. While these cultural conditions are not collectively sufficient for spawning organized crime and may not be strictly necessary for doing so, they were certainly conducive. First, organized crime exploited cultural distrust of extant political and legal institutions. Manly self-respect arose from defending dignity and avenging insults to family personally while ignoring legal authorities. Those who sought protection from or confided in law enforcement authorities were judged dishonorable and feckless.[69] This cultural norm intensified during the period of Italian unification. Second, *l'ordine della famiglia* was well entrenched and impeded regional or national affiliations. The Mafia constructed its code of honor and organizational structure by mirroring these traditional societal accords: venerate the family and celebrate its order; adjudicate personal conflicts without resort to formal, public mechanisms. Third, Sicilian geographical and infrastructural circumstances supported these cultural understandings: "Distances were vast, the roads few, the public institutions practically non-existent, the police and courts impotent, all governments discredited as having been for a long time instruments of foreign oppression, and a man had to look out for himself."[70] Fourth, the Sicilian economy was agricultural and transitioning from feudal to capitalist. Social struggle and economic conflict orbited around land and livestock.⁷¹ Thus, economic conditions promoted the rise of extra-legal protection syndicates to mollify class conflicts and ensure a measure of commercial security. The Mafia matured as a complex conglomerate. As a mirror of traditional society it had a stake in reflecting and preserving established cultural understandings; as a business enterprise the Mafia learned how to corrupt yet cooperate with legal and political institutions while continuing to undermine their full authority; as a social organization it developed regional commissions to oversee crime family disputes; and as a quasi-judicial ordering the Mafia invoked rituals, symbols, and self-serving propaganda as regulatory mechanisms, massively augmented by murderous brutality.⁷²

To understand the Mafia as embracing values subversive of and irreconcilable with the values of the nation is simplistic. Opportunism may be organized crime's highest value. Acting from its collective self-interest, the Mafia has cooperated with, rebelled against, undermined, and corrupted political and legal authorities in turn: "The concept of the Mafia as an antistate is overstated and misleading, and it points us to the theme of the ties linking the Mafia and official power."⁷³ Likewise, to understand the early Mafia as merely a protection agency ensuring the ongoing subordination of the peasants to the hegemony of the ruling classes is also simplistic. As always, opportunism and self-interest guided the Mafia's decision making. The striking consistency in the Mafia's machinations has been its reflecting and reinforcing of cultural understandings, traditions, and behaviors that legitimate and justify the Mafia's existence: "Mafia organization appropriates cultural codes, instrumentalizes them, modifies them, and turns them into an adhesive to ensure that they remain intact . . . it is first and foremost the Mafia that describes itself as a way of life and a form of behavior, as an expression of traditional society."⁷⁴

The results were devastating to the island, particularly in terms of individual achievement and professional desert: "The Mafia in Sicily was cancerous to the society it inhabited. Merit meant nothing. Talent meant nothing. Work meant nothing. The Mafia Godfather gave you your profession as a gift."⁷⁵ Patronage, clientelism, and imperium hijacked the common good, while Might scoffed at the possibility of an independent notion of Right. Meanwhile, the cultural mania of defending oneself only by dint of personal and familial power further undermined governmental and legal authorities, whose ongoing ineffectiveness cruelly reinforced the rationale for the shadow hegemony of the Mafia. A vicious circle chugged along unencumbered by rectitude and the rule of law.⁷⁶

The broad notion of "mafia" in Sicilian culture is unconnected to criminal activity. Mafia implies only the possession and exercise of personal attributes such as refusal to submit to coercion; amplified consciousness of one's own character; inflated sense of honor; steadfast loyalty to family and friends; refusal to accept insults tranquilly; suspicion of institutional authority external to one's family; hostility toward extant law; an openly prideful bearing; and a profound distrust of *stranieri*.

In Sicilian dialect, the term "mafioso" once connoted beautiful or bold or self-confident bearing or action, a kind of self-understanding and presentation that was admirable and rare. Independently of criminal aspirations and schemes, the term suggested general cultural qualities such as mutual aid among friends, collaboration against common enemies, redress of insults and slurs, a principle of silence when dealing with government authorities, and allegiance to rustic chivalry.

Vittorio Emanuele Orlando, Sicilian statesman and Prime Minister of Italy from 1917 to 1919, captured the sentiments of "mafia" understood as excellence of character:

> If by "mafia," they mean having an exaggerated sense of honor; if they mean being furiously intolerant of bullying and injustice, and showing generosity of spirit needed to stand up to the strong and be understanding towards the weak; if they mean having a loyalty to your friends that is stronger than anything, stronger even than death; if by "mafia" they mean feelings like these, attitudes like these . . . then I say to you that what they are talking about are the distinguishing traits of the Sicilian soul.[77]

This cultural ethos or philosophy of life or psychological attitude was the dominant mindset of nineteenth-century Sicily and was transported to America by thousands of Sicilian immigrants. The ethos unwittingly collaborated in sustaining the cultural conditions that permitted the Mafia, in the narrower notion of an organized crime syndicate, to flourish in both countries. On numerous occasions, suspected criminals invoked the widespread understanding of the cultural ethos to deny they were connected to illegal activity. They claimed that their display of the Sicilian philosophy of life was mistakenly taken by the authorities as evidence of illegality. Indeed, some figures muddied the conceptual waters by alleging that government erred systematically in this manner. There was no organized crime syndicate, only the ongoing political blunder. The inability or unwillingness to distinguish the cultural ethos of Sicilians from the practices of the organized crime syndicate spawned a passel of deleterious judgments, not all of which were compatible: the illusion that the Mafia did not exist; the prejudice that Sicilians were by nature and socialization prone to violence and lawlessness; the aspersion that Sicilian immigrants could not assimilate into American society because they were narrowly and incorrigibly tribal; and the fallacy that organized crime was a Sicilian invention.

Those who accepted that *La Mano Nera*, the Mafia, or *Cosa Nostra* did indeed exist in America and who were able to distinguish the cultural ethos of Sicilia from the organized crime syndicate attributed the arrival of the latter to the United States to either (a) the emigration of established members of the mafia from Sicily to America to avoid persecution in the old country or expand their possibilities in the new world, or (b) the emigration of Sicilian peasants, embodying the dominant cultural ethos, from the old world to a harsh new world brandishing urban capitalism, corrupt politics, an Irish-dominated Catholic church, and boundless prejudice toward Mediterranean newcomers. Adapting the imperatives of their cultural ethos to new-world exigencies, a small percentage of these peasants and their children—people of high aggression and accepting of daunting risks—turned to crime, especially in reaction to the ratification of the eighteenth amendment to the U.S. Constitution, which prohibited the manufacture, sale, or transportation of alcohol.[78]

Each of these accounts bears some explanatory currency, but both omit critical details. While a few established gangsters immigrated to America, even some of these returned to their homeland quite rapidly. The early versions of *La Mano Nera* and other incipient Sicilian crime networks were not staffed primarily by veterans from the old country. Moreover, the percentage of Sicilian peasants embracing crime was always minuscule, even though the majority of these *contadini* arrived with a robust dose of the cultural ethos of the homeland. Also, even at the height of the influence of their criminality in the United States, Sicilian and Italian Americans constituted a minority of wrongdoers in the country. In the same vein as H. Rap Brown's intonation in the 1960s that "violence is as American as cherry pie," one might add that a stiff dose of criminality among the latest immigrant group is as American as corn beef and cabbage, matzoh ball soup, and pasta e fagioli ("pasta fazool") would become.

In any case, the fictional Don Vito Corleone embodied the nineteenth-century Sicilian ethos and the enterprising spirit of a steely gangster. At the core of his life was the accumulation and exercise of power. To understand that life we must now examine and evaluate the nature of power and Don Vito's own will to power. That one of Don Vito's core values is amassing and exercising power is undeniable. By philosophically examining the concept of power and will to power, and applying the findings to understand Don Vito, we can interpret *The Godfather*, as a novel and film series, more insightfully.

Chapter Three

Power, Destiny, and Evil

The Godfather is a novel and a film that entertains. It bestows a grand story invoking classical themes of family allegiance, personal betrayal, calculated vengeance, lurid sexuality, merciless violence, peppered with sporadic plot twists. On a surface interpretation, *The Godfather* seemingly romanticizes organized crime, or at least the Corleone family, with scant regard for the pernicious reality of criminal activity.[1] This chapter begins by sketching supposedly subtler metaphors capturing the deeper allegorical meaning of *The Godfather*. All plausible interpretations, however, invoke the notion of power. Accordingly, the chapter continues by explaining why the protagonists of the film regard power as the ultimate prize and not merely as a means of securing wealth; provides a philosophical account of the concept of power; and analyzes Don Vito Corleone's will to power and its connection to his maximally affirmative attitude toward life.

The interplay of human destiny, personal choices, and resulting evil is next on the agenda. In the novel, Don Vito sometimes invokes destiny as the animator of a character's biographical arc. What does he mean? That our paramount life decisions descend from the stars and not from our hearts and souls? That one life-changing choice, sculpted by external circumstances beyond our control, can or must determine our future? Or something else?

Finally, the chapter discusses the personal degeneration of Michael Corleone, the significance of his exile in Sicily after the murders of Sollozzo and McCluskey, how the context and events of *Godfather II* chronicle Michael's increasing alienation and estrangement, and the evanescence of *la via vecchia* in response to American social circumstances hostile to that tradition.

Interpreting *The Godfather*

Interpretations of the supposed deeper meaning of *The Godfather* are plentiful and diverse. Consider a few:

The Godfather as *King Lear* with some quirks. At times, Francis Ford Coppola perceived the movie as a contemporary American rendering of a classical theme, a king coming to grips with mortality and vexed with the problem of succession to the crown: "[*The Godfather*] is a classic story, this is like Shakespeare. [A king] has three sons and each son has gotten some part of his talent. One is cunning and cold and one is violent and emotional and the third is sweet but sort of dumb. And . . . the father had all of those qualities. That's why he was a great king. And I'm going to tell it sort of like a story of succession."[2] In a variation of this theme, Coppola observed, "[The film] is not really about the Mafia. It could just as well be about the Kennedys or the Rothschilds, about a dynasty which demands personal allegiance to a family that transcends even one's obligations to one's country."[3]

The Godfather as a metaphor for the evaporation of the American dream. Coppola also viewed the trilogy as a metaphor for the immigrant's lust for opportunity, enticement into capitalistic values, and ultimate cultural transformation and possible degeneration: "I always wanted to use the Mafia as a metaphor for America . . . Both are totally capitalistic phenomena and basically have a profit motive."[4] [In *The Godfather II*], I wanted to destroy [the family] in the way that I think is most profound—from the inside. And I wanted to punish Michael . . . I don't think anyone in the theater can envy him."[5]

Coppola, on occasion, was more unsparing about the disintegration of the American dream: "I feel that America does not take care of its people. We look to our country as our protector, and it's fooling us, it's lying to us. The reason the book was so popular was that people love to read about an organization that's really going to take care of us."[6]

The Godfather as a metaphor for capitalism and moral disintegration. Closely aligned to but a more specific version of Coppola's second rendering is the notion that the movie celebrates the triumph of twentieth-century American capitalism while castigating its correlated disintegration of salutary moral values. The message seemingly is that capitalism and morality wage their own zero-sum contest. The harsh conclusion is that American capitalism begins with structural advantages virtually ensuring its dominance over rectitude.[7]

Coppola described his cinematic goal as demythologizing the platitude that America is a "pluralistic society living by the rule of law and serving as a model for the rest of the world."[8] The lawlessness of the Corleone family, impossible without a support network including corrupt politicians, disreputable legal authorities, and venal citizens, is nothing less than a microcosm of the American way: aggressive, zero-sum negotiations amplified by violence. David Ray Papke describes this interpretation: "*The Godfather* speaks to and for this skepticism [of legalism] by presenting law and legal institutions as hopelessly biased: police are on the take, judges are in the Mafia's pocket, and family lawyers make offers that cannot be refused."[9]

Mario Puzo adds, "I've wanted to show the parallel between the normal business world and the Mafia . . . these guys know how to use violence as a business tool . . . the old guys were men of honor [with] family values."[10] Of course, Puzo's understanding of "the old guys" is overly approbative.

The Godfather as a chronicling of the immigrant experience in America. On this interpretation, the film evinces the mutual tensions and antagonisms between a capitalist society that both requires and resents fresh immigrants, and the newcomers who fear loss of identity in their struggle to survive yet recognize opportunities for upward mobility in the new world. In the words of Alessia Ricciardi: "reformulating the intense anxieties of late-twentieth century capitalist society with regard to race and immigration in the mythical, supra-historical languages of melodrama and the sublime . . . the passage from the Old to New World . . . is exposed as deeply unnatural and uncanny . . . the desperate search for divine moral absolutes in a profane world . . . the terrifying inevitability of the Law of the Father . . . terrified instinct of self-preservation in the face of a new anthropological and social order . . . the anxiety of exclusion and loss of identity at the root of the immigrant experience."[11]

The Godfather as a reflection of America's economic and political ruthlessness. Overlapping with other interpretations, this explanation indicts the American system as not fundamentally antithetical to organized crime. Movie critic Pauline Kael writes: "[In *The Godfather*] we see organized crime as an obscene symbolic extension of free enterprise and government policy, an extension of the worst in America—its feudal ruthlessness. Organized crime is not the rejection of Americanism, it's what we fear Americanism to be."[12]

The Godfather as a metaphor for contemporary American foreign policy. On this reading, the film provides a vision of America's status in the world in the twenty-first century. Don Vito represents America's power during the Cold War. Vito's sons represent different foreign policy responses to America's decline: Sonny is a neoconservative yearning to attack all foes; Tom Hagen is a liberal, diplomatic internationalist seeking dialogue; Michael is a realist unencumbered by a fixed strategy other than to protect family interests by any means necessary.[13]

A feminist interpretation of *The Godfather* novel and films might highlight the role that the increasing autonomy of women and their reproductive capabilities play in undermining the Corleone crime family's design for economic and functional hegemony. Despite its surface rendering as a paean to *iper virile*, patriarchal prerogatives, *The Godfather* is furtively a canticle to the subversive power of women. A Freudian analysis could focus on the analogical and metaphorical significance of the size and configuration of Sonny Corleone's and Lucy Mancini's sexual organs, as well as the homoerotic dimensions of male solidarity constituting crime syndicate relationships. A cinematic analysis might demonstrate how the two sequels to the initial movie track Francis Ford Coppola's vicissitudes as a Hollywood film maker, how Michael's character development and his collaborations and clashes with mainstream *pezzonovanti* are metaphors for Coppola's own triumphs, debacles, and frustrations: "the higher I go, the crookeder it becomes."

A Marxist examination would insist that internal contradictions plague the Corleone organization, which is thereby a microcosm of capitalism as such. That the Corleone enterprise juggles these contradictions successfully but transiently can forestall but not eradicate its inescapable destiny: the exploitation of and alienation from others, as well as the dissolution of familial intimacy. On this reading, relations within the Corleone family must internally detonate because their foundation, capitalist economics, embodies inherently antagonistic vectors. A conservative business reading, on the contrary, might conclude that Corleone capitalism demonstrates only that intentionally distorting the free market is a recipe for personal and economic disaster. Indirectly, the novel and films support the supreme financial truth: laissez-faire commerce *über alles*.

The inventory of possibilities could continue. My point is that unveiling any sole interpretation and anointing it as capturing the one, true meaning of *The Godfather* novel and films is a mug's game. Although *The Godfather*, like other engrossing novels and films, should not be viewed simply as a mirror reflecting only the projections cast by readers and viewers, and not all readings of the work are equally compelling, a range of interpretations are plausible. My interpretation focuses on what I consider the more vibrant and didactive philosophical and social dimensions of Puzo's novel—the pursuit of power, honor, and respect in the new world through exercise of a specific family and ethnic code imported from the old world. Don Vito is surely a capitalist and a criminal, but he uses business as a tool to attain his higher aims: amassing and exercising power, as well as manifesting and amplifying his honor and respect. His are nineteenth-century Sicilian values struggling mightily for affirmation in twentieth-century America.

Accordingly, my work presents itself for what it is, nothing more and nothing less: an interdisciplinary examination that wields philosophical analyses of concepts such as honor, power, will to power, respect, atonement, repentance, forgiveness, and leading a meaningful human life in service of a distinctive interpretation of *The Godfather* as a novel and film sequence. Applying these analyses to the cultural understandings transported by nineteenth-century Italian immigrants to America casts fresh light on old-world allegiance to *l'ordine della famiglia* (the family order), *la via vecchia* (the old way), and the patriarchal ideal of *uomo di pazienza* (the man of patience), as well as their code of honor.

On my reading, *The Godfather* describes the existential conflict between two sets of values partially constituting competing prescriptive and descriptive visions of the world: a nineteenth-century Sicilian perspective and a twentieth-century American perspective. The two sets of values coalesce uneasily in the same cultural setting and their conflict is irresolvable. Ultimately, the Sicilian perspective must devitalize in the United States because, unlike the old country, the new world lacks its sustaining cultural conditions. I interpret *The Godfather* as, among other things, a commentary on the transformation of personal identity within the Sicilian and Italian immigrant experience.

Seemingly in contrast to part of my thesis, Thomas J. Ferraro argues that in *The Godfather* old-world and new-world cultural values are mutual sustaining, that a nineteenth-century Sicilian ethos and twentieth-century American culture are affable collaborators, not zero-sum antagonists.[14] He argues that group solidarity, ethnic traditions, and protection of turf, all under the purview of family, forms a system that is "one of the primary motors of capitalism, not its antithesis."[15] The challenges of executive succession, family loyalty, and maximizing profits are conjoined. Rather than offering a utopian refuge from capitalism, Don Vito's family and their ethnic structure are absorbed, attenuated, and co-opted by capitalist economics. The Italian American ethnic family flourishes within the American market.[16] To indict capitalism, advises Ferraro, is to "press charges against family and ethnicity, too . . . as Don Vito's business goes, so goes his family: their fates are intertwined."[17] In sum,

> In *The Godfather*, Puzo refashions the gangster genre into a vehicle for overturning the traditional antithesis between ties of blood and the American marketplace. He thus transforms the stock character of the Italian-American outlaw into the representative super (business) man, and transforms the lingering image of immigrant huddled masses into the first family of American capitalism.[18]

Ferraro confines his analysis to the novel, noting that "in *Godfather II*, Michael promotes his criminal enterprise at the expense of his immediate family, group solidarity, and the Italian-American heritage . . . his nuclear family falls apart completely; and the Southern Italian ethos that structured his father's world is vanquished entirely. . . . Michael has Americanized."[19]

That Ferraro's convictions, if persuasive, undermine my thesis is unclear from the outset. I argue that Don Vito's nineteenth-century Sicilian ethos was incompatible with twentieth-century American *culture*. Ferraro argues that the Sicilian ethos coalesced easily and profitably with American *capitalism*. The implorations of doctrinal Marxists that the economic system determines cultural superstructure notwithstanding, one could accept both of our interpretations, distinguishing capitalism as partly constitutive of but not equivalent to culture. Moreover, we may question the identification of the Corleone crime syndicate with capitalism. Are not their accumulating methods, punitive responses, remunerative structures, and hierarchical designs different in kind or at least pivotally different in degree from everyday capitalism? Are not the Corleones a crime syndicate because they lack the prerequisites of flourishing within capitalism's legal contours? Finally, arguing for the fundamental incompatibility of the Sicilian ethos and twentieth-century American culture need not and should not rest upon the bifurcation of the family and culture (or capitalism) into distinctively separate spheres. As I pointed out in my analyses of *l'ordine della famiglia*, the family and its behavioral code were not in Sicily merely an oasis of refuge from the larger culture; their insularity, secrecy, suspicion, and consanguinity also sustained the imperatives and disciplines of the oppressive, broader culture against which they were presumably reacting.

Nudge aside these matters for the moment. Ferraro notes in support of his interpretation of *The Godfather* that Americans have increasingly embraced the compatibility and mutually sustaining dimensions of capitalism and ethnicity. He cites Lee Iacocca, Geraldine Ferrara, and Mario Cuomo as three of numerous Italian Americans who "emphasize the role family values have played in their own success stories."[20]

This evidence, however, wildly misses the mark if directed against my thesis. I argue that the Sicilian ethos and American culture were incompatible, not that ethnicity, Italian or otherwise, coalesces uncomfortably with American capitalism or even American culture. Namely, I argue that a distinctive nineteenth-century Sicilian ethos, grounded in *l'ordine della famiglia, la via vecchia*, and, a stringent code of honor could not endure in twentieth-century America because the new world lacked the cultural conditions required to sustain that ethos. Have Iacocca, Ferrara, or Cuomo ever invoked any of the following precepts, all of which pervaded the immigrant Sicilian ethos and were harnessed in service of organized crime, as critical to their corporate and political success: distrust law enforcement devotedly; categorize and relate to all human beings in accord with the four significant spheres of the family order; regard government as an oppressive alien power; remain silent if interrogated by the authorities; pursue only extralegal methods of resolving personal disputes; respond disproportionately to wrongs perpetrated against yourself or your intimates; prioritize the well-being and judgments of your colleagues within the honor code rather than the well-being and judgments of your immediate family; cling to the efficacy of superstitions and the power of talismanic incantations; seek wealth not as an end but as a means to higher values, such as power and enhanced honor?

The imperatives I list illustrate only a few of the mammoth differences between the nineteenth-century Sicilian ethos and the "family values" presumably underwriting the success of Iacocca, Ferrara, and Cuomo, which values consisted of mutual support, educational advance, tribal love, veneration of hard work, commitment to generational progress, intense hope for the future, and a spirit of vibrant collaboration, to name only a bevy. Extolling the exercise of such "family values" as facilitating success in capitalistic America is judicious but does not sap the energy of my interpretation of the relationship between the dominant nineteenth-century Sicilian ethos and twentieth-century American culture.

Surely, Ferraro is correct in concluding that ethnicity as such is compatible with American capitalism; indeed, understanding oneself as an ethnic is a distinctive way of declaring oneself American. We are a nation of immigrants and their progenies, descendants of slaves, and indigenous peoples now populating sovereign nations within our boundaries. However, countless features of *l'ordine della famiglia, la via vecchja*, and the nineteenth-century Sicilian code jarred twentieth-century American culture and soon shriveled for reasons I have previously adumbrated.

In *Godfather II*, Michael loses his family not only because he rivets his attention on expanding his crime syndicate, retaliating against all perceived enemies, and concocting abstruse intrigues; he surrenders his family in no slight measure because American cultural conditions—social, legal, and educational—gnaw at and diminish the vitality of critical features of *l'ordine della famiglia, la via vecchia*, and allegiance to the Sicilian honor code. Throughout the twentieth century in America, enormously expanding opportunities for mobility, communication, education, and economic advancement; loosening of rigid sexual mores; increased intermingling of ethnicities and races; disaggregating of ethnic ghettos; emerging women's liberation; expanding civil rights; marginalizing appeals to codes of honor; dissipating superstitious commitments; and expanding resort to plea bargaining, generation of witness protection programs, and creation of anti-organized crime legislation mark a cluster of emerging cultural conditions inimical to distinctive aspects of the old-world ethos. Accordingly, Ferraro's explanation of the novel does not sabotage my thesis that aspects of the nineteenth-century Sicilian ethos and twentieth-century American culture waged existential battles.

A Philosophical Analysis of Power

> But his ultimate aim is to enter that society with a certain power since society doesn't really protect its members who do not have their own individual power.
>
> —Michael Corleone to Kay

Don Vito, under cover of old-world family love and loyalty, does not merely exploit but also enhances the corruption and excesses of American institutions. Don Vito grasps intellectually, his way, the old Sicilian fashion, must yield to the exigencies of the new world, which lacks its sustaining conditions. The absent cultural conditions include the following: Sicily endured centuries of foreign invasions and occupations; in the Sicily of Don Vito's day, state authority was perceived as a repository of evil and its power was too frequently brandished unjustly; a code of silence, *omerta*, was the defiant hallmark of the masses; communication, transportation, and mobility were severely restricted, and most people spent their entire lives within their villages and immediate surroundings; competing provincial understandings and prerogatives had solidified; the nation of Italy had materialized only a few decades prior to Vito Andolini's forced immigration to America; that nation continued to be plagued with regionalism and factionalism; a strict extended family order, embodying a narrow blood and soil mentality, prevailed as a counterweight to much of the above; opportunities for upward socioeconomic mobility were scarce; a fierce anti-clericalism coexisted uncomfortably with profound devotion to saints connected to localities and to village priests; and the absence of compulsory public education bred intractable superstitions.

This is also why Sicilian organized crime has largely withered away in the United States—its sustaining cultural understandings are absence in the wider culture. Even if the Racketeer Influenced and Corrupt Organizations Act (RICO) and witness protection programs and plea bargaining did not exist, Sicilian organized crime would have largely evaporated because the new generations were born and raised in the United States. These generations can surely produce criminals but not of the stripe and with the self-understandings of the mythical Corleone family. The time soon arrived when Don Vito's scions confronted stark choices: become the *pezzonovanti*, the hammers of the new world, or resign themselves to subsisting as anvils or nails. The overwhelming majority of Italian immigrants and their descendants, law-abiding and industrious, chose from a far richer array of possibilities.

Viscerally, Don Vito, unlike Amerigo Bonasera, has no inclination for American assimilation. He craves an extralegal Sicilian life obsessed with accumulating power and respect within the boundaries of the new world and its distinctive challenges. Respect and its concomitant rituals are the ballast sustaining Don Vito's social structure and *la via vecchia*.

Intellectually, Don Vito expected Michael, the most American of his offspring, to ascend to the heights of a new-world *pezzonovante*. That Don Vito assuages new-world power-brokers through bribery only reinforces his Sicilian distrust of government. That America celebrates the myth of individualism only underscores his Sicilian reliance on a closely knit social network grounded in blood and sacred pledges of loyalty. That America invokes the rule of law and the common good only energizes Don Vito's

Sicilian conviction that politicians murder millions while supposedly implementing such notions (in effect, "a prime minister kills more victims with one declaration than thousands of criminals with weapons," or in America, "take the money, leave the idealism"). But these competing secular religions, the conflicting descriptive and prescription visions of the two worlds, coalesce uneasily. Intellectually, Don Vito understands that America will compel the offspring of immigrants to relinquish their roots in exchange for exerting their wings. The metaphors of America as a melting pot, salad bowl, or giant stew capture that reality in different ways. Viscerally, Don Vito refuses to go gently into this new world. Intellectually, he envisions corralling power as his ticket out of subservience in America and the voucher for his progeny to enter as American *pezzonovanti*.

The term "power" appropriately refers to a host of different, sometimes overlapping concepts.[21] At its most general, *power is the capability (the disposition) to produce or contribute to the production of outcomes*. Understood at this level, power is not necessarily relational—that is, it does not require at least two parties, one of which is superior in capability to the other; power does not necessarily require a social setting to gain its meaning or to animate its structure; power does not necessarily generate resistance or opposition or a conflict of interests that the agent must overcome; nor does the exercise of power require a demonstrated intention.

This nonsocial rendering of power is crushingly uninteresting, probably because it is the most general concept connoted by the term. But it does illustrate several useful aspects of power: that power is a capability or disposition, thus someone can possess a certain power but not exercise it; that possessing power implies the actualization of a potential—we learn to walk, to speak a language, to sing, and the like by developing our potentials; that power does not automatically translate to wrongful domination, oppression, or subordination; that power is something almost every living and some nonliving things possess to some extent; to exercise power is more than simply producing or contributing to the production of outcomes because results can sometimes be produced accidentally or serendipitously; and that to have power is typically to attain a good in some respect.

Those who study, write about, and argue about power are most concerned with the concept of one entity having *power over* another entity (dyadic relational power) or a significant institution having power over an individual or a class of individuals (general social power). The concern focuses on the effects of wrongful domination, oppression, and subordination in setting the terms of social life—in identifying the agents of power and those whose lives are diminished as a result of the exercise of power. Oppression, however, is only one of at least three ways of exercising power over others.

For example, superiors can exercise power over subordinates without oppressing them. Nothing in my characterization of power-over implies that the exertion of power must be *against* the interests of the subordinate party. On the contrary, superiors can exercise power over subordinates in ways that advance the interests of underlings. This may occur through paternalistic intervention—when a superior exerts power over a subordinate that advances the subordinate's interests in circumstances where the subordinate cannot identity his or her genuine interests through no fault of the superior. The ignorant subordinate may even resist mightily doing what is in his or her interests, but the superior's power may win the day. Thus, wise parents may exercise power over their children and induce them to eat more nutritiously or gain needed bed rest despite the protestations of their offspring.

Moreover, superiors may exert power over subordinates in order to develop the talents of the subordinates to the point where the influence of superiors is no longer required. Again, nurturing parents aspire to transform their children into fully functioning, capable, powerful adults; caring teachers tend to their students with the aim that their tutelage will be rendered obsolete as their pupils become their own best teachers. Although power-over is intuitively understood as wrongful domination or oppression, that should not obscure the fact that power may be exerted over a subordinate in ways that advance their genuine interests or transform their characters beneficially.

Power-over is itself only one manifestation of possessing and exercising power. Most exercises of power are neither social nor relational. However, power-over is the most interesting relational, social rendering of the general notion of power. Such power may be possessed but not exercised. When exercised, power-over may or may not be exerted intentionally; it may or may not involve a relationship between two people or two groups or a social institution and the masses; it may or may not be triggered by a conflict of interests; it may or may not compel the subordinate party to do what it would not otherwise do; it may or may not be met with resistance; it may or may not elicit the consent or acquiescence of the subordinate party; and it may or may not setback the subordinate party's interests. The list could continue. One might well be tempted to conclude that the concept of power-over is either vacuous or too broad to be useful. Such a conclusion is unwarranted.[22]

Power-over is certainly the rendering of power most relevant to Don Vito's biographical arc. Power-over can be used to oppress others or to transform them in positive directions or to treat them paternalistically. To concoct one definition of power-over that fully embodies all these uses is misguided. A better approach is to provide a neutral definition of power-over that is compatible with the three major uses but which requires corollary concepts to distinguish the three uses from each other: *A superior party possesses power over a subordinate party when the superior has the capability (the disposition) to affect the outcomes and/or interests of the subordinate by controlling or limiting the alternative choices or actions available to the subordinate.*

This definition recognizes that the superior party may possess power over the subordinate party but not exercise that power; that when power-over is exercised, the subordinate's outcomes and/or interests may be affected negatively or positively; but in either case exercising power-over involves controlling or restricting, in any of a variety of ways, the choices or actions available to the subordinate. In this fashion, the superior has limited the usual circumstances of agency enjoyed by the subordinate. Moreover, the superior's power vests in a capability or disposition and is thus not merely exerted accidentally or serendipitously: the superior does not affect the outcomes of the subordinate simply by chance or a fluke sequence of events.

The use of "superior party" and "subordinate party" should not mislead us into concluding that power-over is an inherently dyadic notion. The superior party may be an individual or a group (for example, "the ruling class") or a societal institution (for example, the government or an economic system). Likewise, the subordinate party may be an individual or a specific group (for example, "the proletariat") or the body of citizens distinct from the power-holders ("the masses"). Also, the parties need not be superior and subordinate, respectively, in all respects or even in the possession of power generally. Moreover, under this definition the superior party may truncate the subordinate's available choices or actions either structurally or through distinct interventions. Enduring structural relationships embedded in society nurture power as human agents participate in them. In fact, ongoing social relations and social roles—which involve systemic, continual mutual interactions—are often necessary for the more intense and recurrent exercises of power. Also, dyadic power often arises from the actions of third parties, those who are not themselves agents in the dyad. Ongoing social and structural relations can produce a context that promotes various dyadic power combinations. Structural limitations are typically governmental, economic, or ideological and produce systematic power-over that is sometimes oppressive. Distinct interventions are typically more sporadic and overtly intentional.

The first major use of power-over is oppression. *A superior party oppresses a subordinate party when the superior affects wrongfully and adversely the outcomes and/or interests of the subordinate by controlling or limiting the alternative choices or actions available to the subordinate.* This is the most commonly understood use of power-over. Here the superior party controls or limits the available choices or actions of the subordinate party and thereby affects adversely the subordinate's outcomes and/or interests through a host of possible means: force; duress; deception; personal charm; superior economic bargaining power; disseminating ideology that produces false consciousness that impairs the subordinate's ability to identify his or her genuine interests; truncating public debate to include only trivial or uncontroversial issues; through an informational or knowledge advantage; by exploiting psychological and emotional vulnerabilities; by convincing the subordinate that the judgments of the superior embody special authority; and more.

Depending upon the means implemented and the surrounding circumstances, the subordinates may resist the oppression in some cases, especially when they can still identify their genuine interests and the malevolent intentions of their oppressors; in other cases, the subordinates will consent or acquiesce or obey in anticipation, particularly when their wills and judgments have been overborne by social conditioning and structural socialization.

Of course, to *exercise* power-over oppressively (or in other ways), the superior party must *possess* power over a subordinate party. Merely affecting the interests or outcomes of another person adversely is not enough to establish that oppression has occurred or that a relationship of power exists. In addition, exercising power over a subordinate party and adversely affecting the subordinate's interests are not enough to establish oppression. For example, a teacher has power over her students in some respects. Her awarding a student a low grade will, all other things being equal, adversely affect that student's interests. But the teacher has not oppressed the student, at least insofar as her evaluation was unbiased and otherwise reasonable. Thus, oppression requires a wrongful or unjustified setback of the subordinate party's interests.

This use of power is, of course, Don Vito's oyster: extortion, bribery, coercion, and limiting the terms of discourse and action of subordinates define much of his operation. Notably, his closest allies cherish astonishing faith in Don Vito's power for other purposes. In an evocative scene from the novel that is omitted in the film, Genco Abbandando, Don Vito's lifelong friend and consigliere, wails from his deathbed, "Godfather, Godfather . . . save me from death . . . you have the power . . . It is your daughter's wedding day, you cannot refuse me."[23] Don Vito cautions Genco that he possesses no such power but that he and Genco's surviving family will pray for Genco's soul and ensure that all appropriate religious rituals will be observed. Genco takes this as indicative that Don Vito has already negotiated a fix with God: Genco's soul, despite being stained by countless vile deeds and intentions, will rise gloriously to paradise! After Don Vito chastises Genco for blasphemy, Genco fires his final supplication: "Godfather . . . stay here with me and help meet death. Perhaps if He sees you near me, He will be frightened and leave me in peace. Or perhaps you can say a word, pull a few strings . . . We'll outwit the bastard as we've outwitted others."[24] Genco's final earthly gasps portray Don Vito as endowed with power comparable to that of God; as a man whose undraped presence can scare The Grim Reaper; and as a titan who, failing to frighten The Grim Reaper, can surely out-negotiate or out-shrewd Him. Granted, the dying Genco is grasping for hope. Still, his ineffable faith in Don Vito's power is phenomenal.[25]

The second major use of power-over is paternalism: *a superior party acts paternalistically toward a subordinate party when the superior tries to affect positively the outcomes and/or interests of the subordinate by controlling or limiting the alternative choices or actions available to the subordinate.* Paternalism is employed by superiors when subordinates either do not possess the full capabilities of identifying and acting upon their own genuine interests because of age or impairment (for example, they are minors or are mentally or physically challenged) or when subordinates have the capabilities but lack the judgment because of psychological vulnerabilities, the presence of conflicting interests, or weakness of will (for example, adults who act on immediate desires instead of long-term preferences or those who temporarily act in self-destructive or self-undermining ways because of duress or desperate circumstances). The object of the superior's intentional use of power-over here is to promote the objective well-being of subordinates.

Thus, parents supervise and force their children to do and refrain from doing a host of actions; psychiatrists confiscate dangerous objects from patients who are seriously depressed; friends restrain intoxicated comrades from the consumption of additional alcohol and drugs; and the like. The means used can be almost as varied as those employed in oppression: force; rational persuasion; demands of law; personal charm; manipulation of psychological vulnerabilities; outright threat, to name only a few. As noted, power-over wielded paternalistically will always exist in reaction to enduring human tendencies such as weakness of will, knowing genuine interests but not acting to promote them because of laziness or a conflicting immediate desire; self-destructive and self-undermining tendencies arising from alcohol or drug addiction, psychological vulnerabilities, or desperate material circumstances; and the human inclination to seek apparent pleasure in the present to the detriment of long-range preferences and genuine well-being.

Don Vito sometimes conceals his oppressive exercise of power-over as merely paternalistic. His sobriquet "godfather" underscores that masquerade. In fairness, much the same can be said about the actions of many parents regarding their children. This should not obscure the truth, though, that Don Vito did and parents often do act paternalistically in the higher sense.

Subordinates will often initially resist paternalistic efforts, but often ultimately comply because of fear of reprisals, legal or otherwise, if they overtly rebel. Typically, the aspiration of superiors is that subordinates internalize the messages and values disseminated by paternalistic actions; learn to identify their genuine interests; and render future paternalism unnecessary. This, at least, is the hope of most parents, friends, and medical professions who aim at paternalism as a means of positively transforming subordinates. In this manner, the paternalism of superiors facilitates the empowerment of subordinates.

The third major use of power-over is empowerment: *a superior party acts to empower a subordinate party when the superior tries to affect positively the outcomes and/or interests of the subordinate with the aim of favorably transforming the subordinate by controlling or limiting the alternative choices or actions available to the subordinate.* Empowerment is often paternalism with the direct aim of transforming the subordinate to the point where the subordinate is no longer in need of direction. The means of doing so are theoretically as varied as the other two uses of power-over but are practically limited to those that will accomplish the specific mission of empowerment. The harsher means of exerting power-over are generally less useful here. However, this is not always the case. We can imagine parents and professionals who have captured a young adult from the clutches of a manipulative cult that has preyed upon the victim's psychological vulnerabilities. The parents and professionals might need to use relatively stern methods of de-programming the victim in order to nurture the goal of personal empowerment. Still, as a rule the less restrictive and gentlest means of achieving the goal are recommended: the ends will typically be prefigured in the means used. Another example of the use of power-over as empowerment is the re-education of a victim of harmful social conditioning who, because of the pernicious effects of oppression, requires a more acute awareness of his or her genuine interests.

Less dramatic examples of empowerment would include parents who guide their children, whose age and lack of knowledge preclude them temporarily from identifying or pursuing their genuine interests; teachers who tend to their students in ways that restrict the subordinates' freedom in order to facilitate the time when the students can become their own best instructors and the teachers thereby have helped render themselves obsolete; coaches who administer tough love to their players for the purpose of developing and maximizing the athletic talents of their charges; and governmental efforts to ensure that workers develop the habit of saving funds and enjoy pleasant retirements by requiring contributions during their active years to pension systems such as Social Security.

Empowerment is explicitly geared to change: superiors assume that subordinates have the potential to gain, develop, or recapture the capabilities to identify and to act to advance their genuine interests. Thus, empowerment succeeds when superiors and subordinates transcend or transform their relationships. In those cases where subordinates lack the potential to gain, develop, or recapture the capabilities to identify and to act to advance their genuine interests exercising power-over as empowerment is futile. In such cases, enduring paternalism may be required.

Don Vito often exerted his power in service of empowerment, most overtly with Tom Hagen and Michael, in grooming them for positions of authority that would otherwise be unavailable to them. His goal was not oppression or paternalistic control, but the positive transformation of Hagen and Michael.

The three major uses of power-over constitute neither an exhaustive nor necessary catalog. For example, often exercising power-over involves a mixture of more than one of the uses sketched here. Moreover, my definition of the exercise of power-over as oppression could be broken down in several different uses of power differentiated by the means employed and the extent of the use. Some thinkers will prefer to distinguish the use of power-over by force, through social conditioning, by domination, through personal charm, and the like. Finally, at times power-over is exercised in ways that affect the interests of subordinates neither positively nor adversely except insofar as any restriction of freedom narrows autonomous choice and action. Accordingly, my outline of the major uses of power-over is far from sacrosanct; it is only one of numerous reasonable possibilities.

Don Vito's Will to Power

As is well known, Fredrich Nietzsche trumpeted the will to power as the fundamental human drive.[26] I can summarize the various dimensions of will to power in terms of its basic nature, its process and actions, its results, its aftermath, and its measure of value. I will confine my analysis to the psychological version of the doctrine, the one limited to human behavior. Nietzsche does not use "life" univocally in his published work, and he extended will to power to all organic life and was inclined, especially in his notebooks, but at times in his published works, to accept a cosmological version of will to power that included all of nature. In his notebooks, Nietzsche certainly entertains and seemingly endorses a cosmological version of will to power. The world is nothing beyond the totality of its forces, and will to power is nothing other than the play of those forces. In his published work, although will to power is primarily addressed in human psychological contexts, Nietzsche at times attributes will to power to all organic life.[27] Analytic philosophers have found the cosmological version embarrassing. If will to power is to exude persuasive force, we are best advised to address the psychological version of the doctrine.[28]

The *basic nature* of will to power involves a striving for distinction and domination. Nietzsche describes it as an unexhaustive procreative will of life; it is thus insatiable in that it cannot be fulfilled once and forever; it yearns to discharge strength; if exercised properly it enhances life; because of its pervasiveness reality consists of ongoing competition and conflict; one of its goals is mastery and triumph in such competitions. Will to power seeks to command, create, and increase power; it welcomes suffering as necessary for growth and expansion; the strength of will to power is a necessary but not sufficient measure of its value; and the value of will to power is correlated to the rank of the person who embodies it. Will to power as the will of life involves appropriation, injury, overpowering of the weaker by the stronger, suppression, hardness, imposition, incorporation, and exploitation; worthy will to power spurns egalitarian and democratic instincts, but unworthy will to power promotes such instincts.

Will to power requires ongoing action in service of creating and legislating many things, especially values, by interpreting the world; will to power, properly exercised, earns human beings robust freedom by exuding a maximally affirmative attitude toward life and revitalizing and externalizing our basic animal instincts. Unworthy exercises of will to power reflect and sustain physiological decadence, leveling instincts, and disconnect us from vibrant living. We may evaluate the worth of a culture by what it creates and idolizes; and will to power that is feeble, ineffectual, and unrefined mirrors and promotes an unworthy way of life. We must recognize that will to power may grow in strength and value or it may not, but that all human beings possess will to power as their fundamental instinct. Moreover, will to power has an internal and an external dimension. The internal dimension concerns the ongoing struggle within a person as all his or her drives, passions, and affects, embodying will to power, struggle for preeminence. The external dimension relates to the discharge of will to power in our relations with other entities. Finally, on my view, will to power cannot completely evaporate: all human beings retain throughout their lives some measure of will to power bearing some quality and quantity of value.

The *process and actions* of will to power involve agonistic competitions; the tyrannizing over parts of our own natures; sacrificing and risking much to obtain the feeling of power; overcoming obstacles and resistance, and undergoing suffering; crafting an integrated whole from our conflicting drives, instincts, passions, and affects. Healthy will to power embraces and accelerates change while undermining the status quo; recognizes hardship and discipline as requirements of ongoing self-creation, self-destruction, reimagination, and re-creation; and understands that the value of something is connected to the price one pays to attain it. Keeping the most spectacular, possibly calamitous forces in proximity is crucial for robust self-creation as they wage their internal struggle for preeminence; and aligning one's perspectival will to truth with will to power is a natural mission. The process and actions here described are prescriptions for developing a valuable will to power and exercising it in worthy fashions. On my view, a person who follows guidelines to the contrary will retain will to power but diminish its value and exercise it unworthily.

The *results* of exercising will to power worthily are the creation of new, life-affirming values; cultural advances as we seek the feeling of power in sublimated forms; an ordering and structuring of the world as an expression of a most spiritual will to power; and an enhancement of life. We reveal our place in the human rank order by the interpretations we spawn from the perspectives we embody; and we thereby obtain the only happiness worth pursuing, one grounded in feelings that resistance has been overcome, power has increased, and suffering arising from risk has been surmounted. Attaining Nietzsche's highest value, a maximally affirmative attitude toward life, facilitates and sustains meaning and value above the life-denying, leveling instincts of conventional morality. Re-creating an understanding of the world that undermines unworthy second-order epistemological beliefs—such as objectivism, absolutism, dogmatism, and aperspectival interpretation animates self-consciousness. Uniting will to truth, will to power, and a maximally affirmative attitude toward life represents Nietzsche's highest ideal. Acknowledging that the value of an action is measured by the value of the will to power from which it arose; and defining good (what amplifies will to power, feelings of power, and power itself) and bad (what arises from feckless exercise of will to power and weakness) in terms of human excellence, instead of scripting them to the concerns of conventional morality flows from robust will to power. Again, I have sketched the results of exerting will to power worthily; those who embody unworthy will to power and who exercise it unworthily will garner contrary results.

The *aftermath* of the struggle of will to power is ongoing. We reveal and reinforce our value and standing in the rank order of human beings through the will to power we embody and how we exercise it. Those of strong, healthy will to power are inclined to maintain respectful distance, whereas those of weaker, ill will to power will congregate and seek mutual external validation. Those of healthy, robust, active will to power will be less interested in complying with the expectations of others and more interested in earning merited self-approval.

Will to power underscores Nietzsche's appreciation of the three metamorphoses of personal development: construction (the camel), deconstruction (the lion), and reimagination and re-creation (the child). He is clear that "all great things bring about their own destruction through an act of self-overcoming; thus the law of life will have it, the law of the necessity of 'self-overcoming' in the nature of life."[29] Self-overcoming must be distinguished from self-destruction that arises from psychological neurosis, grave insecurities, internal self-contempt, and repressed hostilities. On the contrary, for Nietzsche, self-overcoming is part of self-aggrandizement, not self-destruction. Life is lived at the expense of other lives (because power and identity are relational notions) and at our own expense. Nature and life are dialectical forces, and the value of the self lies primarily in its ability to transcend itself in tacit understanding of the contingency of the ever-changing world. Because the world is in a continuous state of flux, truculent adherence to a fixed self-understanding will interfere with the project of life.

This understanding of Nietzsche's notion of will to power captures well the guiding impulse of Don Vito Corleone. On this reading, Don Vito's distinctive excellence and highest virtue is his voracious will to power understood as a prodigious will to life.[30] I do not take will to power in this sense as necessarily a proclivity to oppress, wrongfully dominate, or subjugate other people, although exercises of wills to power, including Don Vito's, can assume that form. I take will to power in its generic sense to include an affirmative attitude toward life and vigorous pursuit of ongoing activities; will to power describes a general, fundamental desire about desires. The precise activities undertaken pursuant to will to power do not arise from will to power itself but from the first-order desires an agent adopts and embarks upon.

My view, then, is that generic will to power or will to power as such can be described only vaguely: it is a second-order desire (a general, fundamental desire about particular desires) to have, pursue, and fulfill first-order (particular) desires; it bears a relationship to confronting and overcoming resistances and obstacles; and is related to the pursuit of excellence and personal transformation, as well as to experiences of feeling power and strength and enhanced capabilities. In that vein, will to power manifests and is a measure of an agent's attitude toward and visceral connection to life.[31]

Nietzsche's underlying invocation is power-to, not power-over others. The first wall of resistance confronted by will to power is internal: we must master the dwarf within us that seeks comfort, a life of indolence, the accumulation of pleasures obtained passively, and that is inclined toward seeking external validation through conformity with the dominant ideas. Those willing and able to assume the Nietzschean project must, then, assert power over their own tendencies to underachieve, defined as failing to maximize their higher capabilities. Doing so is the first step toward strengthening will to power by increasing our capabilities, actualizing our higher potentials, and risking confrontation with ever-increasing challenges. Although I am firmly convinced that oppression betrays an unworthy underlying psychology that conflicts with Nietzsche's highest value of *amor fati* (love of fate and of life), his notion of will to power does not of itself dictate the first-order desires that should animate human action.

In any event, for Nietzsche will to power includes the exercise of power-over oppressively but is not defined by that use. Will to power encompasses the expansion of capabilities, the striving for excellence— understood as earned, recognized superiority in the development of higher human functions, and uncommon creativity. He relentlessly points out the mendacity of certain exercises of will to power that present themselves other than what they are: charitable acts arising from ego-gratification under the pretense of selfless generosity; subordinates in power relations luring superiors into becoming dependent upon them under cover of loyalty, while in fact aspiring to reverse roles in the power relationship; the enterprise of morality offering itself as universally beneficial while in fact serving mainly to advantage the masses and disadvantage those of potential greatness.

Understood in this spirit, every human being[32] embodies will to power and an attitude toward and visceral connection to life. But the intensity of will to power admits of countless differences in degree. The generic rendering, indeed no specific rendering, describes accurately the level, intensity, and strength of every human being's will to power. In my judgment, Don Vito Corleone's will to power demonstrates a maximally affirmative attitude toward life.

To illustrate this conclusion, I will sketch three versions of will to power: staunch, moderate, and attenuated. This does not constitute an exhaustive catalog of types of will to power. Numerous intermediary versions can be concocted to bridge the gaps between the three types that I identify here.[33]

Staunch will to power requires ever-increasing challenges and confrontation with greater resistance if it is to grow. Staunch will to power cannot be satisfied by recurrently confronting and overcoming the *same* level of resistance or reiterations of power that renege on relentless self-overcoming, the pursuit of excellence, and insatiable growth. Second, staunch will to power pursues an impossible dream: self-perfection, an ideal that cannot be attained but can be approximated through indefatigable strivings. In this respect, self-overcoming is understood as an ongoing process of constructing, reimagining, and re-creating one's self, informed by a standard of excellence. Third, staunch will to power implies the struggle for preeminence, which invokes aspiring for distinction and establishing domination of a sort. Fourth, the activity of staunch will to power results in an increase in power and strength and capability. Understood as an increase in the capability of an agent to affect outcomes—power intensifies only when ever-increasing (or at least different) challenges and confrontations with greater resistances take place. Fifth, staunch will to power reveals and accentuates an affirmative attitude toward life. Staunch will to power invokes the dimensions of self-overcoming, pursuit of excellence, the struggle for preeminence, establishing the foundations for distinction and domination, increasing power and strength and capability, and persistent growth. The activity of staunch will to power so conceived will almost certainly reflect and sustain a maximally affirmative attitude toward life.

Accordingly, staunch will to power is

1. a *strong* second-order desire to have and pursue first-order desires; and

2. a *strong* second-order desire to confront and overcome significant resistance and obstacles, and thereby feel power and strength and increasing capability while satisfying those first-order desires;

3. in service of recurrent self-overcoming and the pursuit of excellence;

4. a process that itself manifests and sustains a maximally affirmative attitude toward and visceral connection to life.

"Satisfying" will to power is thoroughly paradoxical. More specifically, it is transitory, a moment of deserved fulfillment immediately followed by dissatisfaction that spawns ongoing activity. Satisfaction of staunch will to power cannot produce a relatively stable or lingering state of affairs; instead it amounts to a temporary moment or experience that must be immediately followed by additional striving. Although effete forms of will to power may well aspire for lingering contentment or more enduring (and pleasurable) satisfaction, staunch will to power—the version brandished by Don Vito—harbors no such illusions. Value, as always, sparkles most strikingly in the process and recurrent activity of staunch will to power.

On this model, a person's first-order desires are not derived from will to power. First-order desires typically arise from fundamental biological needs (for example, food, clothing, shelter, intimacy, expression), socially situated goals (for example, individual glory, communal benefits, victory in competition, providing succor to the disenfranchised, seeking eternal salvation through religion, serving political parties), and personal aspirations hatched within a social context (for example, striving to become a renowned musician, yearning to become a worthy parent, craving to bowl a perfect game). The point is that will to power, in any of its manifestations, requires but does not produce first-order desires. A person may exercise his or her will to power in countless ways and in pursuit of a myriad of first-order desires. Accordingly, will to power is not inherently a second-order drive to oppress, tyrannize, or destroy other people or things. Will to power can be harnessed to serve, educate, or advance the interests of other people or things, but, again, is not inherently such. Thus, to evaluate both the fictional Vito Corleone and the nonfictional Mother Teresa as evincing staunch will to power is reasonable.

On this rendering, how might staunch will to power not attain (transitory) satisfaction? The possibilities are numerous. Lacking or being unable to pursue first-order desires would stymie the activity of staunch will to power and thereby deny satisfaction. The failure to confront or to overcome resistance while pursuing first-order desires would also chill satisfaction. Thus, if one agent established a monopoly of domination in his or her domain of activity, that agent would not have suitable "enemies" to overcome. The agent's monopoly would be self-defeating to the aspirations of staunch will to power. Therefore preeminence, distinction, and domination should not imply the elimination of worthy competition. Likewise, if the competition is too daunting, the agent will be unlikely to overcome it, and staunch will to power will be frustrated. Another source of frustration arises from overcoming only moderate resistance that does not produce the feelings of power or promote the increase of power. Any of these ways of frustrating staunch will to power is also likely to thwart self-overcoming, the pursuit of excellence, and growth. On this rendering, reflecting and sustaining a maximally affirmative attitude toward life requires ongoing activities and a recurrent, dynamic process, not a final resting point of complacent satiation.

Accordingly, will to power cannot merely be a will to secure more power; we can gain more power without energizing any of the process values critical to the activity of will to power. The currency of will to power is personal transformation, the feelings of power arising from consciously overcoming serious resistance, and the yearning to confront graver challenges and more intense resistance in pursuit of self-overcoming.

Staunch will to power, then, is avaricious, insatiable, and ego-enhancing. The quest for self-perfection involves ruling and dominating in some sense, typically chronicled by the earned recognition of the preeminent in a broad panorama of human enterprises. Nietzsche favors sublimated, spiritual excellence and creativity over brute, physical demonstrations. A salutary solitude is the calling card of staunch will to power; merited self-enjoyment is its hallmark. Although Nietzsche vacillates somewhat, in my view he takes self-enjoyment and feelings of pleasure to accompany the (temporary) satisfaction of will to power and not as the direct end or purpose of its exercise. Joy and the feelings of power flow from the process of striving and creating, but they do not constitute the reason for engaging that process. The triumph of staunch will to power registers in a well-ordered soul.

I propose describing various levels of will to power in terms of the intensity of their desire to overcome serious resistance that directly affects the possibilities for self-overcoming, the pursuit of excellence, and experiencing feelings of power. All human beings embody will to power to some extent. As a fundamental instinct of life, will to power cannot be forfeited or waived by living beings. *Staunch* will to power, among other things, *seeks explicitly* to confront and overcome *serious* resistance. But less intense versions of will to power, among other things, deflate that aspiration.

Following this train of thought, *moderate will to power* is

1. a *measured* second-order desire to have, pursue, and satisfy first-order desires; and

2. a *measured* second order-desire *to be prepared* to overcome (but not seek out) serious resistance and obstacles, and thereby feel some power and strength and increasing capability in satisfying those first-order desires;

3. in service of steady self-overcoming and the pursuit of improvement;

4. a process that itself manifests and sustains an affirmative attitude toward and visceral connection to life.

That is, those embodying moderate will to power will accept and strive to overcome serious resistance if it presents itself but prefer to attain their goals without that challenge. As such, those embodying moderate will to power will experience the feelings of power less frequently and less intensely than those exercising staunch will to power; they will self-overcome and approximate excellence less often and more tepidly. Those exercising moderate will to power embody an affirmative attitude toward and visceral connection to life that is genuine but far from ideal.

Finally, we must account for an attenuated will to power embodied by those who exert themselves minimally and systematically avoid suffering. They typically pursue pleasures that extinguish their possibilities for intense love, creation, longing, striving, and excellence. Their highest ambitions may be comfort and security. In their value system, habit, custom, indolence, self-preservation, and muted will to power prevail. They embody none of the inner tensions and conflicts that spur transformative action: they take no risks, lack dangerous convictions, avoid experimentation, and seek only bland survival.

To continue the caricature: those bearing attenuated will to power often fail to take responsibility for the persons they are becoming; offer facile excuses for their shortcomings; seek only the blandest hedonistic comforts; and conform abjectly to dominant social ideas to highlight their nonthreatening nature and to satisfy their compulsion for external validation. As such, they represent the path of least resistance: easy accommodations and effete aspirations replace the arduous task of self-realization. They are rarely agents of evil. Their attitude toward and visceral connection to life is fragile and tenuous.

Accordingly, *attenuated will to power* is

1. an *enfeebled* second-order desire to have, pursue, and satisfy first-order desires; and

2. a *considerable* second-order desire to avoid confronting serious resistance and obstacles in satisfying those first-order desires;

3. in service of establishing, maintaining, or increasing tepid pleasure, comfort, and communal peace;

4. a process that itself manifests and sustains a fragile, tenuous, marginally affirmative attitude toward and visceral connection to life.

Those harboring attenuated will to power will often abandon the pursuit of their first-order desires if the process of satisfying them is too arduous. Instead, they will conjure and pursue new first-order desires that appear more easily fulfilled. Attenuated will to power still implies the ongoing second-order desire to have, pursue, and fulfill first-order desires, but aspires to avoid facing serious resistance and does not explicitly seek recurrent self-overcoming and excellence. Accordingly, those embodying attenuated will to power experience the feelings of power and strength and increasing capability rarely and fortuitously.

Again, Don Vito's distinctive excellence and grandest virtue is his staunch will to power. Puzo configures him as a bold adventurer embodying a maximally affirmative attitude toward and visceral connection to life. In fairness, Don Vito's first-order desires are too often narrow and unworthy. Excessively tribal, painstakingly focused on zero-sum competitions, and wistfully cynical about the efficacy of social institutions, the source of Don Vito's greatness also underscores his limitations. Still, his staunch will to power and maximally affirmative attitude toward life should not be denied. Don Vito pursues his first-order desires zestfully; he seeks and overcomes significant resistances and obstacles, thereby feeling power, strength, and increasing capabilities; he does so in service of pursuing excellence as defined by the honor code he embodies; and this process demonstrates and reinforces his maximally affirmative attitude toward life. That he departs the earth whispering "Life is so beautiful" attests to Don Vito's staunch will to power and maximally affirmative attitude toward existence. But staunch will to power and existential authenticity are, at most, necessary but never sufficient conditions for leading a valuable and important human life.

Destiny and Evil

Don Vito sometimes interjects that people must follow their destinies. Chris Messenger interprets Don Vito's invocations as implying that "An inescapable slavery dogs man's destiny. An unseen force dictates man's lot, cast as an endless and repetitive coercion that is deterministic, involuntary, and unacceptable."[34] This observation requires refinement. Although people collectively bear the burdens of what is often described as the human condition—our immutable finitude; being forced to take stands on ultimate existential questions that resist definitive answers; an inclination to yearn unrequitedly for an ultimate culmination that will redeem our lives from futility and pointlessness, for a rational and just universe that will bestow meaning and purpose on our strivings and efforts, and for a connection to enduring value that will remove the yoke of impermanence—*The Godfather* does not portray individuals as merely acting out predestined lives. Don Vito did not murder Fanucci because he was destined to be a gangster. He became a gangster after murdering Fanucci and conniving further with Clemenza, Tessio, and Genco Abbandando. Santino Corleone was not predestined to enter the family business. He entered the family business after witnessing his father murder Fanucci and desiring to emulate him. Michael Corleone was not destined to succeed his father. He succeeded his father as leader of the family after murdering McClusky and Sollozzo, after being sent to Sicily for refuge and education, and after the murder of Santino. When Don Vito intones, "Every man has only one destiny,"[35] he is better understood as implying that our prior choices and actions limit our future possibilities than as suggesting our lives are predetermined and merely involuntary responses to cosmic kismet. Don Vito is not a philosophical hard determinist.

Puzo carefully grooms our appreciation of Vito Andolini. He is victimized by unscrupulous thugs who render him an orphan in Sicily; discharged from his job in Abbandando's grocery store because of the exploitive designs of a loutish gangster in America; lured into small-time thievery with two friends to meet the survival needs of his family; and threatened by the same loutish gangster, who demands a percentage of the trio's gains. Does not Fanucci deserve his fate? Is not the soon-to-be Don Vito a praiseworthy avenger? Is he not noble for refusing to cast his lot with Sollozzo's narcotics venture? Is not the entire Corleone family warranted in attacking Sollozzo and his confederates after they tried to murder Don Vito? Should we not celebrate Michael's gritty slaying of the conniving police captain and the repulsive Sollozzo?

Puzo marginalizes Don Vito's disproportionate unwarranted responses to those reticent to comply with his requests (for example, Jack Woltz, the bandleader holding Johnny Fontane's contract, and the labor leader delaying Johnny's movie production) and his daily exploitive activities (prostitution, illegal gambling, extortion, labor racketeering, bribery of government officials, and murders required to sustain those enterprises), while portraying the Corleone family as heroic gangsters repelling their dishonorable enemies. Were any readers of the novel and viewers of the film rooting against Don Vito and his gang? Were Carlo Rizzi fan clubs forming or Virgil Sollozzo memorials erected? The murders perpetrated by the Corleones too often strike us as vindicated as we celebrate the seemingly righteous retaliation and brilliant efficiency of the family. That Don

Vito's life centers on the accumulation and exercise of power and honor generated by enormous evils seemingly evaporates from the audience's consciousness. Embodying a staunch will to power, Don Vito's first-order desires are contaminated by his zero-sum psychology, his disadvantaged background, and the ultimate incompatibility of nineteenth-century Sicilian values and twentieth-century America culture.

The Degeneration of Michael Corleone

Puzo and Coppola offer a bleak, uncompromising portrayal of American business, politics, and legality. All pillars of American self-understanding are corrupt, hypocritical, and self-serving. Jack Woltz curries an expansive reputation as a philanthropist and patriot, but this phony veneer barely conceals the arrogant, preening pedophile lurking beneath. Senator Geary masquerades as a mellifluous champion of the people, but his favors are bestowed on the highest bidder and his private conduct renders him vulnerable to blackmail. Captain McCluskey is renowned as one of New York City's finest policemen, but for sufficient price acts as bodyguard to a notorious mobster orchestrating the narcotics racket. References to the number of judges, politicians, and police officials that Don Vito "has in his pocket" abound. Readers are hard-pressed to find any reputable government or business representatives in the novel, and the few who emerge in the films are ineffective and foolish.

The saga of Michael Corleone's personal degeneration, from idealistic second-generation Sicilian American to money- and power-grubbing renegade who loses his family, orders the murder of his brother, and inadvertently causes the death of his daughter, is a microcosm of the Puzo-Coppola narrative that the United States, grounded in lofty ideology never fully implemented, is collapsing into a rabid corporatism where profit is its sole remaining idol. In his obsession with revenge and victory, Michael loses his soul along with his family, whereas in its mania for global supremacy, America mocks its founding principles in the quest for gold. In the end, both Michael and America are estranged from their original purposes and highest ideals. In this sense, the novel and films are metaphors for American capitalism run amok. Whereas profit and even power were means to an end for Don Vito, for Michael they became his paramount goals. This confusion of instruments and purposes facilitated the collapse of the Corleone family in one generation. With his daughter's death, Michael's destiny is tragically sealed.

By contrast, Don Vito, the criminal-as-hero, resonates with authenticity. Making only incremental adjustments and marginal adaptations, he retains the old ways, remains immersed in Sicilian family values, spends his golden years tending to tomatoes and peppers while ingesting wine, and dies while playing with his grandchild, uttering his own eulogy: "Life is so beautiful." Pushed off the tally sheet are all the murders, corruption, fraud, extortion, and theft for which he was principally responsible. The victims of his relentless illegality evaporate as effortlessly as the colors of a fading rainbow.

We are introduced to Michael as a returning war hero who has distanced himself from his father's criminal enterprises. When Don Vito is shot by Sollozzo's torpedoes and Michael is the only logical candidate to do what must be done to protect the Don—murder Sollozzo and Captain McCluskey—circumstances conspire against his remaining outside the web of his family's criminality. Because he is the most American of his siblings and the only one with whom Sollozzo, wary of his own safety, will meet to discuss peace terms, Michael is the sole person granted the opportunity to eliminate the threat to his father. All agree that Sollozzo must kill Don Vito to substantiate his will regarding the narcotics racket and to avoid reprisals from Sollozzo after his first murder attempt injured the Don severely.

Fred L. Gardaphé notes the wider significance of Michael's murders of Sollozzo and McCluskey:

> In order for Michel to become a man, he must demonstrate the ability to exert power over other men; he must perform his masculinity publicly, for others to see. In order to sustain this power, the other men must see him as someone who has the power to take life. Michael Corleone becomes recognized as a man in his family the day he kills.[36]

Lured into criminality because of circumstances and love of his father, the continuing saga of Michael's life chronicles how his future was prefigured in the means necessitated by his past. Murdering Sollozzo and McCluskey sealed Michael's destiny. He is the loving son committed to retaining family honor, ensuring his father's recovery, and warding off enemies.

Thereafter, much like a person ensnared within a Chinese finger trap, the more forcefully Michael strains to become legitimate, the more deeply he is enmeshed in criminality. Moreover, the means he uses to secure his ends register palpable effects on his soul (understood as his character). Unwittingly providing stark evidence for the adage that "virtue is its own reward and vice is its own punishment," Michael strays incrementally farther from uniting his family and ushering them into legitimate enterprises while simultaneously growing more distant from them. Whereas Don Vito's paternalism, judiciousness, diplomacy, and reasonableness permitted readers of the novel and viewers of the film to marginalize his ongoing criminality and its deleterious effects on countless victims, Michael's cold-blooded brutality, tactlessness, and distance from his immediate family underscore the inherently exploitive texture of his relationships. The Corleone family collapses along with Michael's personal authenticity.

At the end, Michael is bereft of all robust community and exemplifies the worst-case scenario of rampaging individualism untempered by intimacy. At the end, he is nothing more than an isolated, estranged, alienated pseudo–human being. Recalling Aristotle's bromide that humans are social animals and a human being utterly alone is either a god or a beast, Michael degenerates into a pathetic, ineffectual monster.

The Return to Sicily

Prior to the murders of Sollozzo and McCluskey, Michael had distanced himself from the family business and had aspired to a seamless assimilation into American society. His finance, Kay Adams, could not have mirrored more uniformly the stereotype of a cultured, educated WASP.[37] When Michael was forced to leave her and seek refuge in Sicily, his marriage there symbolizes his revitalized heritage. While in Sicily, Michael "understood for the first time why men like his father chose to become thieves and murderers rather than members of the legal society. The poverty and fear and degradation were too awful to be acceptable to any man of spirit. And in America some emigrating Sicilians had assumed there would be an equally cruel authority."[38] Marrying Apollonia confirms Michael's resurrected Sicilian roots.

In the words of Naomi Greene:

> Sicily is not merely a geographical location, an island off the southern coast of Italy; it is, instead, a land ruled by codes of honor, a mythic land where melodramatic dramas of passion and revenge unfold under the sign of destiny . . . the endless

family feuds, the deadly vendettas. . . . A melancholy land of origins and endings . . . It is in Sicily that Michael . . . appears to make contact with his deepest self, to accept the role that fate has ordained for him. . . . Prompted, in part, by [the death of his wife, Apollonia] he finally embraces the family role he has rejected for so long . . . he decides to avenge the family honor . . . he is a changed man . . . a determined, dark-suited son of Sicily.[39]

Apollonia's death, a fate intended for Michael, signals Michael's subsequent cultural and person disintegration. Upon his return to America, he reunites with Kay while simultaneously assuming leadership of the Corleone family. Michael does so because he retains the illusion that he can escort the Corleone family to full legitimacy in a few years: the conflict between his rejuvenated Sicilianism and his vestigial Americanism can be happily resolved. Unfortunately, the new world conspires with Michael to transform his initial devotion to his family to megalomania of the self whereby he obsessively yearns to control everything intruding on his domain. Intimacy, reciprocity, and mutuality vanish when accosted by Michael's lust for utter domination. Michael's assimilation is complete as he instantiates the worst American nightmare: egotistic individualism satiated temporarily and only by victory in zero-sum exertions. Don Vito's invocations of family, honor, respect, and love have putrefied into Michael's deranged vainglory.

The Godfather II

In *The Godfather II*, the Corleone family begins its gradual collapse. Fredo is wed to a flashy, profligate woman who openly mocks him. Connie neglects her children as she desperately pursues *la dolce vita* with a vacuous lover. Michael robotically and uninspiringly enacts the movements and formal rituals of head of the family, but he performs to an unappreciative audience.

Frankie Pentangeli, an old school mobster, represents forcibly three themes: the dissolution of old-world understandings, criminal and legal, in the new world; the lingering power of the honor code; and the possibility of restoring honor after betraying the code. Pentangeli, reminiscent of the Bocchicchios, is neither clever nor discreet. But he is loyal, capable, brave, and resolute. Although not approximating the ideal of the *uomo di pazienza,* Frankie is a man with whom we would eagerly share a foxhole and would not readily groom as an enemy.

At the beginning of the film, after bemoaning the quality of the (non-Italian) food, Pentangeli enthusiastically implores the band to strike up a tarantella, a gesture that signals Frankie's old-world allegiance as he strives mightily to conjure some brio and joy for a celebration that is otherwise lifeless and robotic. The musicians, none of whom are Italian, can do no better than improvise a fatuous version of "Pop goes the Weasel." The distance the Corleone family has fallen, under Michael's leadership, from the unabashed ethnic revelry of Connie's wedding in the first film is unmistakable. Puzo and Coppola use Frankie as the instrument signaling a wider message. Neither Michael's stewardship nor changing times can replicate Don Vito's Sicilian vision.

The distinctively ethnic wedding of Connie and Carlo, framed by gushing wine, plentiful Italian food, earthly old-world music, tarantella dancers, spiced by supplications for Don Vito's merciful intercessions, is replaced by champagne cocktails, tepid appetizers, tasteless sandwiches, achromatic music, tango prancers, laden by clumsy requests for Michael's indulgences. Frankie Pentangeli and Carmela Corleone are the only identifiable, authentic Italian ethnics at the scene. How do they fare? Frank is unable to communicate effectively with the vapid members of the orchestra and prospers no better with Michael. Carmela must tolerate a kiss on the cheek from light-as-a-daisy Merle and absorb the mushy prattle of prodigal daughter, Connie. The spirit of gravity has ejected Sicilian-Dionysian verve. As such, the opening of *Godfather II* screams that old-world cultural sensibilities, understandings, and values are rapidly and irreversibly shrinking.

Just as striking is the contrast between the respect, admiration, fear, and deep devotion generated by Don Vito and the overt hostility endured by Michael from the likes of Senator Geary, sister Connie, and even Frank Pentangeli, all of whom should know better. Despite Michael's masterful defense of the family enterprise and calculated expansion of the business into Nevada, he serves as punching bag for the insecurities and grievances of others. More perilously, he will soon suffer the felonious intrigues of Hyman Roth and Fredo's betrayal. After evading a fusillade of bullets piecing his bedroom window and perceiving the treachery of someone within his inner circle, Michael advises Tom Hagen that the loyalty of their crime associates is based strictly on self-interest and successful business. If any additional evidence was required to conclude that *la via vecchia, l'ordine della famiglia,* and the Sicilian code of honor were recoiling in deference to fluctuating cultural conditions, here it is. Michael did not merely inherit but earned his father's title, yet the precious bounty of the position, the gilded distinctions of honor, bypass him. Whereas Don Vito was feared and loved, Michael is only feared and even loathed by some. His is a recipe for imminent misadventure.

After being deceived by the Rosato brothers, Hyman Roth's allies, being garroted to near death, and concluding that Michael had betrayed him, Frankie breaks faith with the principle of *omertà*. In exchange for leniency on various criminal charges pending against him, Pentangeli offers evidence against Michael. Undoubtedly, he rationalized that Michael's presumed treachery had lifted his obligation to remain true to the principle of silence. As Frankie strides confidently to his seat at a senate investigation of organized crime, he notices his older brother, still residing in Sicily, sitting next to Michael. It is unclear whether Frankie recants the contents of his sworn deposition, information that connected Michael to numerous murders and other crimes, because he feared for his brother's safety or because his brother's presence, radiating the ideal of the *uomo di pazienza*, underscores how Frankie has dishonored himself and his family by squealing to the federal government. I prefer the second possibility because it highlights the lingering power of the honor code and opens prospects for restoring lost honor.

In that vein, Pentangeli denies his written testimony under oath, which voids his contract with the government. The senate investigation ends abruptly, and Frankie is swiftly incarcerated. He is soon visited by Tom Hagen, who reminds Frankie, a connoisseur of ancient history, of a classical Roman solution for restoring lost honor. Pentangeli accepts the invitation and later slices open his veins. His suicide, however, ensures that his surviving family members will be provided for by the Corleone family. In so doing, Frankie Pentangeli dies with restored honor.

In *Godfather II*, the incremental degeneration of Michal Corleone is tied to his loss of tradition, distance from *la va vecchia*, geographical displacement from New York City to Nevada, and estrangement from his family culminating in his ordering the murder of Fredo. Michael remains committed to legitimatizing the family business and entering the wider society on his terms: "I don't trust society to protect us, I have no intention of placing my fate in the hands of men whose only qualification is that they managed to con a block of people to vote for them . . . Whether we like it or not the Corleone family has to join that society. But when they do I'd like us to join it with plenty of our own power."[40]

But Michael's inclinations for gratuitous revenge amplify; the deaths of Fredo, Pentangeli, and even Hyman Roth are not required to advance the interests of the Corleone family.[41] Along the way, Michael recognizes how his relations are changing and that he must save his family. He asks his mother whether it is possible to lose his family. Because she cannot even fathom such a possibility, Carmela Corleone interprets the question as reflecting Michael's sadness at Kay's recent miscarriage (which was in fact an abortion). Michael brushes that aside and repeats the more striking probability that he is losing his family, that changing times open prospects for such a horror. He seems oblivious to the role his own actions and omissions have played in nurturing this peril. What he has done and why and how he has done it have registered their effects on his soul.

In *The Godfather* and in flashbacks in the first sequel, Don Vito embodies "plenitude, nature, and the old country and its accompanying values—vendetta, the don as protector, and a close-knit family."[42] Upon inheriting control of the crime *cosca*, Michael, oozing gelid estrangement, "shares none of these attributes . . . [he] represents a new, internationalized multi-ethnic mafia that could not be more different from the organization Don Vito headed in Little Italy."[43] Michael, however, surely amplifies the value of vendetta and heightens the principle of disproportionately harsh responses to perceived insults and slights. A shrewd, long-range strategist, Michael promotes a ruthless craving for power as an end-in-itself. Coppola administers righteous punishment in *Godfather III*: Michael witnesses the murder of his daughter on the steps of the Teatro Massimo in Palermo with a bullet intended for him and years later dies in Sicily accompanied only by a dog sniffing about his corpse for enhanced symbolism. Whereas Don Vito perishes while playfully chasing his grandson in a vegetable garden, uttering "life is beautiful" with his final breath, Michael departs the earth bestially: alienated from family, disenchanted with the narrative of his biographical life, and bereft of human consolation. He dies alone or dies like (or with) a dog.

John Paul Russo draws the contrast:

> The old dons were not primarily businessmen; their plenitude was satisfied by what they received in goods, in respect, in the acknowledgement of their power over the local territory. . . . This is not the case with . . . Michael, the racketeers, and the Nevada casino owners. In [impersonal, society] culture

one tends to level everything and make structures meritocratic, to rationalize, and to impersonalize. Contracts, laws, and money are the same for everyone; there are ideally no special clientelistic intimacies and favouritisms or even loyalties.[44]

In my view, this analysis tracks the difference between (1) pursuing material wealth as a means or recognition of perceived higher values such as honor, respect, and enhanced power, and (2) thirsting for material wealth as an end-in-itself, which may require the possession and exercise of power oppressively. The former is more in tune with nineteenth-century Sicilian values and culture, whereas the latter reflects the transition of organized crime animated by American capitalistic values and culture.

Michael begins on the cusp of assimilation into the new world, as the upbeat, idealistic Marine defending his country, and devolves into a cold, alienated, heartless, narrow person, one who responds robotically instead of humanely. Forgiveness, mercy, optimism, empathy, and cheerfulness are beyond his emotional range. Vice has brought about its own punishment by altering the typography of Michael's soul. He has created a new essence of character from the choices and deeds predominating within his existence. Michael's will to power is staunch initially, but in *Godfather III* he loses vitality. Worse, his first-order desires have deteriorated. By annihilating so many other human beings, often unnecessarily, Michael has eviscerated his own character and torpedoed his most intimate relationships. He is a parody of American individualism distorted grotesquely. At the conclusion of *Godfather II*, Michael Corleone is no longer one of Aristotle's "social animals." He is supreme in his earthly criminal power yet a wounded beast bereft of salutary, communal attachments. Instantiating the biblical warning, Michael has won his world but lost his soul.

Michael's personal degeneration can be viewed as a metaphor for the enervating of Italian American organized crime in America. The Racketeer Influenced and Corrupt Organization (RICO) section of the Organized Crime Control Act of 1970 permitted prosecutors to indict and potentially convict large numbers of mobsters in one fell swoop by proving they were jointly engaged in a "pattern" of crimes conducted on behalf of a criminal "enterprise." The pattern could be established by at least two specific federal or state offenses connected to the enterprise and committed within a ten-year period. The innovations embodied by RICO opened possibilities for indicting crime bosses, along with lower-level soldiers and associates.

RICO made crime leaders vulnerable when they received a portion of illegal spoils or when they planned or received after-action reports about crimes linked to the illicit "enterprise."

Thus, crime bosses need not commit the crimes in question to be declared guilty as orchestraters of the criminal "enterprise." Connection to any two or more of RICO's specified felonies, including murder, kidnapping, drug trafficking, robbery, loan-sharking, illegal gaming, extortion, bribery, misappropriation of union funds, arson, fraud, and counterfeiting, committed within ten years, was the predicate for indictment. By extending the statute of limitations, RICO also eased prosecutorial burdens. Moreover, RICO allowed the use of previous convictions in state courts as part of its federal case against perpetrators. RICO also authorized stiff punishments such as a maximum of forty years for enterprise leaders and life without parole for murders. RICO seemingly lacked carefully circumscribed bounds, permitting the government to confiscate assets, homes, property, and wealth amassed from the predicate crimes. In a determined effort to dissolve adherence to the principle of *omertà*, RICO inaugurated a witness-protection program that included immunity from prosecution for designated cooperating witnesses. RICO in concert with more liberal employment of sophisticated electronic surveillance and wiretaps was the harbinger of lugubrious tidings for organized crime.[45]

Changing cultural understandings and social conditions were even more critical in undermining Italian American organized crime. The disaggregation of urban Little Italies, the presence of amplified educational opportunities for Italian American youth, the evaporation of honoring the principle of *omertà* by ordinary citizens, the rise of greater trust in law enforcement, and more expansive freedoms to travel and communicate are social conditions that have shriveled the recruitment base for *Cosa Nostra* in the United States. The loosening of blood and cultural bonds among gang members threatened to eviscerate the distinguishing measure of America's most enduring ethnic crime organization. These bonds had hitherto facilitated *Cosa Nostra*'s capability of rebuffing law-enforcement efforts and maintaining its criminal hegemony.

Unsurprisingly, the mob responded by canvassing the old world to replenish its cache of thugs. Results have been mixed. Imports from Sicily are as necessary as they are unsavory. Derided as "Zips" because of their primitiveness and rapid-fire Italian discourse, the old-world auxiliaries exude baroque ferocity, ruthlessness, and resoluteness surpassing their American counterparts. Highly disciplined, intensely secretive, incorrigibly bound, and regarding their Italian American confederates as flaccid by comparison, the Sicilians are especially well versed in the complexities of narcotics trafficking. The unfamiliarity of federal and local law enforcers with the Sicilian imports renders the Zips tantalizing candidates for murder assignments deemed vital for the mob's flourishing. Still, mutual suspicion pervades relationships between new-world criminal entrepreneurs and their old-world cousins.

Moreover, *Cosa Nostra* suffered a gap in leadership in the early 2000s. The most experienced bosses were either dead or imprisoned courtesy of RICO convictions. The principle of *omertà* even among gangsters was disintegrating from the assault of RICO penalties and the allure of witness protection programs. As mentioned, Italian American urban neighborhoods were rarer and no longer provided cover for criminal culture. Longstanding financial honey pots for the mob, such as gambling in Las Vegas and Atlantic City, as well as labor union racketeering, were vanishing under stricter licensing requirements, more diligent legal oversight, and acquisitions by legitimate multinational corporations.

Although I place *Cosa Nostra*'s odds for survival in America as slim to none—and slim is wavering unsteadily—clarification is required as countervailing factors have emerged. The horrifying activity of September 11, 2001, augured a massive reallocation of federal and state legal resources from organized crime to the fight against international terrorism. Looser surveillance by the authorities and lower priority on America's agenda surrendered oxygen for *Cosa Nostra*. Also, technical and social innovations animated new criminal opportunities such as telephone bill frauds, counterfeiting and bootlegging CDs, manufacturing and manipulating credit cards, phone card frauds, and health care extortion and graft.[46]

To ameliorate the dissipation of allegiance to the principle of *omertà*, crime bosses sometimes order the deaths of relatives of informers and reinstate the principle of blood that made men must be of 100 percent Italian or Sicilian descent. The slaughter of innocent relatives of informants is a significant and unwelcome alteration of the traditional honor code. The response smacks of desperation and undermines the pretense of the sanctity of mob women. As intermarriage among ethnic, religious, and racial groups increases, reinvoking the principle of blood further decreases *Cosa Nostra*'s pool for recruitment.

However, that some version of organized crime will exist in the United States is highly probable. One might intone that organized crime is as American as hot dogs, capitalism, and Thanksgiving turkey. That

Cosa Nostra, with its code of honor grounded in the principle of *omertà*, stringent requirements of blood, solidarity of purpose, and arcane initiation rites, will continue to exist in the United States is highly improbable. Along with the pitilessness of RICO, the sophistication of electronic surveillance, and the solace of witness protection programs, dynamic cultural understandings and social conditions are unlikely to sustain sizable crime syndicates populated by Italian Americans.

At his core, Michael Corleone anticipated the need to transcend criminality, the expiration of *la via vecchia*, and the urgency of recapturing family intimacy. Refusing to apologize for the life he had led, he tottered precariously between the Scylla of craving redemption without repentance and the Charybdis of procuring equanimity without forgiveness. To these concerns we must now turn.

Chapter Four

Repentance, Atonement, and Redemption

Much of the substance of Puzo's novel and Coppola's three films transpires from their refashioning of historical events. These virtuosos researched their subject attentively, and their findings stroll into their work. This chapter begins by describing a host of ways that reality configured the novel and the three films. It continues by explaining and examining the role that rustic chivalry assumes in the Godfather genre and the distinctively Sicilian origins and significance of *Cavalleria Rusticana*, the one-act opera that forms the musical backdrop of *Godfather III*. The chapter then registers how the three films constitute a coherent narrative grounded in parallel segments. In the final film, Michael dallies with repentance, atonement, redemption, and spiritual transformation. These phenomena of the soul are often invoked but rarely critically analyzed. To correct this deficiency, this chapter includes philosophical dissections of the concepts of repentance, atonement, and forgiveness, and their connection to salutary personal transformation. Finally, the chapter concludes by demonstrating why Michael Corleone's scattered clutches for personal redemption were futile.

Reality Configures Art

Echoing the concerns of countless Italian patriots, including Dante and Machiavelli, Puzo and Coppola cast suspicious eyes on the temporal power of the Church while affirming its fascinating rituals and spiritual authority over the people. Michael's series of vengeful murders play out as he serves as godfather at his infant nephew's baptism. Prior to gaining criminal preeminence, Vito Corleone kills the disreputable Fanucci during the feast of Saint Rocco. At a celebration of his son's first holy communion in Nevada, Michael schemes with a government official and with fellow mobsters. Vincent Mancini guns down the obnoxious Joey Zasa during the Feast of San Gennaro, a reckless act that places numerous citizens in peril. The plot of the third film revolves around Michael's connivances with officials of the Vatican Bank who are deeply immersed in financial duplicity. Michael's efforts to purchase a major share of *Immobiliare*, the Vatican's real estate holding company, place him in league with Italian *pezzonovanti* who have expertly exploited and oppressed peasants for centuries.[1] When Michael frantically aspires for redemption, he seeks out a Cardinal in Italy after purchasing induction into the Order of Saint Sebastian. At once pathetic and hopeful, Michael's maneuvers reflect a common feature of the human condition: our sense of personal aggrandizement while we engage in our most cherished projects coalesces uneasily with our ruminations that the cosmos may ultimately be meaningless. Michael discovers that the worst demons are those waging sedulous conflict within his own soul. Perhaps only the highest power can forgive Michael's astounding moral excesses and underwrite his transformation.

In the spirit of art mirroring life, Puzo and Coppola borrowed generously from crime chronicles. For example, the interruption of the Rosato brothers garroting of Frankie Pentangeli is extracted in precise detail from an assault on Larry Gallo by Carmine "The Snake" Persico and a confederate in 1961 in South Brooklyn. The Snake's treachery was halted by a police sergeant undertaking a routine inspection of the bar that was the site of the attack. Gallo refused to press charges or identify his assailants, although he and his brothers later undertook an unsuccessful murder attempt on the Snake. Another illustration is featured in *Godfather III* when the Sicilian assassin Mosca masquerades as a priest in his quest to assassinate Michael Corleone. This stratagem mirrors Aniello (Neil) Dellacroce's ruse when discharging a murder ordered by Albert Anastasia. Dellacroce even adopted a pseudonym, Father Timothy O'Neill.

Pentangeli's testimony at a congressional hearing, along with that of Willi Cicci and Michael Corleone, resembles the setting from which Genovese soldier Joe Valachi at a senate committee hearing in 1963 outlined the daily activities, organizational structure, and historical evolution of *Cosa Nostra* in the United States.

The first film is strewn with real and rumored historical vignettes. As is well known, the character Johnny Fontane is shaped from gossip and speculation about the life of Frank Sinatra: his alleged connivance with mobster Willie Moretti to liberate him from his contract with Tommy Dorsey; his ill-fated love affair and marriage to Ava Gardner; and his commercial fall and stunning rise after securing the part of Angelo Maggio in *From Here to Eternity*. Much of Coppola's film and Puzo's book in these regards reinforces fiction (for example, the Moretti intervention and the extortive gaining of the role in *From Here to Eternity* are spurious).

Sollozzo's kidnapping and eventual release of Tom Hagen after the failed assassination of Don Vito mimics the abduction of four Profaci family *caporegimes* and underboss Joe Magliocco by the Gallo brothers in 1961. The return of Luca Brasi's bulletproof vest swaddling a fish emulates the murder of Joseph "Joe Jelly" Gioelli, the Gallo gang's top enforcer. A dead fish enclosed within his suit coat was hurled from a car to a known Gallo-gang hangout. Sollozzo's murder attempt on Don Vito as he purchases fruit from a vender echoes the murder in 1957 of Frank Scalice, underboss of what later became known as the Gambino family, at a produce stand. Even Michael's eventual evisceration of the leaders of the other NYC families hints at the failed plot hatched by Joe Bonanno and Joe Magliocco, acting head of the Profaci family, to murder fellow bosses Carlo Gambino and Tommy Lucchese. The murder of Moe Greene, a character based loosely on mobster Benjamin "Bugsy" Siegel, hints at Siegel's death at his California home. Both Bugsy and the fictional Moe got whacked in the eye.

The major plot in *Godfather III* reflects the shades of a parallel universe as art tracks reality: Michele "The Shark" Sindona (1920–1986) was a Sicilian financier and lawyer with connections to organized crime organizations in the United States and in Italy, to American banks, to Republican party politicians in the United States and Christian Democrats in Italy, to a major lodge of Italian Freemasons, and to Vatican power brokers. Salvatore Lupo remarks:

> Sindona was a man who came out of nowhere and suddenly and rapidly rose to the highest levels of the financial world, international, Italian, and American. He went on to found "one of the largest, indeed perhaps the largest of all of Europe's financial companies," and ultimately attempted to take control of the fundamental institutions of Italian capitalism through his ties to the Andreotti group, the P2 [*Propaganda Due*, a masonic lodge], and the American and Sicilian *Cosa Nostra*.[2]

An expert in shuttling about large amounts of money to avoid taxation, Sindona, given his vast network of connections, would have been better nicknamed "The Octopus." He purchased his first Italian bank allegedly from proceeds gleaned from managing the heroin profits of the Gambino crime family. Sindona befriended Cardinal Giovanni Montini (1897–1978) who would eventually become Pope Paul VI. He parlayed his acquisition of several other Italian banks through a holding company into an association with the Vatican Bank. He laundered enormous sums of money from his illegal activities through the Vatican Bank to Swiss banks, as well as acquiring a significant share of *Società General Immobiliare*, a Vatican held company, which purchased a major share in Paramount Pictures. In effect, Paramount, the film producers of *The Godfather* movies, was at that point mainly owned by the Vatican Bank.

The Shark also purchased controlling interest in the Franklin National Bank in Long Island. Sindona graciously accepted a host of accolades from fawning politicians in Italy and the United States, but his intrigues were stymied by a stock market crash in 1974. His Long Island financial institution lost around $40,000,000. Later that year, as most of his banks collapsed despite Sindona's shuffling of funds to conceal problems, Franklin National was rendered insolvent due to mismanagement and fraud. Sindona was also linked by gossip, rumor, and speculation to the death of Pope John Paul I, Albino Luciani (1912–1978).

Sindona frantically conjured a multidimensional stratagem to secure his freedom, recover lost Mafia monies, and resurrect his financial empire, especially his banks. After orchestrating his fake kidnapping, attempting to blackmail various government officials, including Italian Prime Minister Giulio Andreotti (1919–2013), threatening those who opposed his reorganization schemes, and appointing intermediaries to solicit judicial mercies, The Shark, his possibilities exhausted, finally surrendered to the FBI. In 1980, Sindona was convicted in the United States of more than five dozen counts of fraud and perjury and extradited to Italy in 1984. There he was found guilty of ordering the murder of an attorney, Giorgio Ambrosoli, who had been hired twelve years earlier to examine Sindona's financial records. The Shark died shortly thereafter from swallowing cyanide capsules, a classic Mafia poisoning ritual, while incarcerated in a Milan jail.

Andreotti, Sindona, and Silvio Berlusconi—along with fifty-four representatives of parliament, twelve generals of the carabinieri, fourteen judges, the leaders of all three Italian secret services, leading figures in the finance police, military officials, journalists, and wealthy businessmen—were all members of *Propaganda Due* (P2), a secret Masonic lodge operating out of Rome.

> There was evidence that P2 was plotting a right-wing coup. Seven million dollars had been deposited in a Swiss bank account belonging to Bettino Craxi, who became Italy's first Socialist prime minister. It had been put there by the head of Banco Ambrosiano [whose major stockholder was the Vatican bank], Roberto Calvi, another P2 member. Calvi's connections with the Chicago-born Archbishop Paul Marcinkus at the Vatican bank were so close that he was called "God's banker."[3]

In 1982, Roberto Calvi, the Italian banker with firm ties to organized crime, the Vatican, Italian government officials, and the Freemasons, was discovered hanging under the Blackfriars Bridge in London, presumably slain by the Italian crime family whose drug profits he had unreliably laundered. After an investigation in 1978, Calvi was sentenced to a four-year term and fined almost $20 million for illegally sending the equivalent of $27 million out of the country, as well as authorizing almost $1.5 million in spurious loans. In 1982, Calvi wrote to Pope John Paul II expressing concern for the imminent collapse of Banco Ambrosiano and the harm the Vatican would incur. Within two weeks, Banco Ambrosiano crashed, with much of its debt journeying to the Vatican bank. Two years later, the Vatican bank paid around $224 million to the creditors of Banco Ambrosiano, a suspected launderer of Mafia drug money.

In 1982, after Calvi was murdered and hung underneath the bridge, authorities deemed Archbishop Marcinkus immune from prosecution because he was a citizen of Vatican City. Craxi fled the country and took refuge in Tunis. Licio Gelli, grandmaster of P2, fled to Switzerland, then Uruguay, but was eventually convicted for participating in a Fascist terrorist strike of a Bologna train station in 1980, in which eighty-five people perished. Giuseppe Calò, Mafia financial czar suspected of ordering the murder of Calvi, was convicted and sentenced to life imprisonment on unrelated charges.

Lurking behind and within virtually every major sinister activity in Italy during this period was Andreotti. Seven times prime minister, a paramount force connecting organized crime to the Christian Democracy Party, an intimate ally of Michele Sindona, an unrepentant capitalist, a skilled diplomat, a firmly committed anti-Communist, a crafty navigator of unfavorable political seas, and the steward of a major boom in the Italian economy, Andreotti led a colorful life. He endured criminal indictments and prosecutions for collusion with organized crime, federal corruption, and ordering the murder of a journalist. Artfully invoking the statute of limitations, Andreotti avoided final determinations of guilt in all cases, even where a trial court declared him guilty of murder and sentenced him to twenty-four years in prison.

Clearly, much of the story line of *Godfather III was* inspired by affairs involving Pope John Paul I, Sindona, Calvi, Archbishop Marcinkus, and Andreotti. Their shadows haunt characters such as Cardinal Lamberto, Archbishop Gilday, Frederick Keinszig, and Don Licio Lucchesi. When Michael Corleone laments the outrageous corruptness infecting institutions "the higher he goes up," he was not merely blowing smoke. History wrote much of Francis Ford Coppola's screenplay.

Rustic Chivalry

Anthony Corleone, having forsaken law school for a singing career, meteorically earns the role of Turiddu in *Cavalleria Rusticana* ("Rustic Chivalry") (1890), a one-act opera by Pietro Mascagni based on a short story by Giovanni Verga. Giovanni Targioni-Tozzetti and Guido Menasci composed the libretto. Anthony's performance occurs in Palermo at the legendary Teatro Massimo, the third-largest opera facility in Europe.

Set in a nineteenth-century Sicilian village on Easter morning, the plot centers on love, sex, betrayal, revenge, and death. Turiddu, son of tavern owner Mamma Lucia, returns from military service only to discover that his betrothed, Lola, has married Alfio, a wagon owner and operator. Turiddu seduces a peasant girl, Santuzza, aspiring to stir Lola's jealousies. In an odd way, the strategy works: Lola begins an adulterous affair with Turiddu. Santuzza is heartbroken. Songs celebrating love, purity, the sweet-scented air, and the Blessed Virgin Mary abound.

Santuzza approaches Lucia's home and asks for Turiddu. Lucia lies and tells her he has left the village to secure some wine. Santuzza senses deception and insists that Turiddu was seen in the village that evening. Lucia invites her inside her home. Alfio arrives on his cart, accompanied by townspeople. He sings and celebrates the wonder of his job and the beauty of his bride, Lola. Alfio asks Lucia for some of her finest wine. Lucia tells him she has none left but Turiddu has left to purchase more. Alfio responds that he had seen Turiddu early that morning. Lucia feigns surprise, but Santuzza stops her. Alfio leaves, while the villagers and churchgoers sing paeans to Easter. Santuzza informs Lucia of her seduction by Turiddu and his adulterous affair with Lola. Lucia sympathizes with Santuzza, who insists because of her dishonor she should not enter the church. She asks Lucia to pray for her. Santuzza then confronts Turiddu, begging him to return to her and abandon Lola. She scolds Turiddu for pretending to be out of town when in fact he was romancing Lola, who suddenly appears singing happily. Lola ridicules Santuzza and enters the church. Turiddu pushes Santuzza to the ground and enters the church. Alfio arrives seeking his bride; Santuzza rats out Turiddu and Lola, detailing their betrayals to Alfio, who, of course, swears vendetta. Santuzza repents her indiscretion and begs Alfio to refrain. The village square is vacant as the orchestra plays the renowned *Intermezzo*.

The church service ends. Turiddu invites friends to Lucia's tavern where he sings an ode to drinking. Alfio joins them but refuses Turiddu's offer of wine. The air is redolent with impending menace.

> The little love-triangle that is *Cavalleria rusticana* reaches its climax in a Sicilian town square when the tough cart driver, Alfio, refuses a drink offered by a young soldier, Turiddu. No explicit accusations are exchanged, but both men know that this little slight will have deadly consequences, for Alfio has been told that Turiddu has dishonest intentions toward his wife. A whole primitive value system is compressed into their brief exchange. Both men recognize that honor has been offended, that vendetta is a right, and that a duel is the only way to settle the debt.[4]

The women leave with Lola. Alfio challenges Turiddu to a duel. Following Sicilian tradition, the two pugilists embrace. Turiddu bites Alfio's ear, signaling a fight to the death. Alfio departs. Turiddu tells Lucia that he is going outside for some air and implores her to be kind to Santuzza should he fail to return. Turiddu leaves for battle. Lucia weeps and embraces Santuzza. The villagers gather; voices resound in the distance. Someone screams, "They have murdered Turiddu!" Santuzza faints, and Lucia collapses into the arms of some of the women.

> Mascagni's audience would have viewed Turiddu, and particularly the cart driver Alfio—for all the countrified pathos of their tale—not just as typical Sicilians, but as typical mafiosi.

> For "mafia" was widely taken to refer not to an organization, but to a mixture of violent passion and "Arabic" pride that supposedly dictated Sicilian behavior. "Mafia" . . . was a primitive notion of honor, a rudimentary code of chivalry obeyed by the backward people of the Sicilian countryside.[5]

John Paul Russo refuses to recognize a close connection between the themes of the opera and those of *Godfather III*.

> [The themes of *Cavalleria Rusticana*] are love, betrayal, religion, sacrilege, and violent death. There is a challenge scene with a ritual biting of the ear, an action that connects the opera back to the main plotline and that Coppola underscores heavily by cutting to Vincent, who nods and smiles. Taking place on Easter Sunday, the opera conveys the idea of redemption, which the film's preceding scenes had stressed, most notably in Michael's confession. On the other hand, the opera plot does not sufficiently mirror the film . . . [which] is not a film about love, betrayal, and revenge, but about Michael's search for inner peace.[6]

I perceive a wider bond between the opera and the film sequence. As a depiction of nineteenth-century Sicilian cultural understandings and social conditions, the opera underscores the background from which Don Vito emerged and the psychology animating much of his activity in America. Don Vito's life initiates the causal chain that leads to Michael's biographical arc, which culminates with his ill-fated flirtation with spiritual redemption, the only transformation of his soul that might facilitate "inner peace."

The Godfather Trilogy

The Godfather films are strikingly parallel, even formulaic in their production. Almost a score of coextensive scenes graces the three movies.

Family and Religious Ceremonies Seasoned with Music

The first film spurts with an Italian old-world ethos permeating the wedding of Constanzia Corleone and Carlo Rizzi. Romance, dancing, food, family, and robust community overwhelm the screen, punctuated by the sexually suggestive Sicilian folksong, *Che la luna mezzo mare*,[7] as Don Vito fields a series of requests from friends. Johnny Fontane croons an appropriately romantic Italian favorite. The second film opens in sterile Nevada, the barren southwest, with a senator mispronouncing Michael's surname, musicians who cannot even simulate a tarantella, a whitebread boys' choir chanting passionless tunes, and a fractured family coolly welcoming its prodigal daughter. Alessia Ricciardi notes, "The barren deserts of Nevada and the disquieting stillness of Lake Tahoe thus mirror the frozen interior landscape of Michael's psyche as he solidifies his position as his father's successor."[8] The third film begins with overt hypocrisy as Michael, desperately trying to purchase redemption from the avaricious hierarchy of the Roman Catholic Church, is inducted at St. Patrick's Cathedral into the order of St. Sebastian. Puzo and Coppola link the Church with the other unholy members of the American trinity: business, politics, and law. Michael has returned to his American roots geographically, but his decaying relationship with his family and his genetic origins are underscored. Corruption, treachery, and frenetic capitalism have eviscerated traditional family values. After Michael's induction ceremony, Connie unsuccessfully tries to inspire communal vocalizing of "Eh, Cumpari," Julius LaRosa's adaptation of an Italian folk song, an effort rudely interrupted by Joey Zasa and his enforcer, Anthony "The Ant" Squigliaro.

The three films take viewers from Corleone, Sicily, to New York City's Little Italy to the family compound in Long Island to Las Vegas and Lake Tahoe, then back to New York City, with business and revenge visits in Sicily. But the old world is yesterday's news. The opening scenes in each case fix the opposition between old-world family values and new-world upward mobility punctuated by business and political corruption.

The trajectory of the three films chronicles the journey from robust tribal community within a dangerous, often hostile America extolling grand individualism; to capitulation to America values signaling the gradual collapse of robust community; to realization that radical return to founding communal principles is required for personal redemption and familial reconfiguration; to tragic consciousness that genuine opportunities for actualizing such possibilities have expired. Michael as an individual, the Corleones as a family, and the sublime promises of America, suffocated by avarice, zero-sum competition, and the false idols of wealth and wrongful domination as ends-in-themselves, have all dissipated. *Godfather II and III* de-romanticize the mob. The glories of *la via vecchia*, exemplifying the ideal of the *uomo di pazienza*, and remaining true to the requisite code of honor evaporate as unadulterated avarice, arrogance, envy, and gluttony for power as an end-in-itself reign.

Private Meetings with the Head of the Corleone Family

The first film features the classic encounters of Don Vito with petitioners exploiting the Sicilian tradition that fathers of brides cannot refuse any reasonable request from family members and friends. Amerigo Bonasera, Nazorine the Baker, and Johnny Fontane implore Don Vito to solve prickly quandaries impairing their well-being. Don Vito pledges his support, and soon thereafter the challenges are met to the satisfaction of the petitioners. In so doing, Don Vito demonstrates his generosity, power, efficacy, and allegiance to *la via vecchia*, *l'ordine della famiglia*, and the honor code. In the second film, Michael meets with Senator Geary to solicit his help in obtaining gaming licenses for a casino in Nevada. Geary spews personal insults and tries to extort Michael, demanding an exorbitant fee and an ongoing percentage of profits generated by the casino. Michael also parleys with Frankie Pentangeli, longtime Corleone capo, who is outraged at the incursions into his affairs by the Rosato brothers and their patron Hyman Roth. Michael advises Frankie to endure the aggravations and to agree to peace with the Rosatos, as Michael has larger designs planned with Roth. Pentangeli departs thoroughly frustrated but submits to Michael's orders. The third film features an obstreperous conference between Michael, Vincent Mancini, and Joey Zasa. Joey informs Michael that Mancini, who works for Zasa, has been insubordinate and merits reprisal. Vincent alleges that Zasa has been disloyal to Michael and is ruining Little Italy by peddling drugs and through sloppy administrative practices. The personal animosity between the two is palpable. Michael tries to avoid adjudicating their feud and advises that they reconcile, or at least tolerate each other. As the two adversaries disingenuously embrace, neither gangster evidences allegiance to the Dale Carnegie method of dispute resolution: Zasa insults Mancini, calling him a "bastard," and Mancini takes a bite out of one of Zasa's ears.

Again, the sequence of the films chronicles the degeneration of the power and efficiency of the leader of the Corleone family to solve problems readily and to facilitate the well-being of petitioners. Whereas Don Vito's subsequent schemes to fulfill his promises were merely episodes that ended well, Michael's unsuccessful meetings in the second and third films were springboards to the major plots of the movies. The social conflicts between *la via vecchia* and American understandings and values were deepening.

ROMANTIC LIAISONS AND LOST LOVE

The first film sketches the temporarily idyllic wedding of Constanzia Corleone and Carlo Rizzi, a pairing whose violent discord soon thereafter animates the murder of Santino Corleone. The second film begins with Michael's continuing affection for and protection of Kay, but soon degenerates into Kay's estrangement, her choosing an abortion, her excoriation of the person Michael has become, and their eventual divorce. The third film highlights an intrafamilial romance between first cousins, Vincent Mancini and Mary Corleone. The detachment of these two, from a love forbidden from the outset, becomes Michael's condition for appointing Vincent head of the Corleone family. In the first film, Michael loses Apollonia in the automobile explosion. In the second film, Michael and Kay become estranged, argue violently, and eventually divorce. In the third film, the star-crossed romance of Mary and Vincent must end. In contrast to these ill-fated couplings, lurking in the background is the seemingly rewarding marriage of Don Vito and Carmela Corleone. Bereft of marital infidelity, firm in the allocation of social roles, an alliance of immigrants assiduously traversing the perilous paths of the new world, their union oozes common cause, mutual respect, and steely resolve.

GENERATIONAL DISAGREEMENT

In the first film Don Vito is disheartened that after the treachery at Pearl Harbor his youngest son would enlist in the Marines and fight for the faceless glob of strangers. Privately proud of the subsequent heroism Michael displayed, he remained puzzled by Michael's motivation and sense of duty. In the second film, probably because the timeline narrows possibilities for intergenerational strife, the disharmony is intragenerational. Connie seeks funding for her proposed marriage to Merle, which Michael denies; Fredo bumbles into a betrayal of Michael that generates a fatal climax. The third film marks Anthony's rebellion against Michael's design that he should finish his law school studies and assume a legitimate role in the family business. Aided by Kay's forceful intercession, which secures Michael's tolerance, Anthony pursues a musical career. Mary until the moment she is slain by a bullet intended for her father resents his struggles to disjoin her romance with Vincent Mancini.

Business Transactions and Major Trouble

Virgil Sollozzo's overture regarding narcotics trafficking weaves the major plot of the first film. Don Vito's refusal to participate spurs Sollozzo's attempt of his life, Michael's murder of Sollozzo and McCluskey, Michael's exile to Sicily, his return and accession to head of the family, and eventual wholesale vengeance against the other New York crime bosses. In the second film, Michael's ambiguous financial alliance with Hyman Roth, complicated by Castro's successful revolution in Cuba, generates his appearance before a Senate investigation panel, Pentangeli's anticipated betrayal, Pentangeli's recanting, Michael's assassination attempt on Roth, and eventual vengeful spree against Fredo, Roth, and others. The plot of the third film centers on the intricate financial arrangements of assuming control of *Immobiliare*. Church officials, Vatican bankers, politicians, the shadow government of the Roman Masonic lodge are enmeshed in a web of chicanery.

Deceptive Confederates

The first film registers the treachery of Paulie Gatto as the made man who collaborates in Sollozzo's assassination attempt on Don Vito, and Sal Tessio, a caporegime and one of Don Vito's original criminal confederates, as the conniver who aids Don Emilio Barzini's planned murder of Michael. The second film chronicles Fredo's clumsy betrayal of Michael; Pentangeli's misunderstanding that promotes his arranged senate testimony; and Roth's long-range strategy to kill Michael. The third film highlights Joey Zasa and Don Altobello conspiring with Lucchesi to destroy the Corleone family. In *Godfather II*, Michael reports Don Vito's advice to Pentangeli: "keep your friends close but your enemies closer." The three films substantiate that counsel.

Conferences with the Wider Network of Crime Bosses

Prior to arranging for the return of Michael from Sicily, Don Vito addresses a small congress of crime, including the leaders of the other New York City families, as well as the bosses of other prominent municipalities. Pursuant to suing for peace, he pledges to refrain from all vengeance for the murder of Sonny and the assassination attempt on himself and agrees to provide political and legal protection for narcotics trafficking. He insists, however, that these vows are conditioned on Michael's safe return to the United States. In the second film, Michael meets with Roth and other crime leaders, as well as American industry giants, and Cuban dictator, Fulgencio Batista, to cement understandings and to determine financial arrangements. In the third film, Michael travels to Atlantic City to reward his criminal colleagues for their investment in casinos that he has recently sold and to establish his independence from them as he aspires to purchase controlling interest in *Immobiliare*. Unfortunately, his partners want to stay connected so they too can launder their money through *Immobiliare* and reap financial benefits from the real estate holding giant. Altobello and Zasa, under the leadership of Lucchesi, engineer a helicopter attack that annihilates most of the attendees.

Dominant Enemies Shrouded by a Veil of Guile

In the first film, "it was Barzini all along," who was the mastermind of the Corleone family's calamities, but Don Vito was not aware of this until he listened to Barzini during the conference of criminals. Tattaglia and even Sollozzo were the beards who masqueraded as Don Vito's primary enemies. In the second film, Hyman Roth constructs layers of deceit to obscure his control over political stratagems that jeopardize Michael. In the third film, Michael intuits that the level of sophistication of the plots against him are beyond the talents of Joey Zasa and even Don Altobello, but he identifies Lucchesi as the prime architect only after conferring with Don Tommasino in Sicily.

The Vagaries of Illness

Genco Abbandando expires at the outset of the first film; Sollozzo's gunmen seriously injure Don Vito, and his lengthy recovery occurs during Sonny's battles against the other New York City crime families, which triggers a passel of pernicious events. In the second film, Hyman Roth's cardiac ailments occasion a series of schemes and responses. Michael's struggles with diabetes in the third film culminate in a stroke, weakening his resolve and providing an opportunity for Connie to order Vincent to extinguish Joey Zasa, facilitating Vincent's rise to head of the crime family.

Shadow Dons and Questionable Decisions

Don Vito's injuries compel Sonny's ascent to interim leader of the family in the first film. Sonny responds overly aggressively to the attempt of his father's life, and Tom Hagen proves an inept wartime consigliere, allowing himself to become complacent during a lull in hostilities.

In the second film, the failed murder attempt on Michael causes him to depart the compound, and for a brief period Tom Hagen assumes control. In the third film, Michael's diabetic stroke leaves no one formally in charge, but Connie takes the reins. Convinced that the key to security rests with Joey Zasa's death, just as in the first film the family is convinced that killing Sollozzo is necessary for its defense, and Connie gives Vincent the order to execute that design. Michael later rejects the murder of Zasa as untimely.

Vito Corleone slays the rapacious Don Fanucci during the feast of San Rocco but does not sully the religious blessedness and ethnic gravity of the event. Vito murders the gluttonous Don outside of Fanucci's apartment. The festival churns along unimpeded. In *Godfather III*, however, Vincent Mancini executes Joey Zasa during a religious festival in Bensonhurst, while his crew murder Zasa's bodyguards. In an unmistakable display of the descent of the Corleone family, religious and cultural symbols and artifacts are shattered during the assaults. Religious respect, ethnic boundaries, familial values, and honorable consideration for innocent parties can no longer restrain unbridled vengeance and avarice. America's wild west shootout has usurped Sicily's clandestine rustic chivalry.

Return to Sicily and Subsequent Deaths

Michael scampers to Sicily after murdering Sollozzo and McCluskey. There he not only is educated in *la via vecchia* but also marries Apollonia, who is shortly thereafter killed in an automobile explosion intended to annihilate him. In the second film, Don Vito returns to Sicily on business and to avenge the slayings of his father, brother, and mother. He fatally stabs Don Ciccio, Don Vito's friend Don Tommasino is shot in the leg during their escape, and a principle of honor is fulfilled. In the third film, Michael, Kay, and their children travel to Sicily to attend Anthony's performance of *Cavalleria Rusticana* in Palermo. Michael squires Kay about the countryside of the island, attempting to reclaim her affections, or at least achieve a rapprochement. Beginning with the murder of Don

Tommasino by Mosca, the professional assassin from Montelepre and an old friend of Don Altobello's, the tally of killings includes Michael's twin bodyguards at the Teatro Massimo, Don Altobello, Mary Corleone, Mosca, as well as several murders orchestrated by Vincent Mancini and carried out by Calo, Neri, and others in Italy.

Deaths of Valuable Confederates in Crime

Luca Brasi is garroted in Bruno Tattaglia's nightclub, victim of a trap set by Tattaglia and Virgil Sollozzo. In the second film, Rocco Lampone is shot dead after murdering Hyman Roth. In the third film, Don Tommasino is murdered by an assassin disguised as a priest. Mosca also murders the twin bodyguards hired by Vincent to protect Michael at the opera house in Palermo.

Ersatz, Strategic Betrayals

In the first film, Don Vito instructs Luca Brasi to simulate a betrayal, approach the Tattaglia family, and seek employment. This preposterous venture, hatched immediately after Don Vito had declined participation in Sollozzo's drug racket and involving Don Vito's closest henchman, is easily detected by Bruno Tattaglia and Virgil Sollozzo. Brasi's explanation for his defection from the Corleones is anemic. Was Don Vito exhibiting early signs of dementia? How could Brasi, no intellectual but still a cunning, experienced gangster, agree so facilely to a plot that an enemy could see coming miles away?

Here the most striking betrayal is how the film abandons the novel. In the book, Don Vito sets up the scheme more carefully. He instructs Luca Brasi several months earlier to make contact with Tattaglia and Sollozzo, and even then indirectly. Brasi subsequently frequents nightclubs owned by the Tattaglia family, and becomes a client of one of the Tattaglias' most captivating call girls. During their nocturnal liaisons, Brasi sometimes carps about being undervalued by the Corleone family, taking care not to do so inordinately or hostilely—and all the while feigning genuine romantic obsession with the woman. The call girl, sensing an opportunity to garner all she could reap, predictably informs Bruno Tattaglia of Brasi's apparent dissatisfaction. Bruno first approaches Luca with the proposition to become his enforcer. Brasi wisely does not jump immediately at the bait. The negotiations continue for about four weeks; Luca insists that should he accept Tattaglia's offer—he would never betray or violate Don Vito directly; Luca lusts only for an inroad into drug trafficking, perhaps as an independent operator.

> In that fashion [Luca Brasi] might hear something about Sollozzo's plans if the Turk had any, or whether he was getting ready to step on the toes of Don Corleone. After waiting for two months with nothing else happening, Luca reported to the Don that obviously Sollozzo was taking his defeat graciously. The Don had told him to keep trying but merely as a sideline, not to press it.[9]

Bruno Tattaglia, playing his role to perfection, agrees that his family will never call upon or expect Luca to move against Don Vito. Soon thereafter, Bruno invites Luca to meet someone, whom Luca infers is Sollozzo. That set the stage for the murder of Luca Brasi. Sollozzo and Tattaglia played the percentages: slaying Luca would deprive the Corleone family of its greatest enforcer, and Sollozzo and Tattaglia would not have to wonder whether Brasi's partial defection was genuine. On the eve of their assassination attempt on Don Vito, Sollozzo and Tattaglia eliminated a fearsome enemy. Clearly, the novel assembles the feigned betrayal of Luca Brasi and his murder far more credibly than does the film. The Corleone and Tattaglia crime families were not led by simpletons or fools, and Tom Hagen had accurately evaluated Virgil Sollozzo as a Sicilian (in the sense that Jack Woltz was not).

In the third film, Michael orders Vincent to feign a betrayal and approach Don Altobello for his support. Vincent correctly intuits that Altobello would not believe him. Michael implores Vincent to manipulate the romance angle and to gush rabid ambition:

> See if you can learn how high Altobello is connected. Arrange a meeting. You say how devoted you are to me. Tell him your problems. You ask for his help . . . That you want to run away with my daughter. Only you know that if you do, I will become your enemy. . . . You ask Altobello to speak to me. To further the marriage. . . . Explain to him how, you can never be part of my legitimate world. That you want your own family. . . . Remember, if he hints that he wants you to betray me, get insulted. Because that's his trap.[10]

Vincent dutifully approaches Don Altobello with these implausible rationales, assuring the aging crime boss that should he intercede with Michael on Vincent's behalf, Vincent would consider that an act of friendship (loyalty) upon which he would place great value. Don Altobello takes a leap of faith and infers that Vincent would then work for him. Vincent confirms Altobello's inference. Not yet certifiably senile, Altobello conjures a deeper reason for Vincent's solicitation: "You're not telling me the whole truth, Vincenzo. Isn't it true, with Michael gone, the girl controls everything?"

Vincent feigns outrage and demands Altobello "leave the girl out of this." Altobello gently prods, exalts the mutual love of Vincent and Mary, and elicits the confession he seeks.

Asking, again, whether he had discerned Vincent's deepest motivation, Vincent replies softly: "You're a wise man. Don Altobello. I'm going to be learning a lot from you." Altobello rejoins with an epigram, "The richest man is the one with the most powerful friends," and introduces Vincent to Don Lucchesi, who begins informing Vincent of his broader associations and schemes.

Unfortunately, the clumsy feigned betrayal of the third film cannot be redeemed by the novel. Why would Altobello's intercession cut any emotional ice with Michael? Michael knows that his daughter and Vincent are first cousins. Nothing Altobello can advance changes biological fact. Michael's business affairs are far from fully legitimate, and given Lucchesi's ongoing machinations that Michael will ever attain that goal is highly improbable. What does Mary control when Michael is dead? She does not ascend to leadership of a crime family. She, along with her brother, would probably inherit scads of money and, probably, leadership of the Vito Andolini Charitable Foundation. Still, what could Altobello say that would erase Michael's recalcitrance about the romance of Mary and Vincent? Moreover, why is Lucchesi confiding in Vincent prior to Altobello's efforts on Vincent's behalf? Without knowing whether Altobello can coo magic words that might transform Michael's heart and win Vincent's allegiance to the Altobello-Lucchesi axis of power, Lucchesi, a razor-sharp international swindler, readily reveals economic mysteries, political strategies, and clandestine associations to Vincent. Vincent Mancini seemingly whispers talismanic incantations that render Osvaldo Altobello and Licio Lucchesi as vulnerable as snow floating on the equator. Credibility evaporates in the cauldron of the dramatic requirements of cinema.

The second film lacks the stark feigned betrayals of its siblings. Michael does solicit the cooperation of Frankie Pentangeli in a rudimentary con of the Rosato brothers, but that thin artifice is stymied by Hyman Roth's broader subterfuge.

Distinctly Formidable Antagonists

In each film, the Corleone family confronts powerful, crafty enemies. Don Emilio Barzini and Virgil Sollozzo are ruthless, cunning, and foresighted. They are Sicilians in the requisite sense: they would willingly risk everything on a matter of principle, on a matter of honor, for revenge. As easily as the banality, "it is just business, not personal," flows from their lips, as devotees of an honor code they profoundly comprehend that their enterprises transcend the terms of contractual agreements and the accumulation of profit. Sollozzo detects Don Vito's contrivance with Luca Brasi and arranges an attempt on Don Vito's life. Barzini lulls Tom Hagen and Sonny into complacency and then snaps the trap that results in Sonny's murder on the causeway. If the measure of people resides partly in the quality of the obstacles and challenges they withstand and overcome then Don Vito and Michael were well served by the resistance sustained by Sollozzo and Barzini.

In the second film, Michael waltzes violently with a master of layered deception, Hyman Roth. Orchestrating the Pentangeli-Rosato feud, exploiting the senate hearing on crime to his advantage, and devising the assassination attempt on Michael, Roth shrewdly masks his designs with unctuous avuncularity and false rectitude. Much of his conniving, however, is undermined by the success of Castro's revolution. Nevertheless, overcoming the intricate treacheries of Hyman Roth is no small matter.

In the third film, the Corleone family meets an enemy with the widest and deepest network of confederates: Licio Lucchesi. Moreover, the Corleones meet Lucchesi on his home turf. In a swirl of American gangsters, fraudulent European bankers, avaricious prelates, occult Masonics, and unscrupulous Italian politicians, the Corleones are hard-pressed to discern the identity of the leader of this multinational conglomerate. Meanwhile, Lucchesi engineers a preposterous yet breath-taking helicopter assault in Atlantic City, directs the perfidiousness revolving around *Immobiliare*, and concocts with Don Altobello a blueprint to murder Michael. Lucchesi's fatal error is his inexplicable willingness to confide in Vincent Mancini despite sparse evidence warranting such action. The smug manipulator inexplicably morphs into a guileless, disclosing chatterbox.

Other antagonists also present reasonably strong resistance to overcome. The likes of Bruno Tattaglia, Osvaldo Altobello, and the other leaders of crime families pose serious opposition. However, the primary enemies of the Corleone family comprise the highest rank of encumbrances to conquer.

Passing of the Torch

In order to fulfill his pledge not to disturb the truce forged between crime families and to facilitate the eventual revenge his family must exact upon those families, Don Vito bequeaths leadership of the Corleone syndicate to his youngest son Michael. Don Vito's lengthy recovery from the murder attempt on him, the need to forge a peace to ensure the safe return of Michael from Sicily, and the duty to comply with the honor imperative of vengeance conspire to this end.

Don Vito has no aspiration to transform the family business to full legitimacy during his lifetime, although he accepts rationally that this will be ultimately necessary.

In the third film, Michael's struggles with diabetes, culminating in a stroke, as well as his unrequited determination for full legitimacy, his disappointment at the quality of the person he has become, and the stark threat of imminent widespread violence augured by the murder of Don Tommasino. These conflicts converge and facilitate his bequeathing his leadership position to nephew Vincent Mancini.

In both cases, the transfer of power implies a new style of hegemony. A young Michael is more ruthless, less diplomatic, and less versed in *la via vecchia* than his father but blessed with a keener comprehension of American business. Predictably, he grows colder and more alienated as the effects of time and evil-doing exact their tariffs. Ceding leadership to Vincent heralds a return to the administrative style of the early Michael imbued with the wrathful violence of Sonny, Vincent's biological father. Unless Coppola conjures a fourth *Godfather* movie, we will not learn how Vincent develops, but early returns suggest that a long, tranquil life consummated by a serene death at home surrounded by family, capped by the words "Life is so beautiful," is highly unlikely.

Bloody, Vengeful Climax

The denouement of the first film is the murder of the bosses of the other four New York City crime families, along with the killings of Carlo Rizzi, Sal Tessio, and Moe Greene (and in the novel Fabrizio, the conniving shepherd from Sicily, is murdered in Buffalo). All family business is settled, intones Michael, which translates to all vengeful murders have taken place.

The second film features the murders of Fredo and Hyman Roth, as well as the shooting of Rocco Lampone, the killer of Roth, and the negotiated suicide of Frankie Pentangeli. Those who betrayed Michael Corleone, whom he assesses as enemies, must be destroyed. The assumption of Lampone of what was in effect an obvious suicide mission goes unexplained.

The third film may have the bloodiest ending of all. Mosca slays the Corleone's twin bodyguards, Connie poisons Don Altobello, Mosca shoots Michael and unintentionally kills Mary, and Vincent murders Mosca. In Italy, Al Neri shoots Archbishop Gilday at the Vatican, two assassins suffocate and then hang Fred Keinszig the Vatican banker, and Calo stabs Don Lucchesi in the throat with his glasses before being shot dead by his bodyguard.

The nature of the family business could not be portrayed more bluntly. Even at the end of the third film, the distance of the Corleone family from full legitimacy remains spectacularly remote.

Parallel Murders

At roughly the same age, Vito Corleone slays Fanucci, and Michael murders Sollozzo and McCluskey. Likewise, Don Vito avenges the deaths of his father, mother, and brother by Don Ciccio in Sicily, and Michael, at a similar age, extinguishes Hyman Roth and Fredo and negotiates the suicide of Frankie Pentangeli.[11] Of course, one glaring difference should not be ignored: "Vito would return, in honor, to the Sicilian village of his boyhood and personally disembowel the village strong man who murdered his family twenty years earlier. Michael would send professional killers to murder his rival [Roth] and his traitorous brother."[12] This signals the attenuation of the honor code.

Michael's Plight

The final scenes of the three films chronicle Michael Corleone's internal condition. In the first film a hysterical Connie confronts her brother accusatorily. Convinced Michael has ordered the murder of her husband, Carlo, Connie's outrage is palpable through her tears. Michael, at once condescending and consoling, neither confirms nor denies her allegations. Instead, he coolly embraces his sister, and then dispatches her to see a physician. Having observed all this, Kay asks Michael if he ordered the murder. Although angry that Kay would inquire about his affairs, he indulges her question. He lies and denies responsibility. Kay is seemingly relieved. She leaves the room. Kay looks back and sees Clemenza, Al Neri, and Rocco Lampone, the three remaining Corleone caporegimes, embracing Michael, kissing his head, and demonstrating their submission to his leadership. Neri moves to the door and shuts it. Kay's relief dissolves into an olio of intractable suspicion and shocking comprehension. She seems marked indelibly as an outsider, a *straniera* in her own home. As Neri closes the door, the demarcation between syndicate business and family intimacy distends.

So ends the first film. Puzo's novel, however, is more nuanced. Kay abandons the Corleone family compound; she returns a few days later with the news that she has sought the services of a priest in order to convert to Catholicism. Kay Adams, quintessential WASP, cannot transform herself genetically into a Sicilian American, but she can alter her faith and connect culturally to a fundamental constitutive of Michael Corleone's identity. Comprehending her husband's unspeakable, mortifying transgressions of God's law and his need for redemption, she attends mass daily and prays for Michael's soul.

In the novel, perhaps incomprehensibly but certainly expeditiously, Kay Adams Corleone has skated from a deceived spouse of a serial murderer to a Roman Catholic convert exercising Sicilian rituals of atonement on his behalf. She has translated her initial alienation and estrangement into spiritual advantage for her betrayer. Had Coppola included this scene in his film, the subsequent and radical transformations Kay undergoes in the two subsequent movies would have formed a more provocative character study.

In any case, Michael has morphed from the American outsider into a crime leader who will desperately and unsuccessfully try to compartmentalize the illegality of his business life from the intimacy of his family life. He has earned the undisputed leadership of his crime syndicate, but he is already putrefying callously and icily.

In the second film, the penultimate scene is a retrospective of a family surprise birthday party for Don Vito on December 7, 1941, a day that still lives in infamy. Sonny has introduced Carlo Rizzi to Connie, and they sit around the kitchen table with Fredo, Michael, Tom Hagen, and Tom's future wife Teresa. Sal Tessio brings in a huge birthday cake. Sonny is outraged to learn that Michael has dropped out of Dartmouth College and enlisted in the Marines. He scolds Michael for risking his life for strangers. He instructs him not to forget that his country is not his blood. Michael observes dryly that Sonny is talking like their father. Michael believes differently from both. Everyone rushes to the door of the room into which Don Vito is entering—everyone but Michael, who sits alone, brooding. Michael is the outsider. He is fully American, distanced from *la via vecchia*, prepared to sacrifice his existence for his nation.

Now as Michael Corleone recalls that scene, we must compare it to his present reality: both of his parents are dead; Fredo has been murdered on Michael's order, as have been Tessio and Rizzi; Apollonia was killed in a car explosion intended to annihilate Michael; he is estranged from Kay, who has aborted their unborn son; Clemenza and Pentangeli are dead; and Sonny was murdered. Several of the departed were perpetrators of treachery against Michael. Who remains? Only Connie, who conspired behind Michael's back to allow Kay to visit the children, and Hagen, who has proven to be an ineffective wartime consigliere and for whom Michael's affections seemingly oscillate between trust and hesitation. Earlier in the film, Michael had asked his mother about losing one's family. So outrageous was that suggestion for Carmela Corleone that she misunderstood the drift of her son's query. That Michael has lost his immediate family is clear, and his crime family has been ravaged by the current of events. He now cogitates alone in the barrenness of his Nevada estate, an alienated criminal power broker who has won the moment of zero-sum struggle but squandered familial intimacy and jeopardized his soul. Michael has become an outsider of a markedly different, despicable, and impoverished configuration.

The third film records the death of Michael Corleone. The penultimate scene recalls Michael in happier times: dancing with Apollonia, Mary, and Kay in turn. Are these images in Michael's aging mind just prior to his passing? In the final scene, aged, isolated in the courtyard of Don Tommasino's villa in Sicily (did he ever make it back to New York City?), covered by a peasant's fedora, Michael congresses only with a small dog. Donning his glasses, he drops an orange (a frequent symbol of danger throughout the *Godfather* trilogy) and slumps to the ground. *Morte!* The dog sniffs about. The *Intermezzo* from Mascagni's *Cavalleria Rusticana* wafts in the background.

Philosophical Analyses of Atonement and Repentance

In *The Godfather III*, Michael recognizes his despondency and thirsts for healthy personal transformation. At the simplest level, Michael dreams for the rejuvenation of luxuriant family relations. At the most general level, he craves peace of mind. Not fathoming precisely how that might be attained given his murderous past and enigmatic present, he oscillates between seeking forgiveness, fantasizing rehabilitation, and toying with redemption. Michael's spiritual quest might have been well served by a consigliere exuding philosophical dexterity. I will try now to saturate that void.[13]

Redemption from wrongdoing arises from fulfilling the elements and effectuating the functions of atonement, which substantiates the forgiveness of the victims of that wrongdoing. From a religious vantage point, redemption signals the reformation of the wrongdoer's character and the salvation of the wrongdoer from the punitive consequences of sin meted out by divine justice. From a secular perspective, redemption acknowledges the wrongdoer's reconfigured moral character and restores the wrongdoer's moral standing in the wider community.

The Functions of Atonement. Redemption, then, is the consequence of successful atonement, which includes at least six functions:

1. Removing or mollifying the harm and other pernicious effects generated by the wrongdoing.

The harm is often material—money, property, loss of entitlement—seized from the victim or destroyed by the perpetrator and is typically accompanied by emotional distress, perceived insult, personal violation, and the humiliation of being treated disrespectfully or as less than an equal subject of experience by the perpetrator.

2. Rectifying the wrongful attitudes of the wrongdoer.

Restoring victims to their status quo ante materially and even emotionally is insufficient for atonement. Perpetrators must alter the attitudes, judgments, and dispositions that underwrote their wrongful actions. Wrongdoers must distance themselves from their wrongful deeds by reconfiguring the character traits and frames of mind that promoted their misbehavior.

3. Realigning perpetrators' desires with moral convictions.

In that vein, the reconfiguration of character includes establishing or restoring wrongdoers' aspirations and desires with appropriate moral principles. Rectifying wrongful attitudes involves more than simply recognizing this or that specific act as inappropriate or imprudent; it requires a more thorough commitment to personal transformation.

4. Repairing relations and self-understandings jeopardized and impaired by wrongdoing.

The self-images and sense of self-worth of perpetrators and victims are typically negatively impacted by wrongdoing. The relationships between wrongdoers and their victims, and wrongdoers and their communities, may suffer. One function of atonement is to facilitate the establishment or restoration of salutary human relationships and more wholesome personal estimations of self-worth. Victims must restore their sense of self-value by regaining their dignity, while wrongdoers must earn self-forgiveness by reestablishing their moral standing through realigning their desires with appropriate moral principles.

5. Restoring perpetrators' moral standing.

Successful atonement reinstates reprobates to full moral standing. Although wrongdoing does not forfeit their perpetrators' moral status—perpetrators remain moral agents—it does diminish their moral standing in the community. Atonement signals the welcoming of the return of prodigals into the community with complete moral standing and restored reputation.

6. Earning the forgiveness of the victims of the wrongdoing.

Whether the victims of their wrongdoing offer forgiveness is not fully under the control of the perpetrators of evil. But sincerely and assiduously pursuing the functions of genuine atonement is under their control. Through their painstaking efforts and attainments in that project, wrongdoers can earn the forgiveness of their victims. Those harmed by wrongdoing may or may not forgive, but if reprobates have successfully fulfilled the elements and effectuated the functions of atonement they deserve to be forgiven.

Moreover, victims cannot legitimately demand wrongdoers atone disproportionately to the harm arising from their offense. Victims must remain reasonable. Under certain circumstances—when perpetrators have fulfilled all other elements of atonement reasonably and proportionately—to withhold forgiveness may even wrong the perpetrator. The point is that wrongdoers can earn forgiveness, but they cannot ensure that they will be forgiven by their victims. The earning of forgiveness is the harvest of atonement.

THE ELEMENTS OF ATONEMENT

The defining characteristics of atonement number five: repentance, apology, reparations, emotional surcharge, and material surcharge. Their requirements converge on the general themes of repairing harms caused by the wrong, distancing the wrongdoer from the inappropriate deed, transforming the wrongdoer's character, communicating remorse, and enduring emotional and material suffering as penance for wrongful activity.

1. The first element of atonement is repentance. I offer the following working analysis of genuine repentance.

    A person (a human agent) *repents* for committing an act or series of acts if and only if:

    a. The person performed the act or series of acts.

    b. The acts or series of acts were morally impermissible.

    c. The person acknowledges (a) and (b).

    d. The person accepts moral responsibility for the act or series of acts.

    e. The person sincerely regrets and is remorseful for having done the act or series of acts because they were morally wrong, and the person performed them without excuse or justification.

    f. The person sincerely resolves not to repeat such acts and disavows the character traits promoting them.

    g. The person expresses that sincere regret and remorse to someone or in some way

A similar analysis would track repentance for omissions: wrongfully failing to perform an act or series of acts. Although not an element in the formal definition, genuine repentance almost always signals or spawns positive reconfiguration of character. Subsequent performances of morally impermissible deeds, especially of the acts at issue, call into question the sincerity and authenticity of the prior "repentance." Accordingly, regret that arises only from calculations of rational self-interest is insufficient to establish repentance.

Repentance requires an expression of regret and remorse to someone or in some way. Typically, this communicative requirement is fulfilled by one of the other elements of atonement such as apology or the making of reparations. But for purposes of repentance alone, the agent's sincere expression to a confessor or intimate friend is sufficient to fulfill this requirement.

Repentance is critical for fulfilling several of the functions of atonement: rectifying the reprobate's wrongful attitudes; distancing wrongdoers from their misdeeds; promoting the reconfiguration of wrongdoers' character; aligning the reprobate desires with moral convictions; and beginning the process of repairing fractured relationships with the victim, the wider community, and animating self-forgiveness.

Suppose a perpetrator of a wrong has sincerely repented. Does this imply that the victim of that wrong is obligated to forgive the perpetrator? From the vantage point of conventional moral wisdom, the answer is "no"—more is needed. Only full atonement triggers the considered judgment that the reprobate has earned the forgiveness of the victim.

> 2. The second element of atonement is apology: if possible, the reprobate must sincerely express regret for having treated the victim as less than a full and equal subject of experience, as in effect a lesser being to whom the reprobate did not owe complete moral respect and concern. Ideally, the wrongdoing should empathize with the victim's loss and emotional suffering arising from the wrong and sincerely strive to restore or establish a salutary human relationship.

Apology is important to communicate and signal the realignment of the perpetrator's desires with appropriate moral convictions; to mollify nonmaterial injuries the victim endured; to distance the wrongdoer from the misbehavior; and to advance the repaired of splintered relationships.

> 3. The third element of atonement is reparations. Reprobates must restore victims to their material status quo ante, thereby rectifying the material injuries arising from the

wrong. Reparations obliterate or mollify material harm arising from the wrongdoing; realign the reprobate's desires to proper moral standards as unjust enrichment is disgorged and material injury is softened; and nurtures future healthy relationships.

4. The fourth element of atonement is the payment of an emotional surcharge. Reprobates should suffer proportionate shame, guilt, remorse, self-recrimination, and heartfelt sorrow from their recognition of their wrongdoing and its effects on victims. Reprobates must recognize and lament the wrongful reasons that animated their deeds. Such emotional distress, a form of self-punishment, is appropriate as penance for their wrongful presumption. Still, the emotional surcharge should fit the evil committed. Excessive guilt bears no honor, while insufficient remorse undermines positive transformation of character. The penance of an emotional surcharge separates the reprobate from the misdeed, cements a reprobate's realignment to appropriate moral standards, and contributes to the process of self-forgiveness

5. The fifth element of atonement is the payment of a material surcharge. If possible, reprobates should extend material recompense that goes beyond restoring victims to their material status quo ante. As an external expression of remorse and good faith, atoning wrongdoers should go beyond the contours of strict restitution. Doing so facilitates the establishment or restoration of relationships and demonstrates a reprobate's praiseworthy understanding of a victim's nonmaterial injuries and the reprobate's reconfiguration of character and realignment to moral convictions. Of course, paying a material surcharge is sometimes impossible because of a reprobate's lack of resources, a victim's death and lack of heirs, or the nature of the wrongdoing itself. But as an element in complete atonement this factor resonates.

I have not included acceptance of proportionate, retributive legal punishment as an element of atonement because much wrongdoing is not subject to criminal prosecution. Where misdeeds are subject to criminal or civil liability, atonement requires that reprobates endure their punishments or civil assessments as the baseline of their penance. The emotional and material surcharges featured in the fourth and fifth elements of atonement remain as additional expiations.

If atonement is successful, then the victim should forgive the perpetrator for the wrongful conduct. In my judgment, earned forgiveness transmits a clearer moral message than forgiveness offered too readily. Immediate forgiveness may speak well of the victim's open heart, but such dispensation invites a host of troubling questions: Does hasty absolution minimize the evil impact of the misdeed? Does it inadvertently fail to regard the perpetrator of the misdeed seriously as a moral agent? Does it trivialize the necessities of healthy human relationships? Might it underestimate the importance of the character traits, dispositions, and attitudes that underwrote the misdeed? Does it thereby obstruct the reprobate's positive character transformation?

At the other end of the spectrum, withholding forgiveness after successful atonement may betray a mean-spiritedness that reflects poorly on the victim. After all, the reprobate has done everything possible under the circumstances to merit forgiveness; to deny absolution is to communicate implicitly that forgiveness was impossible from the outset. Perhaps certain wrongdoing is so horrifying or permanent that such a judgment is warranted. Nazi atrocities during the Holocaust, the institution of slavery, malicious killings, terrifying rapes, and the like may well plummet into that category.

If reprobates murder their victims, atonement is rendered problematic. A murderer can repent but cannot apologize to the victim who cannot forgive the killer. The murderer cannot offer reparations to the victim. Material reparations can be offered only to the victim's' surviving family members or donated to the victim's preferred social causes or charities or in service of memorials promoting the victim's life or values or by fulfilling the victim's transcendent desires, those aspirations that can be gratified or thwarted only posthumously.

The vast majority of living human beings now have desires about numerous events that can occur only after their deaths: the disposition of estates, the care and handling of corpses, their reputation after death, the well-being of their children, the welfare of future generations, the ongoing flourishing of cherished projects, among others. Such desires can be fulfilled or transgressed only after death. I have a stake in such matters, but I cannot know now how they will be affected by posthumous events. Thus, a person's interests are not merely identical to her desires, wants, and preferences occurring during our lifetimes; not all our interests are confined to our earthly lives. Murder victims can no longer gather material reparations, yet their slayers can contribute to advancing their transcendent interests.

Although it falls short of complete atonement, murderers can repent, render a public apology, accept legal guilt, possibly offer material reparations in the fashion sketched, and endure the penance of emotional and material surcharges. That material reparations are appropriate for murder is itself a vexing problem, but alternatives are few, if any. Still, that atonement in many cases will prove impossible should not surprise. Even self-forgiveness is a thorny process. The sheer horror of wrongful, malicious killing disturbs neat conceptual analyses. Perhaps the best to which a murderer might aspire is salutary personal transformation, reconfigured character, and a socially productive and rewarding life thereafter. Still, most evil-doing should admit the possibility of forgiveness in principle and in practice.

A Philosophical Analysis of Forgiveness

In *The Godfather III*, Michael, recognizing all of this, vacillates between seeking personal transformation, forgiveness, and redemption, and recognizing that his conversion is hopeless. Or so it appears. The paramount questions surrounding the concept of forgiveness are these: What is involved when one person forgives another? What is the relationship between wrongdoers and their transgressions? Is forgiving others a moral duty or a supererogatory act? Must the transgressing party repent his wrongful deed in order to earn forgiveness? What sort of attitude is required for one person to forgive another? What is the relationship between retributive justice and forgiveness? Does forgiving wrongdoing condone past and encourage future transgressions? Why should we forgive wrongdoers, and why is forgiveness important? What is the difference, if any, between forgiving a wrongdoer and forgetting his wrong?[14]

Let's begin by describing the elements of forgiveness. For you to forgive me we must identify a wrong. If no wrong has been committed, there is nothing to forgive. Moreover, if you have been wronged, you must be aware of that wrong if you are to forgive. Further, if you have been wronged and you are aware of that wrong but are unaware that I am the perpetrator of the wrong, then you cannot forgive me.

Bear in mind also that not all misdeeds are legal wrongs punishable by the judiciary, nor are all moral wrongs grave and significant. A moral wrong as simple and relatively minor as speaking ill of a friend to another person is a misdeed subject to possible forgiveness.

1. The first element: a transgressor wronged a victim and the victim acknowledges that the transgressor wronged the victim.

Sometimes people transgress against others under circumstances in which they are not fully responsible for their acts. That is, I may have a legitimate excuse or justification for my wrongful action. An excuse would mitigate or erase my moral culpability for the wrongful act. Perhaps I was compelled by an irresistible impulse, or was coerced into acting by an external force, or was deceived into thinking that the act was permissible or was otherwise not fully responsible for what I did.

A justification would demonstrate that the act was not in fact a wrong because I performed it because of a public necessity, in deference to a higher duty, in self-defense, or the like. If I acted justifiably, then I committed no wrong that is subject to forgiveness; if I acted with a legitimate excuse, then I may not be morally culpable for the act and, again, I cannot be forgiven.

2. The second element: the transgressor is fully responsible and morally culpable for the wrongful action and the victim recognizes these facts.

If I am to be forgiven the only person in a position to forgive is the person who was wronged, his or her agents, and, perhaps, those uncommonly close to the victim who were also wronged to some extent. This is the case at least where we are discussing interpersonal forgiveness. In cases of judicial forgiveness, we can view the decision makers as the legal agents of the victim or, probably better, we can consider such instances legal forgiveness independent of the victim. Surely, a judge might forgive a miscreant under circumstances where the victim of the wrongdoer's transgression remains obdurate and vice versa. Moreover, after coming to understand the relevant facts, the public at large may feel sympathy for the wrongdoer, but unaffected third parties are not able to forgive the wrongdoer.

3. The third element: only the victim, the victim's explicitly empowered agents, and, perhaps, those uncommonly close to the victim who were also wronged to some extent by the transgressor can forgive the transgressor.

In order to forgive me, you need not and should not accept or condone the past wrong or encourage future wrongs. Instead, you continue to acknowledge that I am fully responsible for my wrongful action. What forgiveness requires is that, as victim, you surrender all negative feelings and attitudes toward me, the transgressor, that arose from the wrongdoing. Forgiveness, then, is a function of how you regard me.

> 4. The fourth element: in order to forgive the transgressor, the victim must relinquish his or her negative feelings and attitudes toward the transgressor that arose from the transgressor's wrongdoing.

But how can the victim attain such a state? How can victims retain their conviction that they have been wronged and that the perpetrator is fully responsible for that wrong yet relinquish their negative feelings of the perpetrator that sprung from that event?

Victims must distinguish the wrongful deed from the value of the fully responsible agent who performed it. That is, victims cannot *define* the perpetrator by the wrongful deed at issue. Victims must perceive the perpetrator as more and better than the wrongful deed that gave rise to the understandably negative attitudes toward the perpetrator that the victims initially embodied. In effect, victims must *distance* the perpetrator from the wrongful action or, perhaps more precisely, victims must evaluate the perpetrator from a wider, more charitable perspective. At first blush, victims judge the perpetrator only by the instant wrong committed; in order to forgive the perpetrator, victims must either separate the perpetrator from the wrongful deed or assess the perpetrator from a broader, more sympathetic vantage point.

> 5. The fifth element: in order to forgive the transgressor, the victim must distinguish the wrongful deed from the value of the fully responsible person, the transgressor, who performed it.

This is easier stated than achieved. What could lead you to separate so neatly the wrongful deed from the value of the fully responsible perpetrator who performed it? After all, evaluating the perpetrator—in this case, me—from a wider perspective may well result in learning about a host of other, even more horrifying, misdeeds that I have wreaked upon other victims. One possibility is that perhaps I sincerely atone for my wrongdoing or at least repent my wrongdoing. Under such circumstances, I distance myself from my wrongful deed. I invite you to no longer define me by my wrongdoing and, instead, to judge my value as higher than I had demonstrated by my mischief. Here you, as victim, do not need to *create* a distance between me and my wrongful deed, but merely *recognize* the distance that I, as perpetrator, have forged through atonement or repentance.

Genuine repentance almost always signals or spawns positive reconfiguration of character. Subsequent performances of morally impermissible deeds, especially of the wrong that triggered the need to repent, call into question the sincerity and authenticity of the wrongdoer's contrition. Accordingly, regret that arises only from calculations of rational self-interest is insufficient to establish repentance.

> 6. The sixth element: from the standpoint of human conventional moral wisdom, the transgressor's sincere atonement or, at least, repentance is one way that he or she can distance himself or herself from the wrongful action. Under such circumstances, from the standpoint of conventional morality, the victim is often morally required to forgive the wrongdoing, at least in the case of sincere atonement.

But suppose that I neither atone nor repent and thus do not distance myself from my transgression. Is it possible for you to create unilaterally a distance between me and my wrong? If so, how and why?

Perhaps my wrong was sweepingly uncharacteristic. Here you might conclude that the misdeed does not reflect my overall worth because the wrongful action is so stunningly aberrational. For example, suppose my past behavior is unimpeachable and the instant wrong is a first offense. If so, the first offense may well be judged an odd deviation. Under such circumstances, you might create unilaterally a distance between my personal worth and my wrongful deed. Even in the absence of my repentance, you might decide to forgive me even though you continue to hold me fully responsible for wronging you.

But why would I not repent in such a case? At the extreme, a transgressor might have died prior to having the chance to repent. Forgiving the dead for their transgressions remains possible. Even, as here, if I have not died, I might not repent because of a mistaken belief that the act was permissible. Under these circumstances, I would remain fully responsible for the wrong and responsible for the mistaken belief. Moreover, perhaps I do repent the wrong, but you are unaware of that fact and thus cannot take it into account. Another possibility is I embody a fatuous code of imperatives that include never regretting any of my acts and never apologizing for them. Following this stringent principle rigidly, I would not consider repentance a genuine option.

Another example of wrongdoings that seem out of character is the perpetrator who has enjoyed a fulfilling relationship with the victim and whose current wrong seems minor by comparison to the past benefits of the relationship. Even in the absence of repentance, you might well create unilaterally a distance between my overall character and my misdeed and forgive me.

Beyond wrongdoings that seem out of character, other possibilities for forgiving in the absence of repentance are possible. For example, suppose you are having difficulties in an intimate relationship that has hitherto brought you great joy. You have a well-intentioned but somewhat inept friend, me, who is greatly concerned for your well-being. I try to intercede in your problem and facilitate reconciliation between your lover and you. However, by officiously intermeddling in your affairs I exacerbate the problem. I wrong you by insinuating myself into your situation without your permission and by making an unpleasant situation much worse. I remain fully responsible for my wrongful deed—worthy intentions neither excuse nor justify my meddlesomeness. Still, even in the absence of repentance, you may well forgive me because my actions were well intentioned although poorly executed.

Yet another case for forgiving in the absence of repentance centers on the suffering of the perpetrator. If I have already suffered significantly, perhaps even disproportionally to the gravity of the wrong, then you may choose to forgive. For example, suppose a prominent person commits a wrong that becomes highly publicized. As a result, the transgressor suffers a host of humiliations including loss of reputation, fading business opportunities, family dissolution, and the like. As the victim of that wrong, you might well conclude that the transgressor has suffered sufficiently and forgive even in the absence of repentance.

Might forgiving unrepented transgressions unjustifiably condone wrongdoing? Often this is the case, but not always. Remember, by creating a distance between the agent and his wrongful act, the victim can still deplore the wrong but reconcile with the wrongdoer. Remember that in all the cases of the victim unilaterally creating distance between the wrongdoer and his deed that I have presented the perpetrator remains fully responsible for the action that remains a wrong.

However, I do not want to oversell the notion that victims can create unilaterally a distance between wrongdoers and their misdeeds. Clearly, that will depend on the gravity of the misdeed, the antecedent character of the transgressor, what happens after the offense, and the transgressor's future conduct. That the transgressor can repent the wrong but fails to do so cannot, all other things being equal, count in favor of forgiveness.

Moreover, the neat separation of agents from their acts can be dangerous. Just as in the case of unconditional love, when we begin stripping people of their choices, actions, and deeds they begin to fade away as concrete individuals and appear more as abstract exemplars of humanity. To forgive the person requires, among other things, that enough constitutive attributes remain that we can distinguish among individuals. These remarks are intended as cautions to those who are tempted to forgive as a matter of course.

7. The seventh element: even if the transgressor does not repent the wrongful deed, the victim can create unilaterally a distance between the transgressor and the wrong such that the victim can forgive the transgressor. Some relevant circumstances that may energize that unilateral creation: the instant wrong is the perpetrator's first offense; the perpetrator's wrong was grounded in good intentions; the perpetrator and the victim enjoyed a prior fulfilling relationship; or the perpetrator suffered sufficiently in the aftermath of the wrong. Should the victim forgive the transgressor based on the victim's unilateral creation of distance between the transgressor and the transgressor's wrong, then the victim's forgiveness is a supererogatory act.

What is the metaphysical result of forgiving a wrongdoer? Where I, as transgressor, atones and you, as victim, forgives, we can talk in terms of reconciliation. Neither of us views the other as alien or estranged. Each of us has tried to mend the rupture between us. Even if we did not enjoy a prior relationship, once the instant misdeed established us as victim and transgressor, our lives became entwined. At that point, hard feelings ensued: you, understandably, affixed me to my wrongdoing and judged me negatively. Once I atone and you forgive, you relinquish hard feelings toward me because I have separated myself from my wrongful deed. This opens the way for reconciliation and renewal.

But what occurs when you unilaterally create the distance between me and my misdeed, when I have not done so? How can reconciliation and renewal take place unilaterally? A relationship requires at least two parties. Where I refuse to even repent the wrongful act, talk of reconciliation and renewal is misplaced. To be more precise, your forgiveness in the absence of repentance is an offer of reconciliation that can occur only if I reciprocate in kind. In the absence of my repentance, you have relinquished hard feelings toward me, but that is insufficient for reconciliation. I, the wrongdoer, must bring something to the table.

Some reasons why the victim might be inclined to forgive transgressors are epistemological: human beings are flawed, fallible creatures; we all err at times; we cannot know fully the background socialization of transgressors; we cannot arrive at fully accurate judgments about the characters of other people; and we rarely are fully aware of the social circumstances other people endure. A principle of charity suggests that judging other people by their worst moments and by their most immoral acts is unwise. Instead, a wider assessment is recommended and the opportunity to atone for one's worst moments should be offered.

8. The eighth element: should the victim forgive an atoning transgressor the metaphysical result is reconciliation and renewal. Should the victim forgive an unrepentant transgressor, the metaphysical result is an offer of reconciliation and renewal from the victim to the transgressor. To accept that offer, the transgressor must distance himself or herself from the wrongful act or otherwise extend himself or herself to the victim.

What is the relationship between forgiveness and punishment? Is forgiveness compatible with fully exacting the requirements of retributive justice? Or does forgiveness imply the waiving of all punishment?

Forgiveness is personal between the transgressor and the victim (or his or her agents or, perhaps, those especially close to the victim), and involves the victim's positive change of *feelings* toward the transgressor. Punishment is typically a legal notion whereby rightful authorities exact deprivation on the transgressor for a host of purposes: retribution, restitution, deterrence, rehabilitation, or incarceration. Retributive punishment implies depriving transgressors of their freedom and many of their privileges in order to balance moral scales: transgressors deserve retributive punishment because they are responsible for wrongdoing. Restitution implies forcing transgressors to make their victim whole by restoring, to the extent possible, the status quo ante through monetary compensation. Deterrence implies depriving transgressors of their freedom and many of their privileges in order to deter them or others from committing similar offenses. Rehabilitation implies depriving transgressors of their freedom and many of their privileges in order to reform them. Incarceration implies depriving transgressors in order to protect society from their possible mayhem in the future.

Should you forgive me, you relinquish retributive feelings and fantasies of vengeance. That is, you surrender all thoughts of retaliation along with your harsh evaluation of me. You may, however, still conclude that institutional punishment of the (convicted) me is appropriate on grounds of deterrence, rehabilitation, or incarceration. Moreover, your forgiveness of me is compatible with seeking and accepting restitution from me. Indeed, making restitution is one way that I might facilitate the process of reconciliation and renewal.

Consider the following scenario: I wrong you. After I repent the wrong, you forgive me. You plead with legal authorities to forego punishing me because you are convinced that I pose no future danger to others. The court, nevertheless, sentences me, citing retributive grounds. That the court has retributively punished me does not vitiate your forgiveness of me. Your forgiveness is personal and involves surrendering feelings of revenge and retribution. That the rightful authorities decide to punish me need not alter your state of mind toward me.

One might argue that once the offender has served the sentence, once the wrongdoer has "paid his or her debt to society," then the wrong is expunged and there is nothing for the victim to forgive. In my judgment, that view is mistaken. Yes, the offender should now be allowed to rejoin society and enjoy freedom, but the victim's feelings toward the offender are still at issue. For example, suppose I, a negligent or reckless driver of motor vehicles, seriously injures a pedestrian, you. I did not target you for injury; the harm was accidental. But I am still culpable for the wrong and you, we will suppose, are paralyzed by my malfeasance. I sincerely repent my actions, plead guilty, and am sentenced to a significant term in prison. I serve the time as a model prisoner and am eventually released.

Does it follow that the moral universe is now balanced and there is nothing for you to forgive? Hardly. In such a case, restoring the status quo ante is impossible. You were and remain paralyzed. That I have been retributively punished registers no effects on your condition. You could have, of course, forgiven me at the time I repented and pled guilty, but suppose that you did not. Your career as an Olympic skier was ruined and you harbor ill will toward me, the obtuse motorist who was texting while driving at a high speed. Once I serve the sentence and am released, your feelings toward me may or may not change. But the point is that forgiveness is still an option. That I have served my sentence does not imply that the wrongdoing has been fully expunged and that there is no wrong that you might forgive.

This is the case even in those situations where restitution does seem to restore the status quo ante. Suppose a reckless motorist slams into your parked car that is occupied by you and your small child. Miraculously, although your vehicle is severely damaged, you and the child suffer no significant injuries. Neither you nor the reckless driver has car insurance, but he makes full restitution and your car is returned to its former condition. Does it follow that forgiveness is impossible because restitution has expunged the reckless driver's wrong? No. You have still suffered great fear at the time of the collision, terror at the thought of the injuries that might have occurred, and major inconvenience during the period when your car was being repaired. The reckless driver's restitution cannot alter those facts. You may or may not decide to forgive his recklessness, but the point is that the possibility of forgiveness is not eliminated by his act of restitution, which does not expunge the wrong in the sense that there is nothing remaining that might be forgiven. Full atonement has not occurred.

Is it humanely possible to love our unrepentant assailant, seek to advance his or her good, and, perhaps, forget about the transgressions? Imagine a recidivist offender, apparently lacking all redeeming social value, who, after being convicted of a major crime, snarls churlishly and sputters that he or she desires only to inflict more mayhem in the future. Can the mother of the young man, who was the murder victim of this lowlife, genuinely love the murderer, forego feelings of revenge, and seek his good? Although she probably will never forget what the murderer has done and cannot forgive him in the fullest philosophical sense of that term, I must admit that some victims—in this case, the mother of the victim—can love the perpetrator and seek to advance his or her good.

I say this because I was once an attorney in New York City and witnessed precisely such an event on a few occasions. Obviously, this does not occur as a matter of course, but only rarely. But I have seen and heard victims and their parents profess love for those who have grievously transgressed against them; they seemingly surrendered all thoughts of vengeance. Moreover, some of these paragons have tried to advance the good of these offenders after their convictions. Obviously, such a response is wildly counterintuitive, radically at variance with conventional moral wisdom, and fiercely at odds with human instincts. That some victims and their parents acted in such a manner can be explained only by their embrace of a higher religious or moral message. As discussed earlier, forgiveness offered too easily brings with it a host of problems and questions.

We might wonder at the object of love in such cases. Is it the recidivist offender, in all his brutish ignobility? Is it some aura of humanity in which the offender shares by virtue of being a member of the human species? Is it love of God, as a sort of third-party beneficiary?

9. The ninth and final element: should the victim forgive the transgressor, the victim abandons retributive feelings and fantasies of vengeance. The victim would surrender all thoughts of retaliation along with harsh evaluation of the transgressor. However, the victim may still conclude that institutional punishment of the (convicted) transgressor is appropriate on grounds of deterrence, rehabilitation, or incarceration. Moreover, the victim's forgiveness is compatible with seeking and accepting restitution from the transgressor. In fact, the transgressor's restitution is one way that the transgressor can facilitate the processes of atonement and reconciliation, as well as renewal with the victim. Moreover, neither the transgressor's repentance, nor the transgressor's punishment by rightful authorities, nor the transgressor's restitution expunges the wrongdoing such that there is nothing remaining for the victim to forgive.

Perhaps I should not oversell the virtues of forgiveness. I should, at least, reiterate the dangers of forgiveness too easily bestowed. When victims forgive perpetrators of wrongs too facilely, they may increase the possibility of serial transgressions. If we are all free moral agents, responsible for our actions, then we must also accept the consequences of our mistakes.

To be forgiven automatically may encourage wrongdoers to continue or amplify their wayward approach to life. For example, family members who continually forgive a spouse's or parent's abuse or aggressive actions may be unwitting collaborators in or unsuspecting enablers of future escalations of that violence. Moreover, just as we have epistemological problems in determining the mindsets of perpetrators of wrongs, we have similar problems when assessing the sincerity of their repentance. Surely, the chronicle of wrongdoing is replete with fraudulent expressions of remorse by perpetrators who understand well that victims and legal authorities welcome such demonstrations. To reward such false repentance with forgiveness brings no honor to either victim or perpetrator. We might insist on a type of moral symmetry: if we lack epistemological certitude about the intentions and motives of perpetrators of wrongs such that we are in a poor position to judge them, so too, we lack certitude regarding the sincerity of their expressions of repentance and are thus in a poor position to forgive them. Finally, those who forgive too easily might suffer from a lack of self-esteem; because of intense guilt or feelings of inferiority, they may on some level think they deserve to be transgressed upon. Accordingly, to conclude that some instances of forgiving are appropriate while some are inappropriate is reasonable.

From another vantage point, it may seem that those who forgive others arrogate to themselves the positions of judge and moral superior. Forgiving others presupposes that the victim has judged that a perpetrator has wronged him or her and the perpetrator is fully responsible for that transgression. The victim has judged that something bad has happened that might be forgiven. The victim, one might well argue, then places himself or herself in a position of moral superiority: although the victim initially harbors resentment and, probably, thoughts of retaliation, the victim will forego those sentiments magnanimously. In effect, the victim has turned the tables on the perpetrator in that the perpetrator may well sense that the victim believes that the act of forgiveness places the perpetrator in the victim's debt. Behind the apparent purity of the victim's motives may lay a repressed resentment and subtle moral retaliation that is masked by high-minded rhetoric. Perhaps victims who forgive do so in service of their own empowerment: they assume the role of divine judge and generously bestow forgiveness upon their moral subordinates. The act of forgiveness, then, may at least sometimes be laced with moral condescension; to forgive another person may be a way to elevate oneself and to underscore that person's moral inferiority. This is especially true in cases where the quality of the perpetrator's act is somewhat contestable or where the perpetrator's responsibility for that act is ambiguous.

My point is not that all acts of forgiveness mask mendacious motives, but only that not all acts of forgiveness are morally pure. Assuming we had full access to the inner spirits of other people, we would need to evaluate fully the motives and intentions of forgiving people to assess the moral quality of their acts; the act of forgiveness as such is not morally self-ratifying.

The Futility of Michael Corleone's Quest for Redemption

The Godfather III is the narrative of Michael Corleone's final defeat and dissolution. He desperately purchases the trappings of divine forgiveness by being inducted into the Order of Saint Sebastian for his massive donations to charities. He contributed $100,000,000 for the preservation of Sicily, earmarked specifically for advancing the interests of the neediest citizens. Unraveling the multiple deceptions ensnared in this scene is no small undertaking. First, Michael's donation springs from the profits from his illegal rackets and his illegal management of legal enterprises such as casinos: the money is dirty. Second, even Michael knows that his funds are unlikely to reach needy citizens in Sicily: the Archbishop who snatches the check is a representative of the corrupt Vatican Bank suffocating in dire financial muck. Third, Michael has a larger undertaking in mind: buying controlling interest in *Immobiliare*, the Vatican's real estate holding company. His initial donation to Sicily and the resulting church ceremony are prefatory rituals to a more ambitious campaign. Fourth, Michael's past association with and allegiance to the Church have been calculated and transactional. The phrases "Michael Corleone" and "true religious believer" enter the same sentence uncomfortably. Fifth, the Roman Catholic Church does not recognize an Order of Saint Sebastian as an international or national honorific organization. With a footnote to Winston Churchill, Michael's induction into the fictional Order of Saint Sebastian is a charade, encased in a parody, within a pretense. The key, as always, is Michael's self-interest: he thirsts for respectability and craves redemption—but must settle for farcical theological blessings and sham displays of reconciliation. His soul remains dark, his spirit oozes alienation, and his mind documents and monitors his torment.

That Michael cannot atone for his decades of evil-doing should be clear. He cannot genuinely repent because he does not recognize most of his wrongdoing as unjustified. He repeats that he was only protecting his family. He obsesses over the circumstances that led him to criminality. Michael cannot sincerely resolve not to repeat his wrongdoing because, despite frequent declarations that he was leading the family to full legitimacy, he laments: "Just when I thought I was out, they pull me back in!"

The one appalling act that might be a candidate for Michael's repentance is ordering the murder of his brother, Fredo. He understands now that murdering "my mother's son" is ineffably evil. He would never repeat the act and, in any case, has no brothers left who might be candidates for his excessive wrath. Murdering Fredo was not necessary to protect Michael's immediate family. Still, Michael does not genuinely disavow the character traits that promoted his order. Although he is sincerely remorseful and profoundly regrets his decision, and seemingly assesses it as morally indefensible, and assumes responsibility for the despicable deed, he cannot renounce the dispositions of character from which the act arose. In sum, Michael does not fulfill all the elements of repentance even regarding the act for which he is most remorseful: ordering the murder of his brother. Not having satisfied the first and paramount element of atonement, Michael cannot lodge a legitimate claim for forgiveness.

Still, suppose Michael can repudiate and even overcome the dispositions of character that animated his decision to order the murder of his brother, who betrayed him more from stupidity and misplaced hope than from malice. Stipulate, then, that Michael can genuinely repent the murder of Fredo. Can Michael achieve the other elements of atonement, in this case and in general? Can Michael earn forgiveness?

Fredo is dead. No victim and perpetrator interaction is possible. Michael can also offer a public apology of sorts, we can suppose. Fredo has no heirs, and his spouse was a wife in title only. What reparations are appropriate for cold-blooded, pre-mediated murder? Michael could provide virtually unlimited monetary resources, but to whom and for what purpose? Perhaps if Fredo had expressed transcendent interests, those that can be fulfilled only posthumously,[15] Michael could ensure that they be observed. He could advance the well-being of Fredo's heirs if he had any; he could endow causes, sustain projects, and promote purposes that Fredo cherished; he could promote Fredo's enduring legacy if a path to doing so existed. Also, Michael could easily tack on material surcharges, assuming we can estimate the rightful punitive and moral cost. Still, even under the best circumstances, atoning for murdering one's sibling is virtually impossible. Michael's circumstances are far short of the best.

Recall when Michael meets Cardinal Lamberto, renown as a pious, uncommonly honorable prelate, to discuss the *Immobiliare* deal and the intrigues in the Vatican. Lamberto urges Michael to confess his sins. Michael recognizes that he is beyond redemption and wonders what efficacy confession might bear absent repentance. Here Michael expresses his clearest thinking: although viscerally he hungers for legitimacy, redemption, and a reconfigured life, he rationally comprehends why such aspirations must remain unfulfilled. Lamberto appeals to Michael's pragmatic nature and suggests he has nothing to lose by confessing. Michael relents and admits that he betrayed his wife and himself, that he killed men and ordered the killing of other men, including his brother. The Cardinal softly endorses Michael's suffering as Corleone sobs. Although accepting that Michael is not genuinely repentant, the Cardinal absolves him formally of his past wrongs yet ratifies his emotional distress.

The Cardinal, in effect, follows Church doctrine and believes that even so horrifying a deed as murdering one's brother is subject to absolution, but not given the particularities of Michael's current state. In any event, Lamberto understands acutely that the emotional surcharge Michael endures is appropriate: "It is just that you suffer." Lamberto also suspects that Michael will not change. Even Michael doubts that he can repent. Add one more factor: would Michael accept legal punishment for ordering the murder of Fredo? Clearly not. This is also the case for every other crime he has committed.

Michael does not atone for any of his evil doing, even for Fredo's murder, yet he craves personal redemption, his declarations to the contrary to Cardinal Lamberto notwithstanding. After the assassin Mosca murders Don Tommasino, lifelong confederate of the Corleone family, Michael mourns over his corpse; "You were so loved, Don Tommasino. Why was I so feared, and you so loved? What was it? I was no less honorable. I wanted to do good. What betrayed me? My mind? My heart? Why do I condemn myself so? I swear, on the lives of my children: give me a chance to redeem myself, and I will sin, no more."

Michael's supplications—To whom? God? The spirit of Tommasino? Michael's own conscience?—spout a profound pathos that must remain unrequited. In this moment of clarity, he divulges in soliloquy the tumult, guilt, and confusion that reside within him. His desires are aligned neither to moral convictions nor to reality nor to the rigors of logic. Michael's visceral hankerings cannot be satisfied. He can never attain internal peace: estrangement from salutary community, alienation from self, and lingering guilt and suffering must mark his final years. Death is merciful in its debarkation.

The contrast between Don Vito's dying paean "Life is so beautiful"[16] and Michael's final years of alienation, estrangement, and isolated expiration is unmistakable. The Don suffered no emotional surcharge for his life of crime. He registered no guilt, made no apologies, expressed no regrets, and endured no inner torment. Don Vito harbored no hopes of going legitimate and made no overtures pursuant to such aspirations. Michael agonized during his final decade over the life he led, was torn between his visceral hankerings for legitimacy and redemption and his rational comprehension of the impossibility of attaining them, and while never genuinely repenting endured considerable guilt. What accounts for the striking differences between these two lives of criminality?

Don Vito never embodied discordant systems of value. He was fervently committed by character, circumstances, and choice to *la via vecchia*, *l'ordine della famiglia*, and the code of honor to which he subscribed. Don Vito did not aspire to become an American in any profound sense. Although he understood precisely his children could not replicate his methods, self-understandings, and way of life—after all, they were Americans—Don Vito appreciated just as distinctly that he could live out his days on the terms that defined him. Accordingly, Don Vito does not languish with inner conflict between allegiance to the old ways and fidelity to the conventional morality of America. He remains firmly convinced that his honor code is superior to the values of America.

Don Vito insists that had he obediently embraced new-world values he would have been condemned to a life of servitude and deference unbecoming a man of his talents and character. He would have been forced, in effect, to dance at the end of strings manipulated by American *pezzonovanti*. Although he accepts that his family must eventually enter mainstream society and fantasizes that his children might become future American *pezzonovanti*, and the groundwork he establishes in accumulated wealth, power, and connections will facilitate that ascension, Don Vito resolves to remain outside that venture and preserve his authenticity. His reward for this self-understanding is a relatively harmonious, balanced internal condition, at least as assessed by subjective standards, especially given his thoroughly criminal life.

Michael Corleone's narrative is remarkably different. He is an American with less vibrant experience of *la via vecchia* and *l'ordine della famiglia*. He even rushed sacrificially to enlist in the armed forces to risk his life for the mass of *stranieri*! A self-proclaimed outsider to the family business, Michael was drawn into illegality because of circumstances and his passion for protecting his father. This led to his exile to Sicily where he learned the intricacies of the code of honor, the old ways, and the family order. Upon his return, the rise and fall of Michael Corleone corresponds to the internal discord he endures between his allegiance to American legitimacy, his newfound appreciation of old-world values, and the exigencies of running a network of illegality he has inherited.

Unlike Don Vito, Michael never commits unambiguously and completely to one set of cultural understandings and social values. He invokes a batch of rationalizations when pressed, usually by Kay, to justify his way of life: he needed to protect his family, he has tried to segue into full legitimacy, but other forces or circumstances draw him back into criminality; the higher his interactions with supposedly legitimate society—the Church, politics, law enforcement, and jurisprudence—the more deeply immersed in illegality he inadvertently becomes.

For example, in *Godfather III*, when trying to gently woo Kay and win back his ex-wife's affection, he portrays himself as a misunderstood victim of hostile circumstance, his own pure intentions, and his unyielding love and duty to family:

> You couldn't understand, back in those days. I love my father—I *swore* I would never be, a man like him—but I *loved* him. And he was in danger; what could I do? And then later, you were in danger. Our children, we were in danger. Look at it. You were all that I loved, valued, most in the world. And, I'm losing you—I lost you—anyway. You're gone, and it was all for nothing—so—you have to understand, I had a whole different destiny planned. . . . You know, every night here in Sicily, I dream, about my wife and my children. And how I lost them.[17]

On the matter of pervasive corruption, Michael squarely hits the mark. Lucchesi's web of treachery ensnares the Italian government and police, the Church, ambitious thugs such as Joey Zasa, conniving aging crime bosses sniffing for one final big score such as Don Altobello, Archbishop Gilday, swindlers within the Vatican, and the P2 (*Propaganda Due*) Masonic lodge, functioning as a shadow government, in Rome. Michael's control of *Immobiliare* would alter the balance of power and disturb Lucchesi's hegemony. Thus, Michael must be terminated with extreme prejudice. When Cardinal Lamberto is elected Pope, which augurs well for Michael's *Immobiliare* transaction, he, too, must be eliminated, especially after the new Vicar demands a thorough investigation of the skullduggery at the Vatican Bank. Michael is aware of the upcoming showdown: in yet another zero-sum event, either Michael or Lucchesi prevails while the other must die.

Michael concludes that his striving for legitimacy and redemption are not possible "in this world." World-weary, physically debilitated by diabetes, and psychologically distraught, Michael, steered by Connie, bequeaths his position and power to Sonny's illegitimate son, Vincent Mancini, who wants "the power to preserve the family." Given the zero-sum context of the moment, Vincent orders Calo on a suicide mission to murder Lucchesi, directs hitmen to smother and hang Keinzig, commands Al Neri to shoot Gilday at the Vatican, while Connie poisons Altobello, her godfather, with a birthday gift of lethal cannolis.

The inner torment afflicting Michael Corleone, then, arises from his irresolvable embrace of incompatible systems of values, his impenetrable visceral coveting of personal reconfiguration and redemption that seems impossible to attain, and the pervasive guilt he suffers over ordering the murder of his brother. The murder of his daughter by a bullet intended for him only exacerbates Michael's misery. The meaning, purpose, and significance of Michael's life have been hijacked by the unwholesome convergence of tragic circumstances, abominable personal choices, fealty to antithetical value systems, and unforeseen consequences. Thus, Cardinal Lamberto, from a theological perspective, summarizes Michael's quandary: "Your sins are terrible. And it is just that you suffer. Your life could be redeemed. But I know you do not believe that . . . You will not change."

A deeper question emerges: did Don Vito's life contain within it the seeds of the next generation's destruction? Santino is murdered on a causeway. Fredo is murdered on order of his brother. Michael's succession to power ends in utter personal dissolution. Costanzia meanders uneasily from pampered daughter, to bereaved widow, to flighty and profligate party lady, to penitent sister, to gelidly dispassionate murderer. In the end, Connie is much less conflicted than Michael. Connie becomes the camouflaged head of the family who orchestrates the passing of power to nephew Vincenzo Mancini. She rebukes Michael when she learns he has confessed his sins to Cardinal Lamberto, and Connie peddles the fiction that Fredo died from an accidental drowning. Creating comforting illusions and alternate realties as a reverse form of gaslighting, however, provides Michael no succor. She confides to Vincent Mancini that he is "the only one left in this family with my father's strength." Connie's transformation as a shadow don may well be the most surprising aspect of *Godfather III*.

Women are not featured prominently in Puzo's novel or in the three films. They assume ancillary roles except for Constanzia Corleone and Kay Adams Corleone. The three films mark Kay along a plausible character arc. At the end of the first movie, Kay is an estranged outsider to whom Michael's door of intimate associates is closed. In the second, her alienation exacerbates through Michael's increasing preoccupation with avenging perceived wrongs, enlarging his criminal empires, and conjuring recondite subterfuges. She struggles mightily through Michael's senate interrogation; she aborts a potential male heir; excoriates Michael's fealty to "this Sicilian thing"; and separates from the family. In the third, Kay, now long remarried, hostilely indicts Michael for his accelerating hypocrisy and implacable commodification of social life. She presses Michael to permit their son Anthony to withdraw from law school and pursue his dream of an operatic career. When Michael initially resists, Kay sharpens her assault on his disreputable career and shameful parental instincts. Michael relents soon thereafter. When the family travels to Sicily to attend Anthony's operatic debut—we must suspend disbelief about how an unknown musician scores the lead role in a major European production—Michael scrambles to recoup Kay's affections, both as symbolic reunification of the family he has alienated and as once, and hopefully future, paramour. As Michael sweet-talks Kay over lunch, both express their ongoing mutual affection—but just as viewers conjure images of a small cottage by a waterfall, Michael's Sicilian henchman brings news of the murder of Don Tommasino and the unfolding of deeper treacheries. The ferocious intrusion of "this Sicilian thing" vaporizes Kay's emotional pliability. The moment of passionate rapprochement is forever lost. At the end of Anthony's performance and with the killings of Mary and so many others, the estrangement of Kay from Michael is sealed.

Had the first film tracked the ending of the novel more closely, however, Kay's developmental arc would have taken more interesting twists, at least from the first to the second movie. At the end of the novel, Kay takes radical steps to reconcile herself to Michael's familial background and close the gap of her estrangement. By converting to Roman Catholicism and duplicating the religious rituals followed by her mother-in-law, liturgies presumed to facilitate the redemption of reprobates who jeopardize their souls, Kay enlists in the female auxiliaries of "this Sicilian thing." Accordingly, on this scenario, her profound disillusionment in *Godfather II* would have required a fuller and more refined transition.

In the first movie, Connie is the pampered daughter who suffers domestic abuse at the hands of her opportunistic husband, Carlo Rizzi. When Michael orders Carlo's death because of his role in the murder of Sonny, Connie is the hysterical, betrayed sister riling at Michael's violence. In the second film, Connie has transformed into a silly, glitzy, coarse prodigal, who seeks Michael's blessing and funding for what would be her third marriage, in this case to an aging gigolo named "Merle." After Michael disabuses both Connie and Merle of this undertaking, Connie goes off. Through the remainder of the movie, though, we witness her transformation as an advisor to Kay and seeker of rapprochement with Michael. Connie meanders back to her roots, older and wiser. In the third film, Connie's transformation is more striking. She becomes the iron surrogate leader of the family. Michael is seeking redemption and plagued by self-doubt. Connie perceives in Vincent, Sonny's illegitimate son, the future of the clan. Vincent, however, lacks connection to old-world values and stylized, nuanced rhetoric. The phrases "Vincent Mancini" and the "*uomo di pazienza*" coalesce uneasily in the same sentence.

Michael has spiritually stumbled from idealistic American to family protector to estranged and alienated from family and the old ways to an empty shell of a man seeking redemption and reconciliation but utterly clueless on how to attain them. Money, power, and the trappings of success have secured his material fortune but shrunk his soul. The ideal of the *uomo di pazienza* has shriveled into commodification fetishism that objectifies everything and everybody with a price tag.

As Michael struggles with illness, uncertainty, and heightened vulnerability, Connie orders Vincent to slay the obnoxious Joey Zasa and hatches future murderous schemes. Old-world subordination has morphed into new-world female empowerment. Connie even fashions a plan to kill her godfather, the treacherous Don Altobello, by poisoning her gift to him—cannolis, of course—which the aged patriarchy consumes during the opera. Constanzia Corleone, beginning as a symbol of new-world ethnic princess, ends as perhaps the most ruthless, cold-blooded killer and conniver in the family. She fashions herself as a fiercer offshoot of her father.

At the beginning of *Godfather III*, Michael writes assuredly to his offspring that "the only wealth in this world is children, more than all the money and power on Earth." Later, Don Altobello observes to Vincent

Mancini that "the richest man is the one with the most powerful friends." Soon thereafter, Don Lucchesi advises Mancini that "Finance is a gun. Politics is knowing when to pull the trigger." Three aphorisms emit flickers of insight while masquerading as organic truths. Children constitute great social riches only within loving relationships gushing with devoted mutuality and secure personal allegiances. The power of friends is exercised most efficaciously in service of rightfully advancing the interests of colleagues, family, and wider community. The glory of politics is apportioning material and spiritual resources for the common good. Human beings are not consigned to choosing between lives as hammers or as nails. At the end, Michael Corleone apprehended this unvarnished principle intellectually but continued to resist its implications viscerally.

The narrative arc of the Corleone family is clear and compelling: oppressed immigrant, "tired and poor," but among the "huddled masses yearning to breathe free," struggles for success along the mean streets of New York City; through enterprise, guile, and exercise of indomitable will, he and his family stride mightily forward; amid ruthless competition, he earns merited respect and honor from those within his tribal circle; he dies, and the values and ethnic understandings sustaining the triumphs of his family dissipate, while his sins are bequeathed to his youngest son. His heir, even more capable in critical respects than the deceased patriarch, jostling within a cyclone of changing cultural circumstances, loses his way, misconstrues the values of ends and means, becomes a prisoner to the endless accumulation of money, power, preeminence, and the sadistic delights of revenge, and alienates those closest to him. His inner conflicts alienate him from his former ideal vision of his destiny; individual aggrandizement assumes pride of place above *la via vecchia* and *ordine della famiglia*; collaboration with disreputable external institutions, dishonorable government authorities, and capacious impersonal organization intensifies; in the end, isolated, bitter, and desperate, he pathetically aspires to purchase the appearance of spiritual transformation whose substance must elude him. While he abstractly craves repentance, atonement, personal redemption, and familial reunification, his obdurate character and material fortune can generate, at most, only a gauzy mirage of respectability that mocks its patron and fails to beguile its witnesses. Michael is a thespian, a "poor player" who "struts and frets his hour upon the stage," camouflaging his despondency with colorful costumes and disingenuous philanthropy, while encircled by counterfeit theologians, conniving financiers, debauched politicians, and adulterated cronies. He dies, fittingly, as and with an animal. In the shadows, the evangelists of cosmic meaninglessness, Father Time, *Fortuna Mala*, and the Grim Reaper, jeer vehemently.

Appendix A

Summarizing *The Godfather*

The movie begins at the wedding of Constanzia (Connie) Corleone and Carlo Rizzi in the summer of 1945. Vito Corleone (born Andolini), the "godfather," Connie's father, leads a major New York City crime family. He is also the father of three sons: Santino ("Sonny"), hot-headed and aggressive; Frederico ("Fredo"), kindly but ineffectual, and Michael, a Marine hero who has returned from service in World War II. Don Vito's *consigliere* is Tom Hagen, who was orphaned as a youth and taken into the Corleone household at Santino's behest. Raised by the Corleones, Hagen is now a lawyer who understands thoroughly Sicilian familial and extralegal traditions.

One such tradition is that on his daughter's wedding day, a Sicilian father must fulfill all reasonable requests lodged by relatives and friends. Don Vito fields and grants requests from Amerigo Bonasera, an undertaker seeking justice for the brutal beating his daughter has suffered at the hands of two roughnecks after she refused their sexual advances; Nazorine, a baker who petitions for his assistant, Enzo Aguello, who faces deportation; and Johnny Fontane, godson of Don Vito and successful crooner, who wants a certain movie role denied him by the head of the studio, Jack Woltz.

After the wedding, Don Vito sends Hagen to Los Angeles to make Woltz "an offer he cannot refuse." Hagen approaches Woltz with all due respect and courtesy. Woltz responds with a series of ethnic insults and screams that Fontane will never get the role even though he would perform it perfectly. Woltz overflows with venom because Fontane once seduced a young actress whom Woltz was sexually exploiting while training for movie stardom. Hagen returns to New York and informs Don Vito, who conjures a plan. Soon thereafter, Woltz awakens to find the severed head of his prized possession, a race horse, Khartoum, in his bed. After reassessing his position, Woltz casts Fontane in his movie.

Likewise, Enzo the baker gains permanent entry into the United States, and the reprobates who tormented Bonasera's daughter are severely beaten. Don Vito fulfills his promises. Great danger, however, looms in the person of Virgil "Turk" Sollozzo, who, supported by the Tattaglias, a rival crime family, seeks Don Vito's collaboration in a new venture: the importing and distributing of heroin. Sollozzo needs financing and political and legal protection in exchange for a reasonable percentage of the profits. Although Sonny unwisely signals his interest, Don Vito refuses, citing the special dangers of the narcotics trade. Anticipating that Sollozzo will not accept no as an answer, Don Vito summons his most fearsome enforcer, Luca Brasi, to connect with Sollozzo and report back with sound intelligence. During Brasi's first meeting with the Turk and Bruno Tattaglia, he is garroted.

Matters then spiral downward rapidly. Don Vito suffers grave injuries during an attempted assassination while he purchases fruit outside his office. Sollozzo abducts Tom Hagen and, thinking that Don Vito is dead, convinces him to persuade Sonny to accept the deal previously offered. Upon learning that Don Vito has survived, Sollozzo repeats his demand to Hagen and releases him.

An enraged Sonny demands that the Tattaglia family turn over Sollozzo or risk all-out war. They respond by sending the Corleones a dead fish nestled in Luca Brasi's bullet-proof vest, an ancient Sicilian message that informs everyone that Brasi sleeps with the fishes.

The Corleones go on the offensive. After killing Paulie Gatto, a soldier in *caporegime* Peter Clemenza's crew, who had betrayed Don Vito and facilitated the attempt on his life, and after stymieing another possible attempt on Don Vito's life in the hospital, where he was recovering, the Corleones conclude that Sollozzo must be eliminated. But how?

The brutal war is taking a toll on all the crime families in the city. Sollozzo asks for a meeting with Michael, recognized as a civilian, while accompanied by Captain McCluskey, a corrupt policeman serving as the Turk's bodyguard. After considerable deliberation, Michael volunteers to attend the meeting and kill both enemies. By discovering where the meeting was to occur and planting a weapon in the restroom, Sonny, Clemenza, and Salvatore Tessio, another *caporegime*, ease the path for Michael's murders. At a restaurant in the Bronx, Michael slays both men.

The family dispatches Michael to Sicily for protection and for education in the old ways. The Corleones brace for all-out war with the other crime families in New York, who ally against them. Police and government authorities crack down on all crime in response to the murder of one of their own. Newspaper stories written by Corleone family associates, though, portray McCluskey as a corrupt officer who betrayed his duties for monetary gain. Don Vito convalescences at home and is stunned to learn that Michael, whom he had been grooming as a possible senator or governor, is now a murderer.

The marriage of Connie and Carlo, never a mating blessed by heaven, turns ugly. Carlo beats a pregnant Connie, and Sonny responds by severely thrashing Carlo at midday on a crowded public street. Carlo plots his revenge with the Corleone's chief enemies, the Tattaglia and Barzini families. After instigating another argument with Connie, Carlo beats her badly. Connie telephones Sonny. With deranged avidity, Sonny jumps into his automobile and travels toward Connie's residence. At the toll booth on the Long Island Causeway, he is violently gunned down by a host of hitmen spewing a fuselage of bullets.

Don Vito instructs Hagen to arrange a meeting with the heads of the five New York City crime families and other national crime leaders. At that conference, Don Vito forsakes revenge for Sonny's murder and agrees to provide legal and political protection for the narcotic trade, but he demands that Michael must return to the United States without incident. The violence in the city ends as the other crime leaders agree to Don Vito's design. At this conference, Don Vito concludes that Barzini was the prime mover in the treacheries against his family.

In Sicily, Michael falls in love with Apollonia Vitelli, young daughter of a local tavern owner. They court and wed under strict Sicilian traditions and rituals. Soon thereafter, one of his bodyguards betrays Michael. Michael's auto explodes as Apollonia keys the ignition. Although he was the intended target, Michael is unscathed physically. After the conference of crime leaders occurs in America, Michael returns safely to the United States around 1949.

About one year later, Michael reunites with his former love, Kay Adams, with whom he had attended Connie and Carlo's wedding years earlier. After much discussion, they wed. Michael assures her that within five years the Corleone family will conduct only legitimate business.

Don Vito keeps the pledges he made at the conference of crime leaders. Tom Hagen, not an effective war-time *consigliere*, is demoted to family lawyer. Michael rises to head of the family, while Don Vito serves as his *consigliere*. Don Vito educates Michael on the sum and substance of crime management. Meanwhile, Clemenza and Tessio are upset with the encroachments of rival families. Michael declines their invitations to retaliate. Still, he recruits a new regime of hitmen under wounded war veteran turned gangster, Rocco Lampone.

Michael travels to Las Vegas to expand the family casino business. He offers, in truth demands, to buy out Moe Greene, a quick-tempered casino boss with loose ties to the Barzini family. Greene angrily refuses. Fredo, who has been working in Greene's casino, takes Moe's side against Michael. At the conclusion of the meeting, Michael sternly cautions Fredo about his conduct.

Michael returns home. Don Vito falls and dies while playing with his young grandson in his tomato garden. Don Vito had advised Michael that at his death the other families would conspire against him, using a trusted family insider as their precipitating instrument. At Don Vito's internment, Tessio relays to Michael a proposal from Barzini for a meeting on Tessio's territory. In so doing, Tessio unwittingly identifies himself as a traitor.

Having anticipated and prepared for such a conspiracy, Michael agrees to be the godfather of Connie and Carlo's newborn son. During the baptismal ceremony, Michael's gunmen kill the four heads of the other city crime families as well as Moe Greene. After the baptism, Clemenza and his soldiers kill Tessio for his betrayal as well as Carlo Rizzi for his complicity in Sonny's death. After turbulent meetings with Connie and then Kay, in his office Michael welcomes Clemenza and new *caporegimes* Rocco Lampone and Al Neri, who pay their respects to their triumphant leader. The film ends with Clemenza kissing Michael's hand signifying full recognition of his authority. As Kay peers, the office door closes to her and to the external world.

Appendix B

Summarizing *The Godfather II*

The film consists of two parallel dramas. The main narrative focuses on Michael Corleone's struggles to preserve and extend his criminal and business ventures from 1958 through 1960. The ancillary storyline consists of a series of flashbacks of Vito Andolini (Corleone), from his childhood in Corleone, Sicily, in 1901 to his arrival in the United States and eventual rise as leader of one of New York City's five major crime families around 1922. The primary storyline consists of new material crafted by Francis Ford Coppola and Mario Puzo, while the background narrative expands on material contained in Puzo's novel.

The movie begins in Corleone at the funeral of Antonio Andolini, whom local Mafia chief, Don Ciccio, has murdered over a minor personal dispute. As mourners follow the casket to the burial site, Don Ciccio's henchmen kill Antonio's older son, who had publicly sworn to avenge his father's death. Soon thereafter, Antonio's widow meets with Don Ciccio to seek mercy for Vito, her younger son. Ciccio, thoroughly immersed in the requirements of the Sicilian code of honor, knows that Vito will seek vengeance upon reaching maturity. He rejects the widow's pleas. She quickly and adroitly grabs the Don and holds him hostage at knifepoint, while young Vito scampers for safety. Ciccio's thugs fatally shoot the widow. They later canvass the town seeking Vito, but their efforts are stymied by a few citizens who facilitate the boy's voyage to Ellis Island. There bungling, harried immigration officials register him as "Vito Corleone." (In the novel, an older Vito changes his name voluntarily from "Andolini" to "Corleone.") The boy is then quarantined at Ellis Island for several months due to smallpox.

The film segues to 1958, where Michael Corleone oversees a lavish party at his Lake Tahoe, Nevada, compound for his son's first communion. He meets with state senator Pat Geary regarding the cost of gaming licenses for casinos that the Corleones are purchasing. Geary, unctuous and amiable publicly, is contemptuous and insulting, demanding an exorbitant payoff in return for facilitating the licenses. Michael, coldly and menacingly, informs Geary that he will not pay anything but would appreciate it if Geary would pay the fees. Amused, Geary departs. Michael then greets his sister, Connie, whose life has spiraled out of control. Divorced from her second husband, she now seeks funding to marry Merle Johnson, a middle-aged gigolo. Michael registers his disapproval and advises Johnson to sever the relationship. Michael also meets with Johnny Ola, Sicilian satellite for gangster Hyman Roth, who is ostensibly supporting Michael's ambitions in the casino industry. Finally, Michael endures an uneven encounter with Frank Pentangeli, a Corleone capo who assumed control of Peter Clemenza's territory at his death. Pentangeli seeks permission to destroy the Rosato brothers, allied with Roth. Michael refuses.

That evening, two gunmen fail to assassinate Michael. They pepper his bedroom with bullets, but he is unharmed while sheltering his wife. The hitmen are killed prior to escaping from the compound, but not by Michael's soldiers. Michael understands that the enterprise was aided by someone close to him.

Circa 1917, Vito is working in a grocery store owned by the Abbandandos. A sartorially elegant extortionist, Don Fanucci, represents himself as part of *La Mano Nera* (The Black Hand). He coerces protection money from the Abbandandos and demands that the owner hire his nephew. Vito is out of a job. One evening, Peter Clemenza frantically asks Vito to hide a package (several guns) for him. Later, in repayment for Vito's service, he escorts Vito to an elegant home where they steal a beautiful rug. The seeds of Vito's criminality are sown.

Michael visits Hyman Roth in Miami. He tells Roth that Pentangeli orchestrated the assassination attempt and asks Roth's forbearance when he avenges the treachery. Michael then goes to New York City and meets with Pentangeli, informing him that Roth devised the assassination plot and asking Frank to feign cooperation with the Rosato brothers to ease Roth's concerns and to allow Michael to exact his revenge. Pentangeli soon meets with the Rosatos, is told that "Michael Corleone says hello," as a thug garrotes him. A passing policeman accidentally breaks up the murder try. Pentangeli is left for dead.

In Nevada, the Corleone family frames Senator Geary for the murder of a prostitute in a brothel operated by Fredo Corleone. Tom Hagan appears on the scene and assures Geary that he can make the problem disappear in exchange for Geary's pledge of future loyalty.

In Havana, Cuba, Michael, Roth, and the chief officers of several major American corporations meet with dictator Fulgencio Batista to discuss investments. Later, at a birthday party for Roth, Michael suggests that the rebellious guerillas could defeat Batista and American investments would thereby be jeopardized. Roth wonders why Michael has not delivered the $2,000,000 required to cement their business partnership. Fredo has arrived in Havana with that money. Michael informs Fredo that Roth was behind the earlier assassination attempt and that Michael has a plan in place to eliminate Roth. As Michael invokes Roth and Ola, Fredo assures Michael that he has never met them.

Michael and a group including Senator Geary, Johnny Ola, and several American business leaders go off for a night of entertainment in Havana, under the direction of Fredo. During a viewing of a lurid sex show, Fredo lets it drop that Johnny Ola knows these types of places well and had tipped him off about this locale. Michael immediately understands that Fredo had betrayed him and was at least indirectly and partially responsible for the earlier assassination attempt.

Meanwhile, Michael's own revenge on Roth is unsuccessful. Although Ola is killed, Roth was in a hospital under care for a heart condition. Michael's soldier is shot prior to killing Roth. At a Cuban New Year's Eve party, it becomes clear that the forces of the Batista regime have been routed by the rebels. Michael embraces Fredo and tells him he is aware of his betrayal but offers to help him escape from Cuba. Panicked, Fredo flees on his own. Michael returns to Nevada. Hagan informs him that Roth is back in Miami, Fredo is probably in New York City, and Kay has suffered a miscarriage.

Back in 1917, Fanucci tries to extort money from Vito and his partners in small-time thievery, Clemenza and Sal Tessio. While his partners resign themselves, Vito takes the money, confines Fanucci to take less, and then kills Fanucci outside his residence during a neighborhood celebration. Vito earns the respect of the community and holds court in the Genco Pura Olive Oil Company (with his partner, Genco Abbandano), where he manages affairs. Amusingly, he convinces an arrogant landlord to rescind his eviction notice to an elderly woman with a dog and reduce her rent.

In 1959, a Senate committee, including Geary, investigate organized crime. Willie Cicci, one of Pentangeli's soldiers, provides graphic testimony but cannot implicate Michael because many "buffers" insulated Michael's direct orders from Cicci's criminality. Michael refuses to exercise his fifth amendment rights and answers the committee's queries, denying all malfeasance. The committee chairperson informs Michael that an upcoming witness will soon corroborate the allegations against him. Enter Frank Pentangeli, alive and well, convinced that Michael had tried to murder him. Indicted on a host of charges, Pentangeli agreed to a deal with the FBI.

In a private meeting, Fredo, returning to Nevada, tells Michael that he had given the Roth faction some minor information but had never suspected an assassination plot would follow. Humiliated at being passed over in favor of his younger brother and yearning for respect, he fell prey to Roth's overtures. Michael disassociates himself from Fredo and tells soldier Al Neri that nothing should happen to Fredo while their mother was alive.

As Frank Pentangeli begins his testimony, he spots his brother from Sicily seated next to Michael. Frank immediately disavows his written statements implicating Michael directly in a vast criminal enterprise. The committee must adjourn as its design is now in shambles. Michael leaves freely.

Michael soon has an acrimonious encounter with Kay. She declares her desire to take their two children and leave Michael. She tells him that she did not have a miscarriage but, instead, arranged an abortion of their male fetus because she could not provide Michael with another heir for the Corleone crime family. Michael first tries to assuage Kay but then slaps her.

In 1925, Vito takes his immediate family to Sicily for a vacation. At its conclusion, he arranges a meeting with an ancient Don Ciccio, whom he knifes to death. During his escape, his friend Don Tommasino is shot in the leg, an injury that results in an irreparable limp.

In Spring 1959, Michael's mother, Carmela, dies. Fredo returns for the funeral. Michael embraces him and apparently forgives him at the request of Connie. But Michael silently signals Al Neri that Fredo's immunity from revenge of his betrayal has expired.

Hagen tries to convince Michael that the family's political and business positions are secure. Roth is on the run, seeking asylum unsuccessfully from a host of countries. But Michael demands revenge. Hagen visits Pentangeli in prison, convincing him to replicate the example of ancient Rome where unsuccessful connivers would commit suicide in return for the ongoing care of their surviving family.

Kay, in collusion with Connie, visits her children but remains longer than Michael expected. When he arrives, he icily shuts the door on her, once again affirming his estrangement.

The film reaches the revenge culmination. Rocco Lampone, posing as a journalist, kills Roth at an airport, and is immediately slain by Roth's henchmen. Pentangeli, pursuant to his deal with Hagen, is found dead in his bathtub. Neri fatally shoots Fredo while fishing on Lake Tahoe. All accounts are settled.

Flashback: in December 1941, the Corleone family attends a surprise birthday party for Vito. Sonny introduces Carlo Rizzi, Connie's date, to the other members. They discuss the Japanese attack on Pearl Harbor. Sonny scoffs at those enlisting to fight on behalf and at the bequest of strangers. Michael informs everyone that he has just enlisted in the Marine Corps. Sonny rages at his decision. Fredo supports Michael. Tessio arrives with the birthday cake and everyone, except for Michael, leaves the room to greet Vito upon his arrival.

Circa 1960, estranged, desolate, and silent, Michael Corleone sits and broods.

Appendix C

Summarizing *The Godfather III*

A concise flashback of past Corleone criminality prefaces the film's 1979 setting. Michael, approaching sixty years old, is wracked with guilt and seeks redemption for his past excesses. Tom Hagen has died. The family has abandoned the Lake Tahoe compound and has returned to New York City. Michael still apparently loves Kay, whom he divorced over a decade ago and who raised their two children, Mary and Anthony. Michael has softened the violent dimensions of the Corleone enterprise and highlighted American corporate-business features. He now strives to minimize violence, maximize business profits, and purchase redemption through religious and secular philanthropy. Pursuant to that quest, he establishes the Vito Corleone Foundation as a way of laundering his reputation.

At an elaborate ritual at St. Patrick's Cathedral, Archbishop Gilday honors Michael as a Commander of the Order of St. Sebastian. Numerous family members and friends attend, including a remarried Kay, her spouse, Anthony, and Mary. At an extravagant after-party, the unbridled hostility between Vincent Mancini, illegitimate son of Santino Corleone and his mistress Lucy Mancini, and Joey Zasa, who has overseen the criminal side of the Corleone enterprise for two decades, generate fireworks. Michael instructs the two to settle their differences and establish a truce. The two antagonists hug, but Zasa utters "bastardo" to Vincent, who responds by biting off part of Zasa's ear. Vincent perceives Zasa as a profligate hood who is recurrently disloyal to Michael and who has presided over a deteriorating lower east side in Manhattan. Zasa leaves the party. Michael takes Vincent to task but agrees to mentor him, as Vincent's loyalty to Michael is palpable.

Michael and Kay discuss the future of their son Anthony. After excoriating Michael for the hypocrisy of the ceremony at St. Patrick's, she informs him that Anthony aspires to a career as an opera singer. Michael insists that Anthony continue in law school, hoping he will join him in the legitimate aspects of the family business. They spar for several minutes before Michael relents. That evening, two thugs, dispatched by Zasa, break into Vincent's apartment while he is romancing journalist Grace Hamilton, whom he met at his uncle's party. Vincent kills both men, but only after forcing one to reveal that they worked for Zasa.

Pursuant to his quest for respectability and redemption, Michael offers to buy the Vatican's shares in *Immobiliare*, an international realty holding company. The Vatican owns 25 percent of the asset, but Archbishop Gilday's corrupt and ill-advised economic maneuvers have produced excessive debt. Needing an influx of cash, Gilday is receptive to the $600,000,000 offered by Michael and his attorney, B.J. Harrison, to the Vatican Bank. Still, the blackened reputation of the Corleone family generates opposition in Rome and the tenuous health of Pope Paul VI delays ratification of the proposed deal.

Meanwhile, Don Altobello, the elderly, crafty head of one of the NYC crime families, informs Michael that his colleagues want a piece of the *Immobiliare* deal. Fearing their inclusion would plunge the company into explicit criminality, Michael arranges a meeting in Atlantic City. Using funds from liquidated casino sales, Michael bestows generous checks upon the greedy Dons. Joey Zasa, however, receives nothing, declares Michael his enemy, and scampers from the room. Altobello follows him, ostensibly to unruffle Zasa's feathers and broker a peace. Within seconds, the doors of the meeting room lock and a helicopter spatters countless bullets through the ceiling window. Michael, Vincent, and Al Neri escape, while most attendees are killed. At his residence, Michael contemplates his response but suffers a diabetic stroke. During the attack, Michael cries out "Fredo," in remembrance of the brother he murdered.

Along the way, Vincent and Mary, first cousins, develop an intimate relationship. In collaboration with Connie, who is becoming more Don-like by the day, Vincent plots an attack on Zasa. The enterprise takes place at a religious celebration. Disguised as a city policeman, Vincent murders Zasa, and with his comrades also slays Zasa's bodyguards. When Michael discovers this, he scolds Vincent, who points out that he was authorized by Connie and Al Neri.

Michael demands that Vincent end his affair with Mary, a romance that is doubly dangerous: biologically and strategically. Reluctantly, Vincent acquiesces.

The family travels to Sicily for Anthony's operatic debut, rest, recreation, and tactical advantage. Michael dispatches Vincent to Don Altobello, with instructions to feign discontent with Michael's request about Mary and seek protection from and allegiance with Altobello. Vincent cajoles the old Don, who introduces him to Licio Lucchesi, the mastermind of the conspiracy to prevent Michael's acquisition of *Immobiliare*.

In Sicily, Michael reconnects with Kay, asking her forgiveness, recounting how he stumbled into a life of crime, and yet again promising to become entirely legitimate. Using Sicily as his romantic backdrop, Michael renews his courtship of Kay.

To underscore his commitment to redemption, Michael meets Cardinal Lamberto, renown as a pious, uncommonly honorable prelate, to discuss the *Immobiliare* deal and the intrigues in the Vatican. Lamberto urges Michael to confess his sins. Michael admits to several major transgressions, including ordering the murder of his brother. Lamberto softly endorses Michael's suffering as Corleone sobs. Although recognizing that Michael is not genuinely repentant, the Cardinal absolves him of his past wrongs yet ratifies his emotional distress: "It is just that you suffer."

Michael learns that Don Tommasino, his former protector and Vito's lifelong ally, has been slain by a notorious assassin, Mosca of Montelepre, who never fails to bag his prey. After Pope Paul VI dies, Lamberto is elected Pope John Paul I, which augurs well for Michael's *Immobiliare* transaction. With a reputation for impeccable rectitude, the new pope is a threat to Lucchesi and his co-conspirators.

Vincent reports his findings to Michael: Lucchesi is the leader of the *Immobiliare* opposition; Altobello has hired Mosca to murder Michael; and the plot will be executed forthwith. Vincent, with Connie's unrestrained enthusiasm, demands to strike first. Brushing aside Michael's warning that to do so will forge Vincent's destiny in crime, Vincent reiterates his desire. Michael inducts Vincent as head of the Corleone family only after demanding, again, that Vincent end his romance with Mary once and forever.

At Palermo, as Anthony performs the male lead in *Cavalleria Rusticana* at the Teatro Massimo opera house, Vincent executes his vengeful plan while Lucchesi, Altobello, and Mosca are simultaneously carrying out their own treacherous designs. The murders flow quickly. Vincent's soldiers kill Frederick Keinszig, the Swiss chief accountant of the Vatican Bank who tried to swindle Michael, and hang his corpse over a bridge to simulate a suicide; Archbishop Gilday poisons or has some other agent poison the tea of Pope John Paul I, who dies; but Al Neri murders Gilday as he ascends a spiral staircase; Michael's former shepherd-bodyguard, Calo, kills Lucchesi by stabbing him in the throat with his own spectacles while whispering, "Power wears out those who do not have it;" Calo is immediately killed by Lucchesi's soldiers; Connie poisons her godfather, Don Altobello, using a cannoli as her instrument of death as she peers at her victim through opera glasses.

Mosca, dressed as a monk, enters the opera house to kill Michael. Two of Vincent's hitmen, twins, are obstacles that he must kill but which prevent him from murdering Michael during the opera. Mosca sets up outside the opera house staircase and fires his rifle. The first shot grazes Michael's shoulder, but the second fatally wounds Mary, who dies crying out, "Dad." Vincent then kills Mosca, whose undefeated streak perishes with him. Kay cradles her daughter's bloody body, while Michael screams, first silently then with bestial pain.

A remembrance of happier days follows: Michael dancing with Mary, then with his second wife, Apollonia, and finally with Kay. Then in a much later year, Michael, aged, alone, and alienated, slumps out of his chair as he tries to put on a pair of glasses. He dies. A dog lurks about his body. The screen fades to dark as *Intermezzo* from *Cavalleria Rusticana* resounds.

Notes

Notes to the Preface

1. Fred L. Gardaphé, *"Italian Signs, American Streets* (Durham, NC: Duke University Press, 1996), 89.
2. I analyze the most persuasive twentieth-century data on these matters in Raymond Angelo Belliotti, *Seeking Identity: Individualism versus Community in an Ethnic Context* (Lawrence: University Press of Kansas, 1995), 247–248 n54. If we take the lowest figure cited for the Italian American population in the late twentieth century and double the 1967 federal figures on organized crime members and suppose, contrary to fact, that all members of organized crime are Italian American, even with these unsupported assumptions unfavorable to Italian Americans, only 0.001 of the Italian American population would be members of organized crime. More realistically, at the peak of participation in organized crime, around three or four Italian Americans in 10,000 (0.0003 to 0.0004) were members. Moreover, no evidence suggests that Italian Americans are involved in criminality unrelated to organized syndicates in greater proportion than other ethnic and racial groups.

Notes to Chapter 1

1. Throughout this work, I refer to the adult Vito Corleone as "Don Vito," according the fictional character all due respect.
2. Mario Puzo, *The Godfather* (New York: G.P. Putnam's Sons, 1969), 32.
3. In the novel, when a large, dead fish wrapped in Luca Brasi's bulletproof vest is delivered to the Corleone compound, Tom Hagen is the person who recognizes the Sicilian message: Brasi is sleeping with the fishes deep in the ocean. In the film, Clemenza delivers the line. Hagen, lacking blood ties to the Corleone family and of Irish-German descent, is throughout the novel closely attuned to

Sicilian culture—more so than any of Don Vito's sons. How did Hagen learn? Undoubtedly, through direct instruction from Don Vito, perhaps augmented through study. That Don Vito appoints Hagen, a non-Sicilian, *consigliere* is no accident. The appointment signals Don Vito's admission on the intellectual level that the ways of the old world are unsustainable in the United States. Also, a critic might argue that Carlo Rizzi physically abused Connie at least twice without reprisal from Don Vito. The difference is that Carlo and Connie were married, considered a much different context than the case of Bonasera's daughter and my hypothetical example involving Don Vito's daughter.

4. Puzo, *The Godfather*, 59.

5. Puzo, 33.

6. Puzo, 260.

7. Fred L. Gardaphé, *From Wiseguys to Wise Men: The Gangster and Italian American Masculinities* (New York: Routledge, 2006), 33, 37.

8. Raymond Angelo Belliotti, *Why Philosophy Matters: 20 Lessons on Living Large* (Newcastle, UK: Cambridge Scholars Publishing, 2015), 36–46; James Bowman, *Honor: A History* (New York: Encounter Books, 2006); Frank Henderson Stewart, *Honor* (Chicago: University of Chicago Press, 1994); Alexander Welsh, *What is Honor?* (New Haven, CT: Yale University Press, 2008).

9. John Dickie writes:

> The new mafioso swears obedience . . . he never asks, "Why?" . . . eliminating women and children is only deemed dishonorable if it is unnecessary. . . . Honor accumulates through obedience; in return for what they call "availability," individual Mafiosi can increase their stock of honor and in doing so gain access to more money, information, and power. . . . Honor also involves the obligation to tell the truth to other men of honor . . . a way of promoting the kind of mutual trust that is in short supply. . . . Honor is also about loyalty. . . . a Mafioso must put *Cosa Nostra*'s interests above those of his kin. . . . It is crucial that individual Mafiosi make sensible choice of marital partner and behave honorably within marriage . . . his spouse's good behavior feeds back into his stock of honor. . . . So "honor" translates as a sense of professional worth, a value system, and a totem of group identity for an association that regards itself as being beyond good and evil.

Cosa Nostra: A History of the Sicilian Mafia (New York: Palgrave Macmillan, 2004), 29, 30, 31, 32, 33.

10. See, for example, Jerry Capeci, *The Mafia* (Indianapolis, IN: Alpha Books, 2002), 23–28.

11. Dickie: "The code of honor is much more than a list of rules. Becoming a man of honor means taking on a whole new identity, entering a different moral universe. A mafioso's honor is the mark of that new identity, that new moral sensibility." *Cosa Nostra*, 29.

12. "The code produces a proud sense of fellowship . . . to break the code of honor and turn state's evidence . . . means abandoning both an identity and a dense fabric of friendships and family ties . . . it means incurring an automatic death sentence. . . . Men of honor are expected to maintain the dignity of their bearing in prison . . . to be a man of honor means to operate beyond society's measures of right and wrong" (Dickie, 33, 188).

13. Salvatore Lupo notes: "The concept of honor, borrowed from aristocratic language, ideally serves as an expression of pride of membership in an elite, criminal though it may be, with an emphasis on distance from ordinary people. A man is honored precisely to the degree that many others are no so honored and cannot hope to be. This results in an amplification of the effect of identification in a system of norms that expresses "the internal language of the organization and not that of the external legitimatization." *History of the Mafia*, translated by Antony Shugaar (New York: Columbia University Press, 2009), 26–27.

14. Puzo, *The Godfather*, 404.

15. Puzo, 278–280.

16. Raymond Angelo Belliotti, *Dante's Deadly Sins: Moral Philosophy in Hell* (Oxford: Wiley Blackwell, 2014), 127–129.

17. Puzo, *The Godfather*, 147.

18. Francis Ford Coppola, *The Godfather Notebook* (New York: Regan Arts, 2016), 147.

19. Jenny M. Jones, *The Annotated Godfather: The Complete Screenplay* (New York: Black Dog & Leventhal Publishers, 2007), 18.

20. Puzo, *The Godfather*, 294.

21. Puzo, 65–66.

22. Coppola, *The Godfather Notebook*, 66.

23. Puzo, *The Godfather*, 55, 61.

24. Puzo, 67–68.

25. For a catalog of other possible forms and renderings of respect see the essays featured in note 26 below.

26. My understanding of the concept of respect has been influenced by Theodore Benditt, "Why Respect Matters," *Journal of Value Inquiry* 42 (2008): 487–496; Stephen D. Hudson, "The Nature of Respect," *Social Theory and Practice* 6 (1980): 69–90; Joel Feinberg, "The Nature and Value of Rights," *Journal of Value Inquiry* 4 (1970): 243–260; Carla Bagnoli, "Respect and Loving Attention," *Canadian Journal of Philosophy* 33 (2003): 483–516; and "The Mafioso Case: Autonomy and Self-Respect," *Ethical Theory and Moral Practice* 12 (2009): 477–493.

27. See chapter 3 for an explanation of the possession and exercise of power-over.

28. See, for example, Raimondo Catanzaro, *Men of Respect: A Social History of the Sicilian Mafia*, translated by Raymond Rosenthal (New York: The Free Press, 1988), 39.

29. Luigi Barzini, *From Caesar to the Mafia* (New York: Library Press, 1971), 361; Lupo, *History of the Mafia*, ix, 6.

30. Dickie, *Cosa Nostra*, 102.

31. Catanzaro, *Men of Respect*, 45.

32. Barzini, *From Caesar to the Mafia*, 361–362.

33. Barzini, 361.

34. Luigi Barzini, *The Italians* (New York: Atheneum, 1964), 286.

35. Selwyn Raab, *Five Families: The Rise, Decline, and Resurgence of America's Most Powerful Mafia Empires*, 2nd ed. (New York: Thomas Dunne, 2016), 196.

Notes to Chapter 2

1. See, for example, Raymond Angelo Belliotti, *Seeking Identity: Individualism versus Community in an Ethnic Context* (Lawrence: University Press of Kansas, 1995), ix–x, 157–158, 191–193.

2. Luigi Barzini, *The Italians* (New York: Atheneum, 1964), 263. Barzini adds, "In the outside world, amidst the chaos and the disorder of society, [Italians] often feel compelled to employ the wiles of underground fighters in enemy-occupied territory. All official and legal authority is considered hostile by them until proved friendly or harmless: if it cannot, it should be neutralized or deceived if need be." *The Italians*, 202.

3. Raymond Angelo Belliotti, *What is the Meaning of Human Life?* (Amsterdam, Netherlands: Rodopi Publishers, 2001); *Is Human Life Absurd? A Philosophical Inquiry into Finitude, Value, and Meaning* (Leiden, Netherlands: Brill Publishers, 2019).

4. Belliotti, *What is the Meaning of Human Life?*, 85–88.

5. Raymond Angelo Belliotti, *Posthumous Harm: Why the Dead are Still Vulnerable* (Lanham, MD: Lexington Books, 2012), 101–132.

6. Belliotti, What is the *Meaning of Human Life?*, 87–88; *Is Human Life Absurd?*, 147–150.

7. The *Mezzogiorno* refers to the regions of Italy south of Rome: Abruzzi and Molise, Campania, Apulia, Basilicata (Lucania), Calabria, and Sicily. Sardinia is sometimes included in the group. *Mezzogiorno* literally means "middle of the day" but also bears several rich connotations, such as "the land that time forgot" and "where the sun always shines." This region has for centuries been the poorest but most intriguing part of Italy. About 80 percent of the Italian immigrants to the United States came from the *Mezzogiorno*.

8. In sketching the general account of the family structure in Southern Italy and Sicily, I consulted Richard D. Alba, *Italian Americans: Into the Twilight of Ethnicity* (Englewood Cliffs: Prentice-Hall, 1985); Barzini, *The Italians*; Richard Gambino, *Blood of My Blood* (New York: Anchor Books, 1974); Jerre Mangione and Ben Morreale, *La Storia* (New York: Harper Collins, 1992); Belliotti, *Seeking Identity*.

9. Barzini observes: "No Italian who has a family is ever alone. He finds in it a refuge in which to lick his wounds after a defeat, or an arsenal and a staff for his victorious drives. Scholars have always recognized the Italian family as the only fundamental institution in the country, a spontaneous creation of the national genius . . . the real foundation of whichever social order prevails . . . the law, the State and society function only if they do not directly interfere with the family's supreme interests." *The Italians*, 198, 199.

10. John Dickie, *Cosa Nostra: A History of the Sicilian Mafia* (New York: Palgrave Macmillan, 2004), 82.

11. Dickie, 82–83.

12. Raymond Angelo Belliotti, *Roman Philosophy and the Good Life* (Lanham, MD: Lexington Books, 2009), 7–8, 108.

13. Vincent Patrick's *The Pope of Greenwich Village* contains an instructive passage about traditional Italian tribalism. An Irish-American safecracker, Barney, is questioning two Italian Americans, Charlie and Paulie, who are trying to recruit him into their criminal scheme. The Irishman questions Charlie as to his relationship to Paulie: "Paulie tells me you're cousins." Charlie replies, "Fifth. Maybe sixth—I can never figure it out. His father's great-aunt back in Naples was a cousin of someone on my mother's side." Barney nods: "With Italians, that makes you about as close as twin brothers in an Irish family" (New York: Seaview Books, 1979), 31–32.

14. Alba, *Italian Americans*, 30. For example, in Italy universal male suffrage for those aged thirty or older was introduced in 1912. By 1918, the right to vote was extended to males aged twenty-one or older who had served in the military. Universal adult suffrage, including women, did not occur until 1945. In 1975 the age for voting was reduced to eighteen or older. Thus, the vast majority of Italian immigrants to America arriving in the late nineteenth and early twentieth century had never voted in the old country.

15. Barzini, *The Italians*, 201, 211.

16. Barzini, 202.

17. Barzini cautions: "The strength of the family is not only . . . the bulwark against disorder, but, at the same time, one of its principal causes. It has actively fomented chaos in many ways especially by rendering useless the development of strong political institutions." *The Italians*, 199.

18. Barzini, 202. However we evaluate *l'ordine della famiglia* today, its moral code arose from, mollified to an extent, but also unwittingly sustained the brutal life prospects of the subjugated denizens of the *Mezzogiorno*. Booker T. Washington, a

man who knew slavery first-hand and fought against it, visited Italy and concluded: "The Negro is not the man farthest down. The condition of the coloured farmer in the most backward parts of the Southern States in America, even where he has the least education and the least encouragement, is incomparably better than the condition and opportunities of the agricultural population in Sicily." Karl Marx, whose scientific socialism would one day energize over 40 percent of the world's population at the height of his influence, once wrote: "In all human history no country or no people have suffered such terrible slavery, conquest and foreign oppression and no country and no people have struggled so strenuously for their emancipation as Sicily and the Sicilians." Quoted in Mangione and Morreale, *La Storia*, xv, 58; Belliotti, *Seeking Identity*, 30.

19. Gambino, *Blood of My Blood*, 129–131. Vera Dika describes the ideal of the *uomo di pazienza*:

> A man who holds his body erect, but composed, his face impassive, and who plans, waits, and then acts. He is not a man of brash impulse, or of too many, or of ill-chosen, words. Nor is he a man of public romantic or sexual display . . . far from being an indicator of vacuity, or of shallowness of feeling. . . . The depth of passion is here controlled and then directed, and so results in power.

"The Representation of Ethnicity in *The Godfather*" in *Francis Ford Coppola's The Godfather Trilogy*, ed. Nick Browne (New York: Cambridge University Press, 2000), 89.

20. Mario Puzo, *The Godfather* (New York: G.P. Putnam's Sons, 1969), 37.
21. Puzo, 38.
22. Puzo, 404.
23. Puzo, 55–56.
24. Puzo, 292, 293.
25. Puzo, 426.
26. Puzo, 365.
27. Puzo, 221.
28. Puzo, 19.
29. Puzo, 327. Concerning religion, Thomas J. Ferraro observes: "[*The Godfather*] is in fact organized around the sacramental activities for which Italians are renowned: weddings, funerals, baptisms, the communion of the dinner table, and various implicit versions of confession (Amerigo Bonasera to Don Vito Corleone), last rites (over the body of Sonny Corleone), and priestly vows ("Father, I am with you now!"). The central plot is the salvific one, of Michael Corleone's renunciation of his Emersonian American Destiny to fulfill the bidding of his (holy) father; and the pagan Catholic identification with the redemptive possibilities of

violence—stylized blood and gore in vengeance's name—overrides our moralism." "My Way" in "Our America": Art, Ethnicity, Profession," *American Literary History* 12 (3) (2000): 499–522, 512. I would caution, however, against interpreting so many scenes as "implicit versions" of Roman Catholic sacramental activities. For example, sometimes a commitment from son to parent is only that and not a "priestly vow," and a father's rendering of "Look, how they have massacred my son," may be only an expression of parental anguish and understated outrage and not a religious pontification of "last rites."

30. Puzo, 213.
31. Puzo, 216.
32. Gambino, *Blood of My Blood*, 131. Also, "The traditional *mafioso* had no love of ostentation. His power, like his consumption, was characteristically discreet and reserved. To say little, to keep a low profile, to disparage the extent of one's influence—these were the rules the mafia followed in its appearance in public life. . . . The *Mafioso* made no display of superfluous consumption, because none was necessary to establish his respectability." Pino Arlacchi, *Mafia Business: The Mafia Ethic and the Spirit of Capitalism* (Lindon: Verso, 1986), 117.
33. Puzo, *The Godfather*, 254, 269.
34. Selwyn Raab reports:

> The *Cosa Nostra*'s variegated crimes—its murders, loan-sharking, extortions, gambling, brutal beatings, prostitution, political fixes, police corruption, and union and industrial racketeering—created immeasurable costs and pain for America. None of these illicit activities, however, inflicted more lasting distress on American society and damaged quality of life more than the Mafia's large-scale introduction of heroin. In the decades following the Palermo agreement [a 1957 pact between the Sicilian Mafia and the American *Cosa Nostra* to import huge quantities of heroin into the United States], the Sicilian Mafia and its American helpers inundated the United States with the drug. An estimated 50,000 Americans were addicted in the late 1950s. By the mid-1970s, according to studies by government and private groups, at least 500,000 were hooked.

Five Families: The Rise, Decline, and Resurgence of America's Most Powerful Mafia Empires. 2nd edition (New York: Thomas Dunne Books, 2016), 114.

35. Jerry Capeci, *The Mafia* (Indianapolis, IN: Alpha Books, 2002), 7–13.
36. Raab, *Five Families*, 60–62, 65.
37. Raab, 201–202.
38. Salvatore Lupo, *History of the Mafia*, translated by Antony Shugaar (New York: Columbia University Press, 2009), 146–149.

39. Barzini, *The Italians*, 273, 275.
40. Dickie, *Cosa Nostra*, 156, 157.
41. Dickie, 276.
42. Barzini, *The Italians*, 279, 280.
43. Dickie, *Cosa Nostra*, 204–205.
44. Dickie, 205.
45. Dickie
46. Michael Goodwin and Naomi Wise. *On the Edge: The Life & Times of Francis Coppola* (New York: William Morrow and Company, 1989), 118.
47. "Whenever the Godfather opened his mouth, in my mind I heard the voice of my mother. I heard her wisdom, her ruthlessness, and her unconquerable love for her family and for life itself, qualities not valued in women at the time. The Don's courage and loyalty came from her; his humanity came from her." Mario Puzo, *The Fortunate Pilgrim* (New York: Random House, 1997), xii.
48. Lupo, *History of the Mafia*, 32; Belliotti, *Roman Philosophy*, 2.
49. Lupo, *History of the Mafia*; Belliotti, *Roman Philosophy*.
50. Alessia Ricciardi, "Toward an Italian-American Sublime: The Case of *The Godfather*." *Voices in Italian Americana* 11 (1) (2000): 15–27, 23.
51. Barzini, *The Italians*, 264.
52. Lupo, *History of the Mafia*, 6–7.
53. Lupo, *History of the Mafia*, 3.
54. Dickie, *Cosa Nostra*, 60; Barzini, *The Italians*, 263.
55. Lupo, *History of the Mafia*, 12.
56. Lupo, *History of the Mafia*, 33.
57. Barzini, *The Italians*, 286.
58. Dickie, *Cosa Nostra*, 132–133. Also, "This culture is said to be characterized by a mistrust of the state and therefore by a habit of taking justice into one's own hands, be a sense of honor, by clientelism, by a familism that exempts the individual from a perception of his own responsibilities in the face of a larger collective than his immediate surroundings." Lupo, *History of the Mafia*, 11. Rejection of the concept of the impersonal nature of the law as well as scorn for police and for those who collaborate with them were critical.
59. Alessandro Camon, "*The Godfather* and the Mythology of the Mafia," in *Francis Ford Coppola's The Godfather Trilogy*, ed. Nick Browne (New York: Cambridge University Press, 2000), 61. "The basic function of the Mafia, can be identified in the racket that protects a legal institution, the business enterprise, using violence to ensure a monopoly for itself—specifically, the verbal and physical intimidation of thieves, traitors, witnesses, and competitors. Mafia wars are largely waged among aspiring protectors." Lupo, *History of the Mafia*, 15.
60. Dickie, *Cosa Nostra*, 38, 42, 21.
61. Lupo, *History of the Mafia*, 15. In the early twentieth century, Ermanno Sangiorgi, administrative director of the district police of Palermo, clearly stated

the principle of reciprocity binding the Mafia to the political establishment: "the *caporioni* [ringleaders] of the Mafia are under the protection of senators, members of parliament, and other influential figures who protect them and defend them, only to be protected and defended by them in turn" (cited in Lupo, 17).

62. Raimondo Catanzaro, *Men of Respect: A Social History of the Sicilian Mafia*, translated by Raymond Rosenthal (New York: The Free Press, 1988), 4. "The Mafia was traditionally a geographic phenomenon characteristic of Palermo and nearly all of the Palermo province, Naples and certain districts of the Neapolitan hinterland, the province of Reggio Calabria, part of the province of Trapani, the inland Sicilian area of the sulphur mines and the large landholdings, with the exclusion of the eastern section of the island. Only in the past thirty years has the infection spread until it covered with some homogeneity three Italian regions, or states—Sicily, Campania, and Calabria—as well as a fourth region, Puglia (Apulia)." Lupo, *History of the Mafia*, 11.

Today, organized crime in Southern Italy and Sicily assumes distinct organizational networks: the Mafia plies its trade in Sicily, the Camorra in the province of Campania, and the 'ndrangheta in Calabria.

63. Cited in Catanzaro, *Men of Respect*, 5.

64. Diego Gambetta, "*The Sicilian Mafia: The Business of Private Protection* (Cambridge, MA: Harvard University Press, 1993), 3.

65. Gambetta, 79.

66. Gambetta, 91.

67. Gambetta, 97, 99.

68. Lupo, *History of the Mafia*, 29. All the figures listed below revealed copious inside information about *Cosa Nostra* and the Mafia, thereby violating the principle of *omertà*.

Joseph Bonanno ("Joe Bananas") (1905–2002) was born into a Mafia family in Castellammare del Golfo, Sicily, virtually a cradle of organized crime activity. His family immigrated to America around 1908, but Joe returned to Sicily ten years later. He re-entered the United States in 1924 and joined the crime family of Salvatore Maranzano. After the Castellammarese Crime War, which featured the murders of both Joe Masseria and Maranzano, in 1931 Bonanno took control of his crime family, which assumed his surname. His family prospered for decades. In 1963, Bonanno conspired unsuccessfully with Joe Magliocco, acting boss of the Profaci family, to murder *Cosa Nostra* Commission members Tommy Lucchese and Carlo Gambino. Profaci soldier Joe Columbo was given the contract. Weighing the percentages, Columbo revealed the plot to Gambino. The Commission ordered Bonanno and Magliocco to appear before it. Magliocco complied and was forced to retire. Bonanno scurried to Canada, then New York, and later engineered a fake kidnapping to avoid repercussions from The Commission. From 1966 through 1968, "The Banana War" raged within the Bonanno family, culminating with Bonanno's retirement to Arizona. In 1983, Bonanno published A *Man of Honor:*

The Autobiography of Joseph Bonanno, a self-serving tome that added to the myth of a once golden age of honorable, judicious mobsters.

Joe Valachi (1903–1971) was a soldier in the Genovese crime family. In 1962, while serving a fifteen-year sentence for drug trafficking, he killed an inmate whom he suspected was ordered by Genovese to murder him. Upon being sentenced to life imprisonment, he agreed to testify at a United States Senate committee hearing in 1963. His testimony was televised nationally as he disclosed details about the Italian American *Cosa Nostra*. After witnessing his narrative, that an organized crime syndicate existed in America was no longer plausibly deniable. In 1968, he collaborated with writer Peter Maas on his memoir, *The Valachi Papers*. A movie with the same title was produced in 1972.

Nicola Gentile (1885–1966) built his career in America, where he first arrived from his birthplace of Siculiana in the province of Agrigento in 1903 at the age of eighteen. He returned to Sicily in 1909, 1913, 1919, 1925, and 1927–1930, and then, for good, in 1937, while free on bail after an arrest for heroin trafficking in the United States. He became boss of a Sicilian *cosca* upon his arrival. Throughout his time in America, he participated in political elections in his native land and in import-export projects, as well as ordering murders. Although indicted several times, he evaded incarceration through his rich network of political contacts, which extended even among the Fascists. Known in Sicily as Zu Cola, in 1963 he collaborated with an Italian journalist in composing his memoirs, *Vita di capomafia*, the first reliable and comprehensive account of the Mafia as an organization and the life of a crime boss in it.

Tommaso Buscetta (1928–2000) was an international mob figure, plying his trade in Brazil, the United States, and Sicily. Around 1982, a major intramural Mafia war resulted in the deaths of his sons and other family members, most of whom were not connected to organized crime. After being arrested in Brazil the following year, Buscetta requested a session with anti-Mafia jurist Giovanni Falcone and agreed to act as a *pentito* (informant). For years he provided precise details of the intricacies of the Mafia's organization, honor code, and daily activities. In 1984, he was extradited to the United States under the Witness Protection Program. He testified in the Pizza Connection Trial in New York in 1985 and the Maxi Trial of Sicilian gangsters in 1986. After the assassinations of righteous judges, Falcone and Paolo Borsellino, Buscetta offered testimony to the Antimafia Commission in Sicily regarding connections between prominent Italian politicians and organized crime. He lived out his days in Florida under assumed identities. Several movies have been made about his life, including the 2019 offering *Il traditore* (The Traitor) by Marco Bellocchio.

Antonino Calderone (1935–2013) was born in Catania. His brother, Giuseppe, was the boss of the local crime family. From 1978 until around 1983, the Corleonesi gang waged brutal war against the Calderone family. Antonino fled to Nice. He was arrested there in 1986.While incarcerated, he suspected that a contract for his murder had been given to some of the imprisoned Sicilians. He offered to consult with Judge Falcone. Their discussions spanned over a year. By 1988, more than 150 arrest warrants had been issued pursuant to Calderone's disclosures. He lived out his days overseas under assumed identities. In 1992, Antonino collaborated with sociologist Pino Arlacchi, composing *Men of Dishonor: Inside the Sicilian Mafia*.

     69. Luigi Barzini, *From Caesar to the Mafia* (New York: Library Press, 1971), 361.

     70. Barzini.

     71. Camon, "*The Godfather* and the Mythology of the Mafia," 61.

     72. Lupo, *History of the Mafia*, 8–30.

     73. Lupo, 25.

     74. Lupo, 11, 12.

     75. Mario Puzo *The Godfather* (New York: G.P. Putnam's Sons, 1969), 327.

     76. Barzini, *The Italians*, 286.

     77. Cited in Dickie, *Cosa Nostra*, 153; Francesco Renda, *Storia della mafia* (Palermo: Sigma Edizione, 1997), 26.

     78. Dickie, 161–162.

Notes to Chapter 3

     1. Mario Puzo, at times, confessed to the distortions in his novel: "The Mafia is certainly romanticized. They are much worse guys than [as depicted in his book]." Michael Goodwin and Naomi Wise. *On the Edge: The Life & Times of Francis Coppola* (New York: William Morrow and Company, Inc., 1989), 118. In the words of Fred L. Gardaphé: "Don Corleone and his fellow Mafia leaders . . . are depicted as heroic male figures, hypermen or supermen who 'refused the domination of other men. There was no force, no mortal man who could bend them to their will unless they wished it.'" *From Wiseguys to Wise Men: The Gangster and Italian American Masculinities* (New York: Routledge, 2006), 33. Anthony Julian Tamburri astutely identifies visual clues in the films, especially in the dress and manner of the main protagonists, that suggest that Coppola's film softens that romanticism. In his view, these visual clues depict Don Vito more as an Italian grandfather than as a crime czar, whereas Michael is the consummate American businessman qua assassin. "Michael Corleone's Tie: Francis Ford Coppola's *The Godfather*," in Dana Renga, *Mafia Movies: A Reader*. 2nd edition (Toronto: University of Toronto Press, 2019), 70–75.

     2. George De Stefano, *An Offer We Can't Refuse: The Mafia in the Mind of America* (New York: Faber and Faber, Inc., 2006), 103. Mario Puzo wrote

about one half of the screen play of *The Godfather*, but after the initial stages the *pezzonovanti* of Paramount froze him out of the film, not even permitting him to view the final cut. Peter Biskind, *The Godfather Companion* (New York: HarperCollins Publishers, 1990), 25; Mario Puzo, *The Godfather Papers* (New York: Fawcett Crest, 1972), 32, 64.

 3. Chris Messenger, *The Godfather and American Culture* (Albany, NY: SUNY Press, 2002), 8. Coppola's interpretation rings true only in the broadest interpretation of the novel. In its more precise dimensions, the novel focuses on the pursuit of honor, power, and respect within a specific family and ethnic code. Mario Puzo added, "I've wanted to show the parallel between the normal business world and the Mafia . . . these guys know how to use violence as a business tool . . . the old guys were men of honor [with] family values" (Messenger, 291). Puzo here should make clearer how Don Vito also uses business as a tool to attain his higher aims: amassing and exercising power, as well as manifesting and amplifying his honor. Also, Puzo's understanding of "the old guys" is overly sanguine.

 4. Stephen Farber, "Coppola and *The Godfather*," in *Sight and Sound* 41 (4) (Autumn 1972): 217–223, 223.

 5. Stephen Farber, "They Made Him Two Offers He Couldn't Refuse," in *New York Times* (22 December 1974), Section 2: 1, 19.

 6. Goodwin and Wise, *On the Edge*, 119.

 7. Fredric Jameson, *Signatures of the Visible* (New York: Routledge, 1992), 224–226.

 8. David Ray Papke, "Myth and Meaning," in John Denvir, ed., *Legal Realism: Movies as Legal Texts* (Urbana: University of Illinois Press, 1996), 1.

 9. Papke, 8.

 10. Messenger, *The Godfather*, 291.

 11. Alessia Ricciardi, "Toward an Italian-American Sublime: The Case of *The Godfather*." *Voices in Italian Americana* 11 (1) (2000): 15–16.

 12. Pauline Kael, "Alchemy," *The New Yorker* (March 18, 1972): 132–138, 137.

 13. John C. Hulsman and A. Wess Mitchell, *The Godfather Doctrine: A Foreign Policy Parable* (Princeton, NJ: Princeton University Press, 2009).

 14. Thomas J. Ferraro, *Ethnic Passages: Literary Immigrants in Twentieth-Century America* (Chicago: University of Chicago Press, 1993), 18–52. Writing almost thirty years prior to the publication of my work, Ferraro, obviously, did not intend his interpretation to engage a thesis released far in the future. However, an anonymous reviewer of my book prudently suggested that I address Ferraro's reading of the novel to sharpen and distinguish my own, a recommendation for which I am grateful.

 15. Ferraro, 24.

 16. Ferraro, 37.

 17. Ferraro, 38, 40.

 18. Ferraro, 52.

 19. Ferraro, 40, 41.

20. Ferraro, 36.

21. See, for example, Steven Lukes, *Power: A Radical View*, 2nd edition (New York: Palgrave Macmillan, 2005); Thomas E. Wartenberg, *The Forms of Power* (Philadelphia: Temple University Press, 1990); Jeffrey C. Isaac, *Power and Marxist Theory* (Ithaca, NY: Cornell University Press, 1987); Robert A. Dahl, "The Concept of Power," *Behavioral Science* 2 (1975): 201–215; Peter Morriss, *Power: A Philosophical Analysis*, 2nd edition (Manchester: Manchester University Press, 2002); Raymond Angelo Belliotti, *Power: Oppression, Subservience, and Resistance* (Albany, NY: SUNY Press, 2016).

22. Belliotti, *Power*, 26–27.

23. Mario Puzo, *The Godfather* (New York: G.P. Putnam's Sons, 1969), 46.

24. Puzo, 46–47.

25. See also Fred L. Gardaphé, *Italian Signs, American Streets* (Durham, NC: Duke University, Press, 1996), 91.

26. Friedrich Nietzsche, *Beyond Good and Evil*, trans. Walter Kaufmann (New York: Random House, 1966); *On the Genealogy of Morals*, trans. Walter Kaufmann (New York: Random House, 1967); *Thus Spoke Zarathustra* in *The Portable Nietzsche*, trans. Walter Kaufmann (New York: The Viking Press, 1954); *The Will to Power*, trans. Walter Kaufmann and R.J. Hollingdale (New York: Random House, 1967); Raymond Angelo Belliotti, *Nietzsche's Will to Power: Eagles, Lions, and Serpents* (Newcastle: Cambridge Scholars Publishing, 2017), 163–169.

27. Nietzsche, *Beyond Good and Evil* 13; *Zarathustra*, II "On Self-Overcoming"; *On the Genealogy of Morals*, II 12.

28. Belliotti, *Will to Power*, 140–153.

29. Nietzsche, *On the Genealogy of Morals*, III 27.

30. Nietzsche's description of his overman in his unpublished notebooks as "A Roman Caesar with Christ's soul" is instructive. *The Will to Power* (from unpublished notebooks), 983.

31. Belliotti, *Will to Power*, 163–166.

32. Although Nietzsche suggests that all living entities have will to power, my purposes do not require addressing that issue. My analysis is restricted to only human will to power.

33. Belliotti, *Will to Power*, 163–175.

34. Messenger, *The Godfather*, 188.

35. Puzo, *The Godfather*, 188.

36. Gardaphé, *From Wiseguys to Wise Men*, 34.

37. Whether coincidental or not, the Italian alphabet does not contain the letter "K." Puzo may have dubbed Michael's wife as "Kay" to underscore her "otherness."

38. Puzo, *The Godfather*, 327.

39. Naomi Greene, "Family Ceremonies: or, Opera in *The Godfather* Trilogy," in *Francis Ford Coppola's The Godfather Trilogy*, ed. Nick Browne (New York: Cambridge University Press, 2000), 140–141.

40. Puzo, *The Godfather*, 365.
41. Anthony Ambrogio, "*The Godfather*, I and II: Patterns of Corruption." *Film Criticism* 3 (1) (Fall 1978): 35–44, 38–39.
42. John Paul Russo, "Thematic Patterns in Francis Ford Coppola's *The Godfather: Part II*," In Dana Renga. *Mafia Movies: A Reader*. 2nd edition (Toronto: University of Toronto Press, 2019), 82.
43. Russo.
44. Russo.
45. Selwyn Raab, *Five Families: The Rise, Decline, and Resurgence of America's Most Powerful Mafia Empires*. 2nd edition (New York: Thomas Dunne Books, 2016), 177–179. "Mafia-type organized crime depends in part on a social consensus made up of tacit acquaintance, a culture of silence, and a mixture of fear and respect, mingled with suspicion of legal authorities." Alexander Stille, "Breaking the Silence in Calabria," *New York Review of Books* 66 (16) (October 24, 2019): 49–52, 49.
46. Raab, 696–697.

Notes to Chapter 4

1. This plot line of the third film mirrors the connivances of Italian financier Michele "The Shark" Sindona (1920–1986) with the Italian government and the Vatican. Salvatore Lupo remarks: "Sindona was supported by Andreotti and by [his followers] even after he had been indicted by the Italian justice system, and even after the murder of the lawyer Ambrosoli at Sindona's orders. Sindona came out of age-old ties with the Gambinos of New York . . . he had other ties with Rosario Spatola . . . Sindona represented the Bontate-Inzerillo group the financial channel that the head of the P2 Masonic lodge Licio Gelli (and with him, perhaps, Roberto Calvi, president of the Banco Ambrosiano) constituted for the Corleonese" (Lupo 264). Spatola was a Mafia entrepreneur and a leading money launderer of profits from narcotics trafficking in the late 1970s. *History of the Mafia*, translated by Antony Shugaar (New York: Columbia University Press, 2009), 12. For an excellent, comprehensive chronicle of the Italian government and Vatican banking scandal that forms the background of *Godfather III*, see Carlo Testa, "Threads of Political Violence in Italy's Spiderweb: Giorgio Ambrosoli's Murder in Michele Placido's *A Bourgeois Hero*," in Dana Renga. *Mafia Movies: A Reader*. 2nd edition. Toronto: University of Toronto Press, 2019: 236–241.
2. Lupo, *History of the Mafia*, 274.
3. Nigel Cawthorne, *The History of the Mafia* (London: Arcturus Publishing Limited, 2011), 150–151.
4. John Dickie, *Cosa Nostra: A History of the Sicilian Mafia* (New York: Palgrave Macmillan, 2004), 15.

5. Dickie, *Cosa Nostra*.

6. John Paul Russo, "Redemption in Francis Ford Coppola's *The Godfather: Part III*," in Renga. *Mafia Movies*, 109–113, 112.

7. *Che La Luna Mezzo Mare* is a romping Sicilian folksong with Neapolitan seasoning, bearing a traditional tarantella beat. With the moon casting a glow in the middle of the sea, a young woman ponders marriage, bouncing ideas with her mother. Each illustration of a potential suitor looking in the window exudes phallic imagery: the fisherman with "come and go, go and come" with his fish in his hands; the baker boy will have a cannoli in his hands; the musician will have his trumpet; and so on. The possibilities are limitless, and the song invites multiple vocalists to offer new examples. Invariably, performers underscore the oral imagery with suggestive body language. In my experience, older Sicilian women consistently design the most sexual and comedic scenarios.

8. Alessia Ricciardi, "Toward an Italian-American Sublime: The Case of *The Godfather*," *Voices in Italian Americana* 11 (1) (2000): 15–27, 24.

9. Mario Puzo, *The Godfather* (New York: G.P. Putnam's Sons, 1969), 108.

10. From the script of *Godfather III*.

11. See, for example, John Paul Russo, "Thematic Patterns in Francis Ford Coppola's *The Godfather: Part II*," in Renga. *Mafia Movies*, 82–86, 83.

12. Michael Goodwin and Naomi Wise. *On the Edge: The Life & Times of Francis Coppola* (New York: William Morrow and Company, Inc., 1989), 163.

13. This section has been influenced by Richard Swinburne, *Responsibility and Atonement* (New York: Oxford University Press, 1989); Linda Radzik, *Making Amends* (New York: Oxford University Press, 2009); Jeffrie G. Murphy, *Getting Even: Forgiveness and Its Limits* (New York: Oxford University Press, 2003).

14. This section has been influenced by Lucy Allais, "Forgiveness and Mercy," 27 *South African Journal of Philosophy* (2008): 1–9; Nicholas Wolterstorff, "Jesus and Forgiveness," in *Jesus and Philosophy*, ed. Paul K. Moser (Cambridge: Cambridge University Press, 2009); "Does Forgiveness Undermine Justice," in *God and the Ethics of Belief*, ed. Andrew Dole and Andrew Chignell (Cambridge: Cambridge University Press, 2005); Jeffrie G. Murphy, "Remorse, Apology, and Mercy," 4 *Ohio State Journal of Criminal Law* (2007): 423–449; Jeffrie G. Murphy and Jean Hampton, *Forgiveness and Mercy* (Cambridge: Cambridge University Press, 1988); Raymond Angelo Belliotti, *Jesus the Radical: The Parables and Modern Morality* (Lanham, MD: Lexington Books, 2013), 83–97.

15. Raymond Angelo Belliotti, *Posthumous Harm: Why the Dead are Still Vulnerable* (Lanham, MD: Lexington Books, 2012), 17–37, 49–50, 74–75, 94–95, 165–166.

16. Puzo, *The Godfather*, 409.

17. From the script of *Godfather III*.

Bibliography

Alba, Richard D. *Italian Americans: Into the Twilight of Ethnicity.* Englewood Cliffs: Prentice-Hall, 1985.

Allais, Lucy. "Forgiveness and Mercy." *South African Journal of Philosophy* 27:1 (2008): 1–9.

Ambrogio, Anthony. "*The Godfather*, I and II: Patterns of Corruption." *Film Criticism* 3:1 (Fall 1978): 35–44.

Arlacchi, Pino. *Mafia Business: The Mafia Ethic and the Spirit of Capitalism.* London: Verso, 1986.

Bagnoli, Carla. "The Mafioso Case: Autonomy and Self-Respect." *Ethical Theory and Moral Practice* 12 (2009): 477–493.

———. "Respect and Loving Attention." *Canadian Journal of Philosophy* 33 (2003): 483–516.

Barzini, Luigi. *From Caesar to the Mafia.* New York: Library Press, 1971.

———. *The Italians.* New York: Atheneum, 1964.

Belliotti, Raymond Angelo. *Dante's Deadly Sins: Moral Philosophy in Hell.* Oxford: Wiley Blackwell, 2014.

———. *Is Human Life Absurd? A Philosophical Inquiry into Finitude, Value, and Meaning.* Leiden, Netherlands: Brill Publishers, 2019.

———. *Jesus the Radical: The Parables and Modern Morality.* Lanham, MD: Lexington Books, 2013.

———. *Nietzsche's Will to Power: Eagles, Lions, and Serpents.* Newcastle: Cambridge Scholars Publishing, 2017.

———. *Posthumous Harm: Why the Dead are Still Vulnerable.* Lanham, MD: Lexington Books, 2012.

———. *Power: Oppression, Subservience, and Resistance.* Albany, NY: SUNY Press, 2016.

———. *Roman Philosophy and the Good Life.* Lanham, MD: Lexington Books, 2009.

———. *Seeking Identity: Individualism versus Community in an Ethnic Context.* Lawrence: University Press of Kansas, 1995.

———. *What Is the Meaning of Human Life?* Amsterdam, Netherlands: Value Inquiry Book Series, Rodopi Publishers, 2001.
———. *Why Philosophy Matters: 20 Lessons on Living Large.* Newcastle, UK: Cambridge Scholars Publishing, 2015.
Benditt, Theodore. "Why Respect Matters." *Journal of Value Inquiry* 42 (2008): 487–496.
Biskind, Peter. *The Godfather Companion.* New York: HarperCollins Publishers, 1990.
Bonanno, Joseph (with Sergio Lalli). *A Man of Honor: The Autobiography of Joseph Bonanno.* New York: Simon and Schuster, 1985.
Bowman, James. *Honor: A History.* New York: Encounter Books, 2006.
Browne, Nick, ed. *Francis Ford Coppola's The Godfather Trilogy.* New York: Cambridge University Press, 2000.
Camon, Alessandro. "*The Godfather* and the Mythology of Mafia." In *Francis Ford Coppola's The Godfather Trilogy*, ed. Nick Browne. New York: Cambridge University Press, 2000.
Capeci, Jerry. *The Mafia.* Indianapolis, IN: Alpha Books, 2002.
Catanzaro, Raimondo. *Men of Respect: A Social History of the Sicilian Mafia.* Translated by Raymond Rosenthal. New York: The Free Press, 1988.
Cawthorne, Nigel. *The History of the Mafia.* London: Arcturus Publishing Limited, 2011.
Chiampi, Thomas. "Resurrecting *The Godfather*." *MELUS* 5:4 (Winter 1978): 18–31.
Coppola, Francis Ford. *The Godfather Notebook.* New York: Regan Arts, 2016.
Dahl, Robert A. "The Concept of Power," *Behavioral Science* 2 (1975): 201–215.
De Stefano, George. *An Offer We Can't Refuse: The Mafia in the Mind of America.* New York: Faber and Faber, 2006.
Denvir, John, ed. *Legal Realism: Movies as Legal Texts.* Urbana: University of Illinois Press, 1996.
Dickie, John. *Blood Brotherhoods: A History of Italy's Three Mafias.* New York: PublicAffairs, 2014.
———. *Cosa Nostra: A History of the Sicilian Mafia.* New York: Palgrave Macmillan, 2004.
Dika, Vera. "The Representation of Ethnicity in *The Godfather*." In *Francis Ford Coppola's The Godfather Trilogy*, ed. Nick Browne. New York: Cambridge University Press, 2000.
Dole, Andrew, and Andrew Chignell, eds. *God and the Ethics of Belief.* Cambridge, UK: Cambridge University Press, 2005.
Falcone, Giovanni (with Marcelle Padovani). *Men of Honour: The Truth about the Mafia.* Translated by Edward Farrelly. London. Fourth Estate Ltd., 1992.
Farber, Stephen. "Coppola and *The Godfather*." *Sight and Sound* 41:4 (Autumn 1972): 217–223.
———. "They Made Him Two Offers He Couldn't Refuse." In *New York Times* (22 December, 1974), Section 2: 1, 19.

Feinberg, Joel. "The Nature and Value of Rights." *Journal of Value Inquiry* 4 (1970): 243–260.
Ferraro. Thomas J. *Ethnic Passages: Literary Immigrants in Twentieth-Century America*. Chicago: University of Chicago Press, 1993.
———. " 'My Way' in 'Our America': Art, Ethnicity, Profession." *American Literary History* 12:3 (2000): 499–522.
Gambetta, Diego. *The Sicilian Mafia: The Business of Private Protection*. Cambridge, MA: Harvard University Press, 1993.
Gambino, Richard. *Blood of My Blood*. New York: Anchor Books, 1974.
Gardaphé, Fred L. *From Wiseguys to Wise Men: The Gangster and Italian American Masculinities*. New York: Routledge, 2006.
———. *Italian Signs, American Streets*. Durham, NC: Duke University, Press, 1996.
Goodwin, Michael, and Naomi Wise. *On the Edge: The Life & Times of Francis Coppola*. New York: William Morrow and Company, Inc., 1989.
Greene, Naomi. "Family Ceremonies: or, Opera in *The Godfather* Trilogy." In *Francis Ford Coppola's The Godfather Trilogy*, ed. Nick Browne. New York: Cambridge University Press, 2000.
Hudson, Stephen D. "The Nature of Respect." *Social Theory and Practice* 6 (1980): 69–90.
Hulsman, John C., and A. Wess Mitchell. *The Godfather Doctrine: A Foreign Policy Parable*. Princeton, NJ: Princeton University Press, 2009.
Isaac, Jeffrey C. *Power and Marxist Theory*. Ithaca, NY: Cornell University Press, 1987.
Jameson, Fredric. *Signatures of the Visible*. New York: Routledge, 1992.
Jones, Jenny M. *The Annotated Godfather: The Complete Screenplay*. New York: Black Dog & Leventhal Publishers, 2007.
Kael, Pauline. "Alchemy." *The New Yorker* (March 18, 1972): 132–138.
———. "Vanity, Vanities." *The New Yorker* 66 (48) (January 14, 1991): 76–79.
Kauffmann, Stanley. "*The Godfather* and the Decline of Marlon Brando." *The New Republic* (April 1, 1972): 1–3.
Krause, Paul. "Family, Love, and Tragedy in 'The Godfather.' " *The Imaginative Conservative* (November 22, 2018). www.theimaginativeconservative.org/2018/11/family-love-tragedy-godfather-paul-krause.html
Lukes, Steve. *Power: A Radical View*. 2nd edition. New York: Palgrave MacMillan, 2005.
Lupo, Salvatore. *History of the Mafia*. Translated by Antony Shugaar. New York: Columbia University Press, 2009.
Mangione, Jerre, and Ben Morreale. *La Storia*. New York: Harper Collins, 1992.
Messenger, Chris. *The Godfather and American Culture*. Albany, NY: SUNY Press, 2002.
Morriss, Peter. *Power: A Philosophical Analysis*. 2nd edition. Manchester: Manchester University Press, 2002.
Moser, Paul, ed. *Jesus and Philosophy*. Cambridge: Cambridge University Press, 2009.

Murphy, Jeffrie G. *Getting Even: Forgiveness and Its Limits*. New York: Oxford University Press, 2003.

———. "Remorse, Apology, and Mercy," *Ohio State Journal of Criminal Law* 4:2 (2007): 423–453.

Murphy, Jeffrie G., and Jean Hampton. *Forgiveness and Mercy*. Cambridge: Cambridge University Press, 1988.

Murray, William. "Interview: Francis Ford Coppola." *Playboy* 22 (7) (July 1975): 53–68, 184–185.

Nelli, Humbert S. *The Business of Crime: Italians and Syndicate Crime in the United States*. New York: Oxford University Press, 1976.

Nietzsche, Friedrich. *Beyond Good and Evil*. Translated by Walter Kaufmann. New York: Random House, 1966.

———. *On the Genealogy of Morals*. Translated by Walter Kaufmann. New York: Random House, 1967.

———. *Thus Spoke Zarathustra* in *The Portable Nietzsche*. Translated by Walter Kaufmann. New York: The Viking Press, 1954.

———. *The Will to Power*. Translated by Walter Kaufmann and R.J. Hollingdale. New York: Random House, 1967.

Papke, David Ray. "Myth and Meaning." In *Legal Realism: Movies as Legal Texts*, ed. John Denvir. Urbana: University of Illinois Press, 1996.

Patrick, Vincent. *The Pope of Greenwich Village*. New York: Seaview Books, 1979.

Porter, Ethan. "*The Godfather Doctrine* and American Foreign Policy." *Dissent* (April 2, 2009). www.dissentmagazine.org/online_articles/the-godfather-doctrine-and-american-foreign-policy

Puzo, Mario. *The Godfather*. New York: G.P. Putnam's Sons, 1969.

———. *The Godfather Papers*. New York: Fawcett Crest, 1972.

———. *The Fortunate Pilgrim*. New York: Random House, 1997. (First published 1965.)

Raab, Selwyn. *Five Families: The Rise, Decline, and Resurgence of America's Most Powerful Mafia Empires*. 2nd edition. New York: Thomas Dunne Books, 2016.

Radzik, Linda. *Making Amends*. New York: Oxford University Press, 2009.

Renda, Francesco, *Storia della mafia*. Palermo: Sigma Edizione, 1997.

Renga, Dana. *Mafia Movies: A Reader*. 2nd edition. Toronto: University of Toronto Press, 2019.

Ricciardi, Alessia. "Toward an Italian-American Sublime: The Case of *The Godfather*." *Voices in Italian Americana* 11:1 (2000): 15–27.

Russo, John Paul. "The Hidden Godfather." In *Support and Struggle: Italians and Italian Americans in a Comparative Perspective*, ed. Joseph L. Tropea, James E. Miller, and Cheryl Beattle-Repetti. Staten Island, New York: The American Italian Historical Association, 1986.

———. "Redemption in Francis Ford Coppola's *The Godfather: Part III*." In Dana Renga, *Mafia Movies: A Reader*. 2nd edition. Toronto: University of Toronto Press, 2019, 109–113.

———. "Thematic Patterns in Francis Ford Coppola's *The Godfather: Part II.*" In Dana Renga, *Mafia Movies: A Reader*. 2nd edition. Toronto: University of Toronto Press, 2019, 82–86.
Santopietro, Tom. *The Godfather Effect: Changing Hollywood, America, and Me*. New York: St. Martin's Press, 2012.
Simon, John. "The Mob and the Family." *National Review* 43:1 (January 28, 1991): 63–65.
Sterling, Claire. *Octopus: The Long Reach of the International Sicilian Mafia*. New York: W.W. Norton, 1990.
Stewart, Frank Henderson. *Honor*. Chicago: University of Chicago Press, 1994.
Stille, Alexander. "Breaking the Silence in Calabria." *New York Review of Books* 66:16 (October 24, 2019): 49–52.
Swinburne, Richard. *Responsibility and Atonement*. New York: Oxford University Press, 1989.
Talese, Gay. *Honor Thy Father*. New York: World Publishing, 1971.
Tamburri, Anthony Julian. "Michael Corleone's Tie: Francis Ford Coppola's *The Godfather*." In Dana Renga, *Mafia Movies: A Reader*. 2nd edition. Toronto: University of Toronto Press, 2019, 70–75.
Testa, Carlo. "Threads of Political Violence in Italy's Spiderweb: Giorgio Ambrosoli's Murder in Michele Placido's *A Bourgeois Hero*." In Dana Renga, *Mafia Movies: A Reader*. 2nd edition. Toronto: University of Toronto Press, 2019, 236–241.
Wartenberg, Thomas E. *The Forms of Power*. Philadelphia: Temple University Press, 1990.
Welsh, Alexander. *What is Honor?* New Haven, CT: Yale University Press, 2008.
Wolterstorff, Nicholas. "Does Forgiveness Undermine Justice." In *God and the Ethics of Belief*, ed. Andrew Dole and Andrew Chignell. Cambridge: Cambridge University Press, 2005, 219–247.
———. "Jesus and Forgiveness." In *Jesus and Philosophy*, ed. Paul K. Moser. Cambridge: Cambridge University Press, 2009, 194–214.

Index

Abbandando, Genco, 103, 127; death of, 90
Adams, Kay, 106, 110, 125, 128; character development of, 135–36, 160–61
Altobello, Don Osvaldo, 126, 127, 129, 133, 158; death of, 134, 159, 161; treachery of, 130–31
Ambrosoli, Giorgio, 118, 192n1
amici di cappello, 45, 46, 49
amicitia, 46
amor fati, 97
Anastasia, Albert, 58, 116
Andolini, Vito. *See* Corleone, Don Vito
Andreotti, Prime Minister Giulio, 117, 118–20, 192n1
Aristotle, 106, 111
Arlacchi, Pino, 185n32, 189n68
arrogance, 124; contrasted with pride, 25
art, and reality in *Godfather*, 115–20
atonement, 115, 146, 148, 149, 151; and Michael Corleone, 155–56, 162; philosophical analysis of, 137–43

Banco Ambrosiano, 119, 192n1
Barzini, crime family of, 37
Barzini, Don Emilio, 55, 126, 127, 132

Barzini, Luigi, 35–36, 41, 47, 59–60, 61–62, 64
Basilone, John, 56
Batista, Fulgencio, 127
Berlusconi, Silvio, 118
Bible: and pride, 25–26
Bocchicchio, family of, 107; and honor, 21–23
Bonanno, Joseph, 71, 117, 187–88n68
Bonasera, Amerigo, 5, 180n3, 184n29; and assimilation, 7, 85; and daughter, 6–8, 20, 46; and Don Vito Corleone, 6–11, 17; and honor, 9, 19
Borsellino, Paolo, 188n68
Brasi, Luca, 9, 117, 129–30, 132
Brown, H. Rap, 74
Buscetta, Tommaso, 71, 188n68

Cabrini, Francesca Saverio ("Mother Cabrini"), 56
Calderone, Antonino, 71, 189n68
Calo, 129, 134, 159
Calvi, Roberto, 119, 120, 192n1
Camon, Alessandro, 66
Carnegie, Dale, 124
Cascio Ferro, Don Vito, 59, 60, 62, 63
Castiglia, Francesco ("Frank Costello"), 57–58, 62, 63

Catanzaro, Raimondo, 35, 68
Cavalleria Rusticana, 120–22, 128, 136
Che la luna mezzo mare, 123, 193n7
Christian Democrats, party of, 61, 62, 117, 119
Churchill, Winston, 154
Cicci, Willie, 116
Ciccio, Don, 128, 134
Cicero, Marcus Tullius, 63; and Sicily, 63
chivalry, rustic, 120–22, 128
Clemenza, Peter, 103, 135, 136, 179n3
clientele, 46
commare, 7, 10, 45
community, 39–41, 106; and individualism, 25, 53, 65, 85, 107, 111, 123
comparaggio, 45–46
compare, 10, 45
Coppola, Francis Ford, 53, 80, 108, 110, 115, 116, 122; and Don Vito Corleone, 55, 62; interpretation of novel, 78–79, 104, 123, 135, 189n1, 190n3; notes on novel, 27, 28
Corleone, Anthony, 120, 125, 128, 160
Corleone, Carmela, 108, 110, 125, 136; and Amerigo Bonasera, 9, 46
Corleone, Constanzia ("Connie'), 6, 9, 11, 122, 125; and *Godfather II*, 53, 107–08, 125, 136; and *Godfather III*, 123, 127, 128, 134, 158, 159–60, 161; character development of, 159–60, 161
Corleone, Don Vito: and Amerigo Bonasera, 6–11, 17; and death, 16, 90, 134, 157; and destiny, 77, 102–4; and evil, 16, 102–4; and family, 7, 9–11, 29, 33, 37, 41; and Genco Abbandando, 90, 103, 127; historical roots of, 56–63; and honor, 9, 19, 13, 15–16, 19–20, 27, 28–30, 45–49; and ideal of *uomo di pazienza*, 50–54, 56; and Jack Woltz, 28–30, 103; and justice, 6–8, 9, 11, 12, 54; and narcotics, 35, 55, 56, 103, 104, 105, 126, 127; and nineteenth-century Sicilian values, 2, 5, 9, 33, 41, 45–49, 81; and power, 8, 9, 12, 29, 32–33, 36–37, 41, 49, 51, 90–93; and respect, 7–9, 17, 30–33; and will to power, 93–102
Corleone, Frederico ("Fredo"), 53, 54, 107, 108, 109, 125, 134, 136, 155
Corleone, Mary, 125–26, 129, 131, 134, 136, 160
Corleone, Michael: and Americanism, 12, 53, 84, 85, 105, 107; and atonement, 137–43; 155–56, 162; and Cardinal Lamberto, 156, 159, 160; contrast with Don Vito Corleone, 157–58, 159, 162; and death, 104, 107, 136, 163; degeneration of, 104–6; and exile in Sicily, 77, 126, 158; and forgiveness, 154–55; and Frank Pentangeli, 107–10, 116, 124, 126, 131–32, 134; and Fredo Corleone, 108, 110, 125, 126, 136, 155, 159, 160; and Hyman Roth, 108, 109, 110, 124, 126, 127, 132, 134; and *la via vecchia*, 77, 84, 108, 114, 125, 128, 133, 136, 158, 162; and loss of family, 84, 110, 114; and murders of Sollozzo and McCluskey 22, 27, 37, 55, 103, 105, 126, 134; and redemption, 116, 154–63; and repentance, 137, 139–40, 155–56, 162; and return to Sicily, 106–7
Corleone, Santino ("Sonny"), 37, 53, 103, 135–36, 159; character of, 52, 54, 80, 128, 133; death of, 11, 20, 55, 125, 127, 132; and narcotics, 55
Cosa Nostra, 57, 58, 71, 74, 112–14, 117, 180n9, 185n34, 187–88n68; rules of, 15–16

cosca, 15, 58, 110, 188n68
Craxi, Bettino, 119

Dellacroce, Aniello, 116
destiny, 77, 80, 102–4, 106, 158, 162
Dickie, John, 46, 64–65, 67, 180n9, 181n11, 181n12
Dika, Vera, 184n19
DiMaggio, Joe, 56

Falcone, Giovanni, 188–89n68
Fanucci, Don, 54, 59, 103, 116, 128, 134
Feast days, Italian: and Saint Rocco, 116, 128; and San Gennaro, 116
Fontane, Johnny, 116–17, 123; and Don Vito Corleone, 9, 10, 103, 124; and Jack Woltz, 28, 29, 30
forgiveness, 137, 138–39, 140; and Michael Corleone, 154–55; philosophical analysis of, 143–54

Gallo, Albert, 117
Gallo, Joey, 117
Gallo, Larry, 116, 117
Gambetta, Diego, 69–70
Gambino, Carlo, 57, 58, 62, 63, 117, 118, 187n68, 192n1
Gambino, Richard, 50, 52
Gardaphé, Fred L., x, 11, 105, 189n1
Gardner, Ava, 117
Gatto, Paulie, 126
Geary, Senator Patrick, 104, 108, 124
Gelli. Lucio, 119, 192n1
Genovese, Vito, 62, 116, 188n68
Gentile, Nicola, 71, 188n68
Gilday, Archbishop, 120, 134, 158, 159
Gioelli, Joseph ("Joe Jelly"), 117
The Godfather: as conflict of value systems, 81–84; as chronicling immigrant experience, 79; feminist analysis of, 80; Freudian analysis of, 80; interpretations of, 78–84; as *King Lear* metaphor, 78; Marxist analysis of, 80; as metaphor for American foreign policy, 79–80; as metaphor for capitalism, 78–79; as reflection of American economics and politics, 79; summary of 165–68; as trilogy, 78
The Godfather II, summary of, 169–73
The Godfather III, summary of, 175–78
Greene, Moe, 54, 117, 133
Greene, Naomi, 106–7

Hagen, Tom, 27, 52, 80, 108, 109, 117, 128, 130, 132; and Don Vito Corleone, 28–29, 53, 54, 55, 92; and Jack Woltz, 10, 28–29
honor: and canon of behavior, 12–13; and capitalism, 26–28; case favoring, 23–26; and *Cosa Nostra*, 15–16; and Don Vito Corleone, 9, 13, 15–16, 19–20, 27, 28–30, 45–49; and internalization of values, 18–20; limitations of, 33–37; and organized crime, 15–16, 21–23; and personal identity, 13, 17, 23, 24, 44; philosophical analysis of, 12–23; and principle of redress, 20–21; and sense of belonging, 14–15
human life, meaningful, 26; philosophical analysis of, 39–44
human lives: autobiographical, 41, 42, 43, 44; biographical, 43–44, 110; biological, 42, 43, 44

Immobiliare, 116, 117, 118, 126, 132, 154, 156, 159
individualism: and community continuum, 39–41
"Is he a Sicilian?," 28

Johnson, Merle, 108, 125, 161

Kael, Pauline, 79
Keinszig, Frederick, 120, 134

LaGuardia, Fiorello, 56, 57
La Mano Nera, 56–57, 50, 74
Lamberto, Cardinal, 120; and Michael Corleone, 156, 159, 160
Lampone, Rocco, 129, 134, 135
LaRosa, Julius, 123
la via vecchia, 55, 81, 123, 125, 157; and honor, 44; and living meaningfully, 41; and Michael Corleone, 77, 84, 108, 114, 125, 128, 133, 136, 158, 162; waning of, 77, 83, 84, 108, 114
Lazarus, Emma, 55
l'ordine della famiglia, 45–49; and *amici di cappello*, 45, 46, 49; and *amicitia*, 46; and *clientele*, 46; and *compareggio*, 45–46; and Don Vito Corleone, 7, 9–11, 29, 33, 37, 41; and *madrine*, 45, 46; and *padrini*, 45, 46; and *stranieri*, 45, 46, 49, 50, 73
Lucania, Salvatore ("Lucky Luciano"), 56, 57
Lucchese, Tommy, 117, 187n68
Lucchesi, Don Licio, 120, 126, 127, 131, 132, 134, 158, 159, 162
Luciani, Cardinal Albino (Pope John Paul I), 118, 120
Lupo, Salvatore, 64, 67–68, 71, 117, 181n13, 186n58, 186n59, 187n62, 192n1

madrine, 45, 46
Mafia: historical development of, 71–74: origins of, 63–70; self-image, 70–75; two meanings of, 73–74
Magliocco, Joe, 117, 187n68
Mancini, Vincent, 116, 122; assuming control of crime family, 133, 160, 161; feigning betrayal, 130–31, 162; murder of Joey Zasa, 127, 128, 161; murders of others, 129, 134, 159; private meetings, 124; romance with Mary Corleone, 125–26, 131
Maranzano, Salvatore, 57, 187n68
Marciano, Rocky, 56
Marcinkus, Archbishop Paul, 119, 120
Marxism, 80, 82, 184n18
Mascagni, Pietro, 120, 121, 136
Masseria, Joe, 187n68
McCluskey, Captain, 22, 27, 77, 104, 105, 106, 126, 128, 134
meaningful human life, 26; philosophical analysis of, 39–44
Menasci, Guido, 120
Messenger, Chris, 102, 190n3
Mezzogiorno, 47, 48, 49, 52, 182n7, 183n18
Montini, Cardinal Giovanni (Pope Paul VI), 118
Moonan, Kevin, 8, 9
Morello, Giuseppe, 59, 60
Mori, Cesare, 21, 60
Mosca, of Montelepre, 116, 129, 134, 156
Mother Teresa, 99
Mussolini, Benito, 21, 60

narcotics, 21; and Don Vito Corleone, 35, 55, 56, 103, 104, 105, 126, 127; and organized crime, 16, 56, 57, 113, 192n1
Neri, Al, 129, 134, 135, 159
Nietzsche, Friedrich, 93–97, 100, 191n30, 191n32

omertà, principle of, 13, 21, 56, 85, 109, 187n68; defined and applied, 15, 35, 51–52; waning of, 112, 113, 114
Orlando, Vittorio Emanuele, 73

padrini, 45, 46
parallels within *Godfather* trilogy, theatrical, 122–36; bloody, vengeful climax, 133–34; business transactions and trouble, 126; conferences with crime bosses, 126–27; deaths of valuable confederates, 129; deceptive confederates, 126; distinctively formidable antagonists, 132–33; dominant enemies, 127; ersatz betrayals, 129–32; family and religious ceremonies, 122–24; generational disagreement, 125–26; Michael's plight, 134–36; parallel murders, 134; passing of the torch, 133; private meetings, 124–25; return to Sicily, 128–29; romantic liaisons and lost love, 125; shadow dons, 128; vagaries of illness, 127
Paramount Pictures, 118, 190n2
Patrick, Vincent, 183n13
Papke, David Ray, 79
Pentangeli, Frank, 107, 108, 124, 131; death of, 110, 116, 134, 136; testimony against Michael Corleone, 109, 116, 126
Persico, Carmine ("The Snake"), 116
Petrosino, Giuseppe, 59, 60
pezzonovanti (pezzi da novanta), 51, 80, 85, 116, 190n2; in America, 12, 50, 55, 86, 157
power: and Don Vito Corleone, 8, 9, 12, 29, 32–33, 36–37, 41, 49, 51, 90–93; and empowerment, 91–92, 153, 161; and oppression, 86–87, 89–91, 92, 96; and paternalism, 90–91, 92, 106; philosophical analysis of, 84–93; as power-over, 31, 32–33, 36, 87–93
pride: and Bible, 25–26; contrasted with arrogance, 25

Profaci, Joseph, 62, 117, 187n68
Propaganda Due (P2), 117, 119, 158, 192n1
punishment, 19, 42, 106, 110, 111, 112, 156; and atonement, 141, 142; and forgiveness, 149–52
Puzo, Mario: and his novel, 21, 27, 29, 30, 56, 135, 160; and interpreting his novel, 79, 82, 189n1, 190n3; and Michael Corleone, 104, 108; and use of historical criminals, 57–63, 115–20; and Vito Corleone, 50–53, 54, 55, 102, 103, 186n47

Raab, Selwyn, 185n34
Racketeer Influenced and Corrupt Organizations Act (RICO), 15, 85, 114; application of, 113; elements of, 111–12
redemption, 137, 154–63; and Michael Corleone, 116, 154–63
repentance, 115, 146–47, 149, 153, 155–56; and Michael Corleone, 137, 139–40, 155–56, 162; philosophical analysis of, 139–40
respect, 6–8, 9, 14, 15–16, 19, 51, 55, 81; philosophical analysis of, 30–33
Ricciardi, Alessia, 79, 123
Risorgimento, 67–69
Rizzi, Carlo, 55, 103, 122, 125, 133, 135, 161
Rosato, Anthony, 109, 116, 124, 132
Rosato, Carmine, 109, 116, 124, 132
Roth, Hyman, 124, 126, 132; death of, 110, 129, 134; treachery of, 108, 126, 127, 132
Russo, John Paul, 110–11

Saint Sebastian, Order of, 116, 154
Scalice, Frank, 117
Scialo, Dominick, 58

sfregio, 35
Sicily: and heroic ethos, 41; and Mafia, 63–75; nineteenth century values of, 5, 33, 35, 41, 45–56; and Sicilian Vespers, 63–65
Sicilian Vespers, 63–65
Siegel, Benjamin, 117
Sindona, Michele, 117–19, 120, 192n1
Società General Immobiliare, 116, 117, 118, 126, 132, 154, 156, 159
Sollozzo, Virgil, 22, 37, 117, 126; capabilities of, 55, 127, 129–30, 132; death of, 22, 27, 77, 103, 105, 106, 126, 128; narcotics scheme, 55, 103, 126
Spatola, Rosario, 192n1
Squigliaro, Anthony, 123
Stille, Alexander, 192n45
stranieri, 45, 46, 49, 50, 73

Targioni-Tozzetti, Giovanni, 120
Tattaglia, Bruno, 127, 129–30, 132
Tattaglia, crime family of, 37, 129
Teatro Massimo, 110, 120, 129
Tessio, Salvatore, 103, 136; and betrayal, 126, and death, 133
"This is business, not personal," 26–27, 28, 132
Tommasino, Don, 127, 128, 136, 156; death of, 129, 133, 156, 160

Unione Siciliana, 57
uomo di pazienza, ideal of the, 41, 44, 50–55, 81, 107–8, 109; defined, 50–55, 184n19; and twentieth-century gangsters, 58–59; waning of the ideal, 124, 161

Valachi, Joe, 71, 116, 188n68
values: nineteenth-century Sicilian, 5, 33, 35, 41, 45–56, 81–84; twentieth-century American, 5, 33, 55, 78–80, 81–84
Verga, Giovanni, 120
Vitelli, Apollonia, 106–7, 136; death of, 107, 125, 128, 136
Vizzini, Don Calogero, 61–62, 63

Wagner, Jerry, 8, 9
Washington, Booker T., 183n18
will to power, 93–102, 191n30, 191n32; and *amor fati*, 97; attenuated, 101–2; and Don Vito Corleone, 93–102; and Friedrich Nietzsche, 93–97, 100, 191n30, 191n32; moderate, 100–1; philosophical analysis of, 93–102; staunch, 97–100
witness protection program, 15, 84, 85, 113, 114
Woltz, Jack, 130; as businessman, 28–29, 30; and Don Vito Corleone, 28–30, 103; and Johnny Fontane, 28, 29, 30; and sexual perversion, 29, 54, 55, 104; and Tom Hagen, 10, 28–29

Zamperini, Louis, 56
Zasa, Joey, 123, 158; confrontation with Vincent Mancini, 124; death of, 116, 127, 128, 161; treachery of, 126, 127
"Zips" (imported Sicilian gangsters), 112, 113

About the Author

Raymond Angelo Belliotti is SUNY Distinguished Teaching Professor of Philosophy Emeritus. He received his undergraduate degree from Union College in 1970, after which he served three years in military intelligence units of the United States Army during the Vietnam War. Upon his discharge, he enrolled at the University of Miami where he earned his Master of Arts in 1976 and his doctorate in 1977. After teaching at Florida International University and Virginia Commonwealth University, he entered Harvard University as a law student and teaching fellow. After receiving a juris doctorate from Harvard Law School, he practiced law in New York City with the firm of Barrett Smith Schapiro Simon & Armstrong. In 1984, he joined the faculty of the State University of New York. He retired from SUNY in 2018.

Belliotti is the author of twenty-three other books: *Justifying Law* (1992); *Good Sex* (1993); *Seeking Identity* (1995); *Stalking Nietzsche* (1998); *What is the Meaning of Human Life?* (2001); *Happiness is Overrated* (2004); *The Philosophy of Baseball* (2006); *Watching Baseball Seeing Philosophy* (2008); *Niccolò Machiavelli* (2008); *Roman Philosophy and the Good Life* (2009); *Dante's Deadly Sins: Moral Philosophy in Hell* (2011); *Posthumous Harm: Why the Dead are Still Vulnerable* (2011); *Shakespeare and Philosophy* (2012); *Jesus or Nietzsche: How Should We Live Our Lives?* (2013); *Jesus the Radical: The Parables and Modern Morality* (2014); *Why Philosophy Matters: 20 Lessons on Living Large* (2015); *Machiavelli's Secret: The Soul of the Statesman* (2015); *Power: Oppression, Subservience, and Resistance* (2016); *Dostoevsky's Legal and Moral Philosophy: The Trial of Dmitri Karamazov* (2016); *Nietzsche's Will to Power* (2017); *Is Human Life Absurd?* (2019); *Dante's Inferno: Moral Lessons from Hell* (2020); and *Values, Virtues, and Vices, Italian Style* (2020). *Good Sex* and *Power* were both later translated into Korean and published in Asia.

He has also published ninety-four articles and reviews in the areas of ethics, jurisprudence, sexual morality, medicine, politics, education, feminism, sports, Marxism, and legal ethics. These essays have appeared in scholarly journals based in Australia, Canada, Great Britain, Italy, Mexico, South Africa, Sweden, and the United States. Belliotti has also made numerous presentations at philosophical conferences, including the 18th World Congress of Philosophy in England, and has been honored as a featured lecturer on the *Queen Elizabeth 2* ocean liner.

While at SUNY Belliotti served extensively on campus committees, including as the chairperson of the Department of Philosophy, as the chairperson of the University Senate, and as director of General Education. Belliotti also served as Vice President for Academics for the local United University Professions. For six years he was faculty advisor to two undergraduate student clubs: The Philosophical Society and *Il Circolo Italiano*. Belliotti has been the recipient of the SUNY Chancellor's Award for Excellence in Teaching, the William T. Hagan Young Scholar/Artist Award, the Kasling Lecture Award for Excellence in Research and Scholarship, and the SUNY Foundation Research & Scholarship Recognition Award. He was also a member of the New York State *Speakers in the Humanities* Program from 2006 to 2014. Belliotti is currently a member of the SUNY Distinguished Academy Visiting Scholars Program.

www.ingramcontent.com/pod-product-compliance
Lightning Source LLC
Chambersburg PA
CBHW020329240426
43665CB00044B/1047